PAT GARRETT

PAT GARRETT

The Man Behind the Badge

W.C. Jameson

TAYLOR TRADE PUBLISHING
Lanham • Boulder • New York • London

Published by Taylor Trade Publishing
An imprint of The Rowman & Littlefield Publishing Group, Inc.
4501 Forbes Boulevard, Suite 200, Lanham, Maryland 20706
www.rowman.com

Unit A, Whitacre Mews, 26-34 Stannary Street, London SE11 4AB

Distributed by NATIONAL BOOK NETWORK

British Library Cataloguing in Publication Information Available

Library of Congress Cataloging-in-Publication Data

Jameson, W. C., 1942– author.
Pat Garrett : the man behind the badge / W. C. Jameson.
pages cm
Includes bibliographical references.
ISBN 978-1-63076-104-2 (cloth : alk. paper) — ISBN 978-1-63076-105-9
(electronic)
1. Garrett, Pat F. (Pat Floyd), 1850-1908. 2. Sheriffs—New Mexico—Lincoln
County—Biography. 3. Frontier and pioneer life—Southwest, New. 4. Lincoln
County (N.M.)—Biography. 5. Southwest, New—Biography. 6. Billy, the Kid.
I. Title.
F801.G3J36 2016
978.9'04092—dc23[B]   2015029038

∞™ The paper used in this publication meets the minimum requirements of
American National Standard for Information Sciences—Permanence of Paper
for Printed Library Materials, ANSI/NISO Z39.48-1992.

Printed in the United States of America

There is nothing concealed that will not be disclosed, or hidden that will not be made known.

—Matthew 10:26

Contents

Prologue

◆◆◆

Close to midnight, July 14, 1881.

Pat Garrett, the sheriff of Lincoln County, New Mexico, was moments away from telling the biggest lie of his life. It would not be his first lie, nor would it be his last, but it would be, by far, the most prominent.

The night sky was illuminated by a young waning moon as Garrett was seated on the edge of Pete Maxwell's bed in the rancher's Fort Sumner house. The sheriff was searching for the outlaw Billy the Kid, and had received information that his quarry was in the area. The Kid had been sentenced to hang for the killing of Sheriff William Brady. While awaiting the gallows, however, the young rustler broke out of jail and in the process killed two more lawmen. Citizens and politicians clamored for Garrett to bring in the outlaw, dead or alive. His career depended on it.

Minutes before, Garrett, along with deputies John Poe and Kip McKinney, had crept from their hiding place near a peach orchard and headed toward the ranch house. Garrett knew his way around the small settlement because he had worked there for Maxwell a few years earlier. He and the rancher were well acquainted.

Maxwell's ranch house was a one-story adobe and wood structure. Prior to the military abandoning Fort Sumner, it served as officer quarters. In addition to six bedrooms, there was a mess hall and three storage rooms. Leaving Poe and McKinney outside on the front porch, Garrett opened the outer door to the building, stepped into a ten-foot-wide hallway, and approached the door to Maxwell's bedroom located five feet down this hall on his left. He entered, awakened the rancher, and settled himself on the edge of the bed to explain why he was there.

From his position on the bed where he sat as he spoke with Maxwell, Garrett could see the layout of the bedroom, which was partly illuminated by moonlight passing through the open windows. Only three

minated by moonlight passing through the open windows. Only three nights earlier, a full moon shone over the Fort Sumner landscape. On this clear night, the moon was in a waning phase and provided 87 percent of full brightness.

Maxwell's bed was against the wall opposite the door, the headboard toward the southeast corner of the room. In the northeast corner stood a wooden washstand. The washstand was painted black, was thirty inches tall, twenty-eight inches long, and sixteen inches wide. The front of the washstand, which contained three drawers, faced Maxwell's bed. In the southwest corner of the room was a doorway into the adjoining one. A blanket hanging from the top of the doorframe served as a door. Located in the middle of the southwest wall was a fireplace.

Garrett was nervous. He had heard from sources that the Kid wanted to kill him if given the opportunity. The sheriff fingered the handle of his .44-.40 Colt revolver. As the sheriff and Maxwell conversed in the dark room, a man suddenly stepped though the open doorway and asked the rancher about the identities of the men outside. Caught by surprise, his heart rate surging, Garrett raised his weapon and shot the intruder in the chest, the bullet passing close to the heart. The man dropped to the floor, falling next to the fireplace.

Panicked, and with adrenaline coursing through his veins, Garrett leaped from the bed and made an attempt to flee from the room. Blinded by the flash of his weapon, he crashed into the wall to the left of the doorway. Believing he was on the right side of the opening, Garrett hurriedly felt his way toward the left in the darkness along the wall in an attempt to locate the door. He suddenly came to the blanket that hung in the entrance to the adjacent room. The unexpected contact with the object further alarmed the sheriff and with his rushed movements he got tangled up in it and fell to the floor. With both knees and his left hand on the wooden floor of the bedroom, the confused and unnerved lawman, not knowing if the man he shot was dead or alive, raised his revolver and fired a second time at what he thought was the outlaw, Billy the Kid. The bullet passed through the washstand.

Crawling along the floor, Garrett finally reached the open doorway, dashed out into the hall, and then out the front door of the ranch house. On reaching the porch, he encountered deputies Poe and McKinney. Breathing heavily, Garrett told them, "That was the Kid that came in there, and I think I have got him." Poe replied, "Pat, the Kid would not come to this place; you have shot the wrong man." Poe's words would prove to be prophetic.

The sound of Garrett's two shots awakened Fort Sumner residents. Some gathered outside the ranch house in an attempt to discern what was going on. Garrett told them that he had just killed Billy the Kid. The residents, most of them friends of the outlaw, did not contradict the sheriff, but noted that the dead man, who was the same height as the Kid, had a beard and the dark skin of a Mexican. They knew the outlaw was fair complected, had no beard, and boasted only a tiny amount of peach fuzz on his upper lip.

Garrett, however, perpetuated his lie. Later, he manipulated the coroner's report, and saw to it that the body was interred quickly. Garrett, for the rest of his life, maintained his concocted role in ending the career of the famous New Mexico bad man. Law enforcement and politicos, for the most part, bought Garrett's lie because they did not know any better and because it was convenient to do so. Others, however, knew the truth: The Kid escaped. Sheriff Pat Garrett had killed the wrong man.

Pat Garrett's account of what had occurred in Maxwell's room was published months later under his name with the considerable assistance of a ghostwriter. It was a story that has subsequently been characterized by those who have examined it closely as blatantly self-serving and filled with lies, all of which have been documented. Through successive years, however, men who passed themselves off as western historians invariably resorted to retelling Garrett's account in their writings about the lawman and Billy the Kid. Thus, Garrett's lies were perpetuated.

Pat Garrett's lies, the incompetency he demonstrated relative to business and ranching, his inability to repay numerous debts, his drunkenness, his gambling, and his whoring, gained him the reputation of a man who could not be relied on, could not be trusted. This carelessness and recklessness would cost him his life twenty-seven years later.

ONE

◆◆◆

Introduction

The history of the American West, as much or more than the history of anywhere else, is filled with clichés and with hackneyed myths made commonplace as a result of frequent repetition. It is through such notions, as well as through western novels and film, that people are exposed to what they perceive to be history. An entire book could be filled with such historic misperceptions, but a few will suffice for example.

Surveys have shown that most people believe that frontiersman Davy Crockett went down at the Alamo at the hands of General Santa Ana's troops, heroically clubbing away at them with his rifle in defense of Texas liberty. Their knowledge of this event came almost exclusively by way of the Walt Disney film production starring the actor Fess Parker. Disney screenwriters, in fact, made this scene up—it never happened.

What then is the truth? There is compelling evidence that Crockett may have been captured, was brought before Santa Ana where he tearfully pled for his life, and later stood in front of a firing squad to be executed. When this revelation was published in a popular Texas magazine, people turned hostile, wrote angry letters to the publication, and the author of the article received death threats.

Query most people and they will tell you that the outlaw Butch Cassidy perished in a shoot-out with four hundred Bolivian soldiers in 1908. When asked where they derived this information, they will tell you that they got it from the movie starring Paul Newman as Cassidy and Robert Redford playing the part of his pal, the Sundance Kid.

The ending of the movie wherein Cassidy and the Sundance Kid are gunned down made for great cinema. The truth, however, is that this never happened. As I pointed out in *Butch Cassidy: Beyond the Grave* (2013), only three Bolivian gunmen were involved, one of whom was a soldier. Furthermore, no significant evidence whatsoever

1

exists to support the notion that the two men killed in that place were Cassidy and Sundance. Cassidy, as the book points out, returned to the United States, where he lived out the remainder of his life under a different name.

When apprised of a truth that conflicts with common perception, people often get angry. When confronted with both myth and reality, people will often choose the myth, even if the myth is a lie.

Dozens of other examples exist, but we return to Pat Garrett. Garrett, once a sheriff of Lincoln County, New Mexico, has become a cliché. People—historians and enthusiasts alike—do not hesitate to say that Garrett shot and killed the outlaw, Billy the Kid. In fact, if it were not for that one significant claim, Pat Garrett would be little more than a minor footnote in American history.

Over the years, Garrett has been elevated to the position of the stalwart, dependable, unwavering, and conquering lawman. To this day, Lincoln County sheriffs and deputies have an image of Garrett on their shoulder patches. To some, Garrett represented the quintessential sheriff. This reference is a by-product of the mythic and cliché Pat Garrett, not the real man. While occasionally demonstrating some prowess as a lawman, Garrett relentlessly pursued numerous vices that ultimately crippled his standing as a peace officer, a rancher, and as a member of the community. He also claimed, and was afforded by writers who did not do their research, credit for deeds he did not accomplish.

There are three pertinent historic events to which Garrett is linked and for which, to some degree or another, he has become famous. One is the alleged killing of the outlaw Billy the Kid. Another is the book he purportedly authored titled *The Authentic Life of Billy the Kid.* And yet another relates to the mysterious circumstances under which Pat Garrett died.

The standard reference for this controversial and misunderstood sheriff is *Pat Garrett: The Story of a Western Lawman* (1974) by Leon C. Metz. Most western historians and enthusiasts I have encountered over the past five decades derived the bulk of their knowledge of Pat Garrett from this book. To Metz's credit, he did a great deal of important spadework relative to locating documents, newspaper articles, and bringing to light other materials, as well as conducting interviews pertaining to Garrett. Like far too many enthusiasts, however, Metz only repeated what he had read. He applied no investigation into the credibility of his sources and the truth of their content. Though Metz is a fine writer, his book is filled with historic and geographic errors, as well as contrived dialogue. In the end, it does little more than provide support for the myth of Pat Garrett, but contains little of the truth.

History, if approached correctly, should be a quest for the truth. It should not merely repeat what others have already stated or written without offering questions. It must introduce investigation, and provide deconstruction, analysis, and reconstruction.

A biographical writer, on investigating historical subjects such as Pat Garrett, should strive for truth, for reality. Reality, however, does not readily give up its meaning. It is the job of the biographer, as Stacy Schiff writes, "to clobber [meaning] into submission. You're meant not only to tame it but to extract substance, to identify cause and axiomatic effect." Unfortunately, this stance has not been taken with much of America's outlaw and lawman history.

As a young man interested in the outlaw West, I read *The Authentic Life of Billy the Kid.* Pat Garrett was listed as the author. Even as inexperienced as I was, the book deeply troubled and annoyed me. After a third reading, I realized that the book was uncomfortably self-serving. I suspected that truth had given way to Garrett's need to portray himself as the conquering lawman who unselfishly risked his own life to bring a noted outlaw to justice.

Later, I read two biographies of Garrett: John Milton Scanland's *Life of Pat Garrett* (1952) and Leon C. Metz's *Pat Garrett: The Story of a Western Lawman.* These two publications bothered me for the simple reason that they, for the most part, relied heavily on Pat Garrett's published version of what had happened. In other words, the two authors essentially repeated what had already been written by Pat Garrett himself, but with a few furbelows added here and there. That experience left me still wondering what the truth might be. Convinced that Garrett's veracity was suspect, that his word could not be trusted, I became certain that his version of events, particularly the alleged killing of the outlaw Billy the Kid, could bear looking into. I dedicated the next four decades to that search.

Over time, I and others determined, and ultimately proved, that Pat Garrett manufactured significant parts of his own history, that he concocted a tale of adventure, of danger, of devotion to law and justice, and placed himself in the middle of the story as the hero. Little of it, however, was true.

It has been said that history is collective memory. But who decides which story counts? Who chooses what to remember, or what to forget? Pat Garrett chose to manufacture parts of his history, and embellished wildly. He was aided and abetted by so-called historians who simply repeated his lies and exaggerations to the degree that the saga became accepted because that was all that was available. No one seemed to be curious enough to learn the truth.

This book will present evidence that Pat Garrett did *not* kill Billy the Kid, and that he deliberately lied about his role in this event as well as others. Furthermore, it will be shown that the publication that carries his name as author is filled with lies. And last, the mystery of Garrett's death, which has perplexed and confused researchers for over a century, is investigated and brings to light new evidence that explains why he was killed and identifies the man who pulled the trigger.

The truth is, the accepted and published history is wrong. This current age is having a significant impact on perceptions of American history. For one thing, unparalleled access to information on a wide variety of topics and research has become more easily available via the Internet. Thus, more information that heretofore languished in obscurity has come to light. Recently published books and articles illustrate that more and more people are suspect of long-accepted history. As a result, we are discovering that much of what we have long embraced as truth has turned out to be bogus. Oscar Wilde once said, "The details of history . . . are always wearisome and usually inaccurate." Sadly, we are learning this is often true.

The growing desire among enlightened members of the population to learn the truth is a good sign. Happily, some fine publications have helped set history straight. Dee Brown, author of *Bury My Heart at Wounded Knee* (Holt, Rinehart and Winston, 1970), pioneered much of this approach in 1970 by informing us that virtually all of the military and governmental reports pertinent to subduing the American Indian tribes across the West were replete with self-serving deceptions. Tony Horwitz's book, *A Voyage Long and Strange* (2008), relates important, overlooked, and ignored aspects of the settling of America that were left out of our public school and university history books. In my own book, *Billy the Kid: Beyond the Grave* (2005), the long-buried and often suppressed information regarding this famous outlaw conflicted with the prevailing "history," much to the annoyance of the so-called experts. Another Wilde quote: "The one duty we owe history is to rewrite it."

Years ago some wag wrote "The truth will set you free, but before it does it often causes great annoyance." Any newspaper columnist can verify this. Experience has clearly demonstrated that outlaw and lawman buffs and historians are more interested in having their perceptions validated than searching for the truth. A quest for maintaining the status quo predominates to the point where new and relevant information and deductions are squelched, even ridiculed, without providing the opportunity and benefit of discussion and debate that benefits any legitimate historical quest.

It would not be fair or honest to regard what has previously been written about Pat Garrett as accurate history for the simple reason that it was concocted not by historians or anyone remotely connected with the principles, techniques, and aims of historical research, but by enthusiasts and hobbyists. In the world of western lawman and outlaw history, there are precious few legitimate historians, researchers, investigators, and analysts. Robert Utley, the author of *Billy the Kid: A Short and Violent Life* (1989), is one. The vast majority of the others are historians only because they claim to be such. Only a small percentage of them possess legitimate credentials, and they manifest few skills related to research. While there is nothing inherently wrong with this, close examination of their contributions reveals that they do little more than look up information that has already been written and simply repeat it in books, magazines, and on television. Author Tony Horwitz stated, "Much of our past is being preserved less by scholars than by passionate amateurs." Another Oscar Wilde quote: "History never repeats itself. Historians repeat each other."

This brings up the question of research, which is defined by *The New Lexicon Webster's Dictionary* as "A systematic search for facts; scientific investigation." Most hobbyists have little familiarity with research. They undertake little to no investigation; they perpetuate an absence of deconstruction, analysis, and reconstruction. Alarmingly, many degreed academic historians are also guilty of same.

Another troubling aspect of lawman/outlaw history has crippled valid research over the years. Among many of the lawman/outlaw enthusiast cadre, there persists a quest to preserve one's imagined status within the group as an expert. This becomes a quest not for the truth, but one to preserve the ego. No tigress defends her young as ferociously and passionately as the pseudo-historian defending his research or publication. For some, publications and positions become a matter of pride and ego more than a matter of communicating the truth. Gotthold Lessing summed this up perfectly in 1778:

> The true value of a man is not determined by his possessions, supposed
> or real, of truth, but rather by his sincere exertion to get to the truth. It

is not possession of the truth, but rather the pursuit of truth by which he extends his powers and in which his ever-growing perfectibility is to be found. Possession makes one passive, indolent, and proud.

One problem with history is that historians are convinced they own it. The fact is, history belongs to all of us. Historians, if true to their chosen calling, are, or should be, after the truth. In reality, a great many important historical revelations are brought forth not by historians, but by scientists and investigators. When information and truths are discovered, common sense and honor require that they should be shared, discussed, debated, and reexamined in the hope of the emergence of a greater or more accurate truth.

Here is a truth: Pat Garrett was a liar. Some will no doubt blanch at this distinction. They will point out that Garrett has long been regarded as a western hero, a respected icon. This recognition, however, is based entirely on Garrett's word when Garrett seldom told the truth. Nevertheless, because of his proximity to and interaction with significant historical figures and events, Pat Garrett played an important role in shaping an image of the American West. Garrett, of course, should be recognized for his part in the grand setting that was lawless New Mexico. He was only one of many actors in a play, even if drama surrounded him.

It is time to tell the true story about the man behind the badge. What follows is a revisionist biography of Pat Garrett. Put very simply, this topic was professionally and exhaustively researched and involved the contributions of a number of highly qualified participants. Revisionist history has come under attack in recent years by the status quo historians who grow upset because revisionists try to leave no stone unturned—that is, they turned over all of the stones that the traditionalists missed. In the following pages the reader is invited to examine the stones I turned over.

TWO

✦✦✦

Origins

Patrick Floyd Jarvis Garrett was born on a farm in Chambers County, Alabama, on June 5, 1850. His father, John Lumpkin Garrett, knew little else than farming, and managed to grow just enough to sustain his large family through good times and lean. John Lumpkin Garrett was born in either Alabama or Georgia—no one knows for certain—on August 13, 1822. He married Elizabeth Ann Jarvis in Georgia, her home state, when she was eighteen years old.

When Pat was three years old, John Lumpkin Garrett purchased a plantation in Claiborne Parish, Louisiana, and moved the family there. The holding—eighteen hundred acres—was located eight miles east of Homer in the northwestern part of the state. The fertile land provided an abundance of cotton and garden vegetables.

While growing up, young Pat Garrett spent his daylight hours in the fields hoeing, plowing, and picking. On occasion, he worked part-time as a clerk at the plantation store. In Louisiana, Pat was subjected to some formal schooling, though it was spotty. It is suspected his education was supplemented with lessons at home. Examples of Garrett's extant letters suggest a steady and practiced penmanship hand as well as a modicum of literacy. Garrett family lore says Pat read often and possessed a small library.

Life on the Garrett plantation was little different from those of others in that part of Louisiana. Endless days of farm-related chores took up most of the time. With eight children to work on the place, John Lumpkin Garrett got by as well as anyone. Life was good and relatively undisturbed until the onset of the Civil War in 1861.

John Lumpkin Garrett was thirty-nine years old when the war broke out. Because of his age and poor health, according to his descendants, he did not serve in the Confederacy. In one of many lies Pat Garrett told throughout his life, he claimed his father was a colonel in the

Confederate army. This concocted image of his father was perhaps a foreshadowing of things to come.

The war was hard on the Garrett family and the plantation. Yankees confiscated the cotton and produce and John Lumpkin went deeply into debt. There were times when it appeared as though they would have to abandon the farm. Carpetbaggers moved into the area and took advantage of the depressed Garretts. Neighbors, previously friendly to John Lumpkin and his family, aligned themselves with the Northerners, all of them wanting some of his plantation.

John Lumpkin Garrett's wife, Elizabeth, died on March 25, 1867, at thirty-eight years of age. John Lumpkin had suffered much at the hands of the Yankees and began drinking heavily, which took an additional toll on him and the family. One day, on encountering a Northern sympathizer outside the courthouse, John Lumpkin shot him. The Northerner, wounded, fled town shortly after the shooting and no charges were ever filed.

John Lumpkin Garrett's health continued to deteriorate. He died on December 2, 1868. He was forty-six years of age. He left debts amounting to $30,000. His assets totaled just over $23,000. Following some legal and familial difficulties, the settlement of the elder Garrett's estate fell into the hands of son-in-law Larkin Randolph Lay, who had married John Lumpkin's daughter Margaret. At the time, Lay ran a saloon and a brothel in Shongaloo, Louisiana, near the Arkansas border.

In the end, Pat and his siblings received nothing in the estate settlement. It is suspected Lay benefitted the most, but it was never proven. Pat Garrett—tall, angular, and quick-tempered—threatened to kill his brother-in-law, but was talked out of it by sister Margaret. Embittered by the estate squabble, Pat packed his few possessions onto the back of a horse and rode west out of Louisiana on January 25, 1869. He was eighteen years old.

THREE

❖❖❖

Headed West

Following young Pat Garrett's departure from the family holdings in Louisiana, little is known of his wanderings and adventures over the next few years. A cryptic mention of a man indicted for "intent to murder" in Bowie County, Texas, in March 1875 may have involved Garrett. Bowie County is located about one hundred miles northwest of Homer, Louisiana. The name on the indictment is "Pat Garrity," and family lore has Pat killing a black man somewhere near the Texas-Louisiana border region around that time.

"Garrity" escaped from the county jail and fled westward. Allegedly, both Texas and Louisiana law enforcement authorities pursued him for three hundred miles before giving up and turning back. No part of this tale, however, has ever been verified.

In an interview with the *El Paso Herald* on December 13, 1901, Garrett never mentioned the Bowie County incident. He did state, however, that he found work clearing land on a "dirt farm" in Dallas County and eventually entered into a partnership with the owner. Garrett did not take to such work, and after staying for only one growing season, decided he had had enough of the tedium of farming.

A short time later, Garrett hired on with a Louisiana rancher. He was given the job of escorting a herd of cattle northward to Dodge City, Kansas. Some accounts have Garrett completing the trip to Dodge City, others have him leaving the drive at Denison in North Texas, near the Red River, and then continuing westward.

Some time during the mid-1870s, Garrett met Willis Skelton Glenn in Tarrant County, Texas. Glenn was around twenty-eight years old. As a teenager, he had served in the Confederate army. Following the Civil War, he moved to Mount Pleasant, Texas, where he operated a cotton farm and raised cattle while dabbling in real estate. Glenn once drove a herd of cattle from north-central Texas to Florida. During this

time, Glenn had looked long and hard at the possibility of making a
fortune hunting buffalo on the High Plains of Texas. At the time, buffalo hides were bringing high prices in the east.

Glenn hired Luther Duke, Joe Briscoe, and Pat Garrett to serve as
his basic hunting crew. Like Garrett, Briscoe was from Louisiana. At
first, Glenn thought Briscoe, a devout Catholic, was far too young
and naive for the buffalo range, but Garrett argued in his favor.
After loading supplies into a wagon, the four men traveled one hundred miles from Fort Worth to Fort Griffin, located forty-five miles
northeast of Abilene.

FOUR

❖❖❖

The Buffalo Range

Fort Griffin was a rough town, one that was generally avoided by most people, save for buffalo hunters, outlaws, cowboys, current and former soldiers, gamblers, and prostitutes. The buffalo hunters who frequented the adjacent High Plains relied on Fort Griffin for supplies and recreation.

Fort Griffin was established in 1867 on the banks of the Clear Fork of the Brazos River and originally called Camp Wilson. From this location, U.S. Army cavalry patrols ranged out defending buffalo hunters, settlers, and travelers from raiding Comanche and Kiowa Indians. By the time Pat Garrett arrived at Fort Griffin, however, the Plains Indians were, for the most part, subdued and placed on reservations. The hunters spread out across the range believing the chances of Indian attack had been minimized, though some still occurred.

A single buffalo hunter could kill fifty to one hundred animals per day. The skinners followed in the hunter's wake. A good skinner could do sixty to seventy buffalo a day. The work of the skinner was much harder than that of the shooter, but he only made a nickel a day.

Untreated buffalo hides, along with robes, were often seen stacked in and around Fort Griffin, all awaiting shipment to the east. The stink of the hides could be detected from miles away, and flies hovered everywhere. In a single month, as many as 200,000 buffalo hides were traded here. A large buffalo robe in good condition sold for three dollars. After the skinning and the processing of the hide into the robe, the hunter pocketed only twenty-five cents of that amount. An untanned hide would sell for one dollar, and the hunter's share was five cents.

The name for Fort Griffin most often used by the hunters was "Hidetown." For the most part, the town was lawless, and two or three men were hanged each month, some of them legally, some not. What law existed in Fort Griffin was manifested by Sheriff John Larn. Larn, a colorful and somewhat dangerous character, was known to supplement his lawman's income by rustling cattle. Having had enough of Larn's manner of doing business, a group of a half-dozen masked men entered his office one night and shot him to death.

By 1881, a railroad was put through the town of Albany, located twenty miles to the southwest, and all of the buffalo hide business moved in that direction. It spelled the end to Fort Griffin, which exists today as a state park.

When Glenn and his buffalo-hunting party, including Pat Garrett, arrived at Fort Griffin, they went straight to a store owned by Frank Conrad. Conrad was also the town banker. At the store, the men purchased saddles, bridles, harnesses, skinning knives, guns, and ammunition. Garrett selected a Winchester .45-caliber buffalo gun for which he paid fifty dollars. Glenn also purchased 1,000 rounds of ammunition and enough lead and powder for making their own bullets for a long time. The purchases were rounded out with bacon, beans, flour, molasses, coffee, tobacco, and corn for the horses.

Before leaving town, Glenn hired Nick Buck, an accomplished skinner, and Grady Burns, a cook. All of the gear and supplies were loaded onto wagons and strapped onto horses. After spending only one night in town, the men departed for the buffalo range.

The Glenn party headed west from Fort Griffin for the Double Mountains in the southern Panhandle to hunt. At first, some herds of significant size were encountered, but the harvest grew poorer with each passing day. In addition to the Glenn party, there were dozens of other buffalo-hunting bands on that part of the range.

In November 1876, Glenn left the group for Camp Reynolds to have a rifle repaired. Back at the camp, the cold and rainy weather had a depressing effect on the hunters and skinners. It was difficult to find dry wood and buffalo chips for the cook fires, and the men often went hungry.

One morning Burns managed to get a small fire going. As he moved about preparing breakfast, Briscoe finished up washing his clothes in a nearby stream and walked back into the camp. He approached the fire and held out his cold and numb hands to warm them. Garrett, also standing by the fire, made the comment that only an Irishman would be so stupid as to wash clothes in an icy and muddy stream.

Offended, Briscoe advanced on the six-foot-five-inch Garrett, who responded by knocking him to the ground. Briscoe made several attempts to grapple with Garrett only to be knocked down again and again. Refusing to back away, the now enraged Briscoe grabbed an ax and swung at Garrett. Garrett ran around the campsite staying one step ahead of Briscoe. Tiring of the Irishman's tirade, Garrett grabbed his rifle and shot his attacker in the chest. Briscoe staggered and fell into the campfire. He died a few moments later.

Concerned that he might be charged with murder, Garrett packed a few items, saddled his horse, and rode away. Cold, exhausted, and not knowing what to do or where to go, he returned to the camp after two days.

On arriving back at the campsite, Garrett approached Glenn, who had returned from Camp Reynolds the previous day, and explained what happened. Glenn suggested Garrett ride into Fort Griffin, turn himself into the law enforcement authorities, and provide his version of the killing. Garrett balked at the idea, but finally agreed to do so and rode away. He returned to the camp four days later, claiming that the Fort Griffin lawmen decided not to prosecute.

Two months later, Luther Duke resigned and rode away. The buffalo herds had thinned out and the future was beginning to look bleak. The possibilities of earning a living as a buffalo hunter were coming to an end. In spite of the presence of the U.S. Cavalry, more and more Indians were breaking out of the reservations and returning to their hunting grounds. The threat of an Indian attack was growing.

A number of Comanche had escaped from the reservations and were subsisting on some of the few buffalo remaining in the High Plains. The devastation of the herds by the white buffalo hunters, however, angered the Indians. In addition, the bands of Indians were further irritated by the constant pursuit and harassment from the U.S. Cavalry. The Comanche were torn between starving and surrendering, but as their rage grew at what they considered the reckless and wasteful manner of hunting by the white men, they chose instead to fight.

A little-known Comanche named Nigger Horse led a band of forty warriors. On February 1, 1877, while every member of Glenn's party was miles away on the range, they attacked the unmanned camp. During the melee, the Indians destroyed eight hundred buffalo hides by slashing and burning them. In addition, they made off with most of the horses. When the hunters returned and saw the devastation, Glenn fumed and raged and swore revenge. Garrett argued that it was not worth the trouble to go after the Comanche, but Glenn was not persuaded.

In addition to his own men, Glenn talked forty-eight other buffalo hunters into meet at Camp Reynolds and prepare for an attack on the Indians. The hunters packed rifles, ammunition, and kegs of whiskey into wagons and set out after the raiders. Following several days of slow travel and heavy drinking, they located Nigger Horse and his band at Yellow House Canyon near present-day Lubbock. As it turned out, the now hopelessly drunk buffalo hunters were way overmatched by the Indians; they were routed in short order and chased all the way back to Camp Reynolds. Embarrassed by the defeat at the hands of the Comanche, and having consumed all of the liquor, the men decided to return to buffalo hunting.

On May 1, the Comanche were back. They raided several of the hunting camps again, including Glenn's. Glenn was wounded in the leg. A man named Dofflin, a new skinner, grabbed Glenn and dragged him to safety. As Glenn and Dofflin watched, the Indians destroyed the accumulated buffalo hides.

During the raid, Pat Garrett was out on the buffalo range hunting. When informed of the attack, he hurried back to Fort Griffin, believing that Glenn would seek refuge there. After finding Glenn safe, the two men returned to the camp. They salvaged a portion of the hides and sold them for one dollar each. With the money, Glenn and Garrett bought round-trip tickets to St. Louis, where they drank and gambled away what little money they had left.

The two men returned to the buffalo range from St. Louis in November and resumed hunting. By January 1878, it was apparent there were not enough buffalo left on the Texas and New Mexico high plains to provide for a living. While encamped near Yellow House Canyon, Glenn and Garrett decided to part company. The two men, along with the other hunters and skinners, simply mounted their horses and rode away from the wagons, gear, and supplies.

By February, Garrett, in the company of Willis Skelton Glenn and Nick Buck, arrived at Fort Sumner, New Mexico.

Years later, Willis Skelton Glenn decided to sue the U.S. government for the losses incurred as a result of the Indian raids. In 1892, Glenn filed a claim, stating that the Comanche had violated a treaty by attacking his camp and destroying his hides and equipment. He insisted the government was negligent in maintaining the Indians on the reservation. Glenn asked for $15,000 in compensation. The claim dragged on for years, and in 1899 *Willis Skelton Glenn vs. The*

United States Government came to trial. Pat Garrett was called from New Mexico to testify.

Glenn was not prepared for and was entirely surprised by the testimony provided by his former partner. Taking the stand, Garrett, under oath, stated that the total value of destruction amounted to no more than one thousand dollars. Glenn was unable to provide any evidence to dispute Garrett's claim. In spite of that, the case remained in the courts for several more years. In 1912, four years following the death of Garrett, Glenn's strategy was to impugn the integrity and character of his former friend, who by this time had acquired a reputation as a dishonest and untrustworthy individual. He claimed that Garrett had never been one of his partners in the buffalo-hunting enterprise and that he had left the camp following the killing of Briscoe, having been driven away by Glenn himself.

In his search for support for his case, Glenn located a number of people willing to provide testimony relative to Garrett's character. Ed O'Beirne, a Fort Griffin resident, stated under oath that Garrett was less than truthful. A man named Commodore Burge claimed Garrett's honesty was questionable. It was also pointed out that Garrett was a drunk, a womanizer, a gambler, an agnostic, and was slow to pay his debts. More witnesses were called into court who testified that Garrett's capacity for truth was lacking. It should be noted, however, that these witnesses offered solely their opinions and provided no pertinent evidence for their statements. Garrett, who by this time had been in the grave for years, was not present to defend himself.

For every prosecution witness that vilified Garrett's character, the defense provided one that testified to his integrity and honesty, and words such as "truthful," "brave," "unsullied," "first class," "honest," and "honorable" were recorded.

In time, Glenn's case was finally judged. The U.S. Government awarded him $4,140. Of that amount, he had to pay his lawyer $830.

FIVE

✦✦✦

Fort Sumner

Several years prior to the arrival of Pat Garrett in Fort Sumner, the location had served as a compound where thousands of Apache and Navajo Indians had been imprisoned. The cruel and shameful conditions under which the people were kept, along with the inept governmental administration of the site, doomed its continuation. By 1869, the project was abandoned. In 1871, the buildings were sold to Lucien Bonaparte Maxwell. Maxwell established a successful cattle ranch in the area, running thousands of head on the nearby fertile plain.

Lucien passed away in 1875 and the operation of the ranch fell to his son, Pedro, known as "Pete" to the locals. Lucien's widow had a thirteen-room house constructed of adobe a short distance from the old fort. In time, a small Mexican settlement evolved in the area that included a number of residences, a post office, and a church.

On arriving at Fort Sumner, Garrett exhausted what little money he possessed by purchasing a small amount of bacon and flour to feed himself, Glenn, and Burke for a few days. While encamped along the Pecos River, Garrett noticed a herd of cattle being driven from one pasture to another. Garrett, not unfamiliar with livestock, decided to locate the owner and ask for a job. He found Pete Maxwell, explained he was looking for work, and was hired. Within a short time, Glenn and Buck moved on.

When not working cattle, Garrett hung around the settlement and soon became an object of interest among the residents. It was here, it is believed, that he met and became friends with Billy the Kid. When Garrett first came to the small town of Lincoln he had little in the way of possessions and his boots were worn out. The Kid and his gang pooled their money and bought him a pair of new ones.

Because of Garrett's height, they nicknamed him "Juan Largo" (Long John). Several of the young Mexican women found Garrett intriguing but were troubled by tales that he had once had a wife and children in Sweetwater, Texas, whom he allegedly had abandoned. Researcher and author Eve Ball claimed she had evidence of Garrett's marriage in Sweetwater, and even knew the name of his wife, but because her claim carried the possibility of potential embarrassment, she refused to divulge the specifics. Members of Garrett's family claimed the story of the Sweetwater marriage was not true.

Equally confusing, if not more so, is the record of Garrett's marriages in Fort Sumner. An unsubstantiated rumor has him wedding Juanita Gutiérrez in 1877. Gutiérrez was the daughter of the owner of a freighting business. A search for the record of this marriage has yielded nothing, but such is not unusual for the time and place. There exists, however, a reference to the notion that Billy the Kid and his gang paid for the wedding reception. Likewise, there is no date relating to the death of the alleged Mrs. Garrett as a result of miscarriage or childbirth, as one story went, only months following the wedding.

A short time later, Garrett wed Apolonia Gutiérrez, believed to be the sister of Juanita. Apolonia has been described as educated and refined. An oft-told story has Garrett and Thomas L. McKinney joining together to conduct a hog business in Fort Sumner. Garrett was attacked by an angry sow that knocked him down and inflicted some minor wounds. Apolonia took him in, treated his wounds, and nursed him back to health. They were married a few weeks later in Anton Chico, New Mexico. Garrett and Apolonia remained married for the rest of Pat's life despite his well-documented drinking, gambling, and whoring. During the ensuing years, Apolonia bore eight children.

SIX

◆◆◆

The Lincoln County War

Garrett enjoyed his new life in Fort Sumner. He was frequently seen at the community dances and could be counted on to flirt with all of the single women. Though the details are unknown, Garrett and Pete Maxwell fell into disagreement over some matter and Garrett left his job at the ranch. In time, he found employment as a bartender in a Fort Sumner saloon owned by Beaver Smith. Some researchers are convinced Billy the Kid hung around the saloon quite a bit, and some believe he may have owned a share in it. For a time, Garrett and the Kid remained friends.

As Garrett was tending bar and meeting new people all of the time, events were evolving toward what became one of the bloodiest episodes in New Mexico history—the Lincoln County War. The cause of the war was linked to money and who was going to receive most of it.

Around the time of the Civil War, a Texan named John Chisum arrived in eastern New Mexico and established a ranch at Bosque Grande, then later at South Spring, near the Pecos River close to Roswell. He referred to his brand as the Jinglebob and he owned hundreds, if not thousands, of head of cattle that grazed up and down the valley. In time, and because of his success, Chisum became the biggest landowner and rancher in the area.

Such success often breeds jealousy, fear, and enemies. The small ranchers in the region grew nervous over Chisum's growing power and banded together. With Major Lawrence G. Murphy as their leader, they began to feel more secure in obtaining markets for their cattle.

Murphy, a former army officer, had been the post trader at Fort Stanton until he was caught in a number of dishonest transactions, most of them related to placing more money in his pockets. Murphy moved to Lincoln, eighteen miles to the southeast and the county seat at the time. There, he built the House of Murphy—a saloon and store.

Before much more time had passed, Murphy obtained the monopoly on supplying beef and flour to Fort Stanton. Research has shown that most of the beef was stolen and most of the flour was weevil-ridden.

In spite of the poor quality of his products, Murphy's business grew. He added partners—James Dolan, Emil Fritz, and John Riley. Before much more time passed, the four men formed an alliance with Thomas B. Catron, the head of the so-called "Santa Fe Ring." All were also Masonic brothers. Their collective goal was to destroy Chisum and eliminate him as a competitor in providing beef for the fort.

Intruding onto this scene was John Henry Tunstall, an Englishman. Tunstall had inherited a family fortune and had an entrepreneurial bent. Tunstall was a thin man, looked almost fragile, and was given to migraine headaches. With support from John Chisum and a lawyer named Alexander McSween, Tunstall also opened a store in Lincoln a short distance from Murphy's. Tunstall's ambition was to obtain a share of the beef contracts for Fort Sumner, much to the dismay and irritation of Murphy.

Life in Lincoln went along relatively calmly and undisturbed for a period of time until Murphy partner Emil Fritz died in Germany, leaving a $10,000 life insurance policy. Murphy, convinced the money should go to the House of Murphy, hired lawyer McSween to deal with the insurance company. By August 1877, McSween reported that he had collected just over $7,000, the remainder being paid to the New York law firm he had hired to help him with the claim.

Murphy did not entirely believe McSween, but decided to settle for the $7,000. McSween, however, refused to turn over the money, claiming that he was waiting to hear from legitimate Fritz heirs. Rumors circulated that McSween had already spent the money. Murphy filed charges against the lawyer, and on December 24, 1877, McSween was arrested and delivered to the jail in Mesilla. Bond was set at $8,000.

Murphy partner Jimmy Dolan had papers drawn up that claimed property that was in the possession of both McSween and Tunstall. Lincoln County Sheriff William Brady placed a padlock on the Tunstall store and then rode to the Englishman's ranch with papers providing for foreclosure on nine of the rancher's blooded horses. Dolan claimed the horses, in truth, belonged to McSween. Tunstall, outraged at the effrontery of Dolan to suggest such a thing and at the law for being so presumptuous to suggest that it could be true, refused to turn over the stock. Brady, a puppet of the Murphy faction, grew confused, and agreed to meet with Tunstall in town to discuss the problem. Tunstall agreed to bring the horses to Lincoln and surrender them until the case was cleared up.

On the morning of February 28, 1878, Tunstall left his ranch for the meeting with Brady in town. Riding with him were his ranch foreman Dick Brewer and cowhands John Middleton, Bob Widenmann, and a young man who went by the alias of William Bonney and whom people referred to as Billy the Kid. At this time, the Kid was nineteen years old and amounted to little more than a thin young man dressed in ragged work clothes and carrying a .44 caliber revolver. At the time, no one knew his real name. In addition to Bonney, he went by aliases Henry McCarty and Henry Antrim. According to documentation presented in *Billy the Kid: Beyond the Grave*, his given name was William Henry Roberts (see appendix I).

While Tunstall and his cowhands were trailing the nine horses to Lincoln, a posse arrived at his ranch to seize them. Informed that the rancher was on the road to town, some of the posse went in pursuit.

On reaching a wooded area along the road to Ruidoso, Brewer and the Kid spotted the oncoming posse led by Billy Morton and composed, according to some researchers, of Jesse Evans, Frank Baker, Tom Hill, and others closing in at a fast pace behind them. Brewer tried to get Tunstall to make a run for it, but the rancher refused. He said he wanted to stay with the horses and believed he could reason with the posse. Brewer, Middleton, Widenmann, and the Kid were not as confident as Tunstall, so they rode away and concealed themselves in a grove of trees where turkeys roosted one hundred yards away.

In a taped interview conducted in 1949, William Henry Roberts, aka Billy the Kid, described what happened next.

> I could tell by the way the posse came galloping up that there was going to be trouble. We rode off into a part of the woods that was a turkey roost. We sat our horses off in some trees and brush watching Dolan and his boys ride up on Tunstall. They formed a circle around him and then they shot Tunstall in cold blood and then drove the horses to Lincoln. We took off when the shooting started, outnumbered like we were. Later on, the boys went out and got Tunstall's body.

According to some researchers, Tunstall was shot through the chest with a rifle bullet. After he had fallen to the ground face-first, Jesse Evans rode up and shot him in the back of the head. Not content with killing the rancher, Evans allegedly shot Tunstall's horse.

Brewer, Middleton, Widenmann, and the Kid hastened to locate McSween and report the incident. The men were then deputized by Lincoln Justice of the Peace John Wilson. They called themselves "the Regulators," and during the ensuing weeks others were added to the ranks. Wilson wrote up warrants for the members of the posse responsible for killing Tunstall, all of whom were appointed by Brady. Lincoln now had two opposing law enforcement groups.

In March, the Regulators encountered two members of the posse—Billy Morton and Frank Baker—working cattle near the Pecos River. The two men were placed under arrest. The two prisoners were being escorted to Lincoln where they were to be tried for the killing of Tunstall. Some have theorized that the two men were executed along the way. According to William Henry Roberts, the Regulators took a roundabout route to Lincoln, because they feared the Murphy gang would be waiting for them somewhere along the main road. According to Roberts, "We stopped at Agua Negra in the [Capitan M]ountains], when an argument broke out between one of our posse and Frank McNab." During the heated discussion, Morton and Baker attempted to escape and Roberts shot them.

On April 1, Sheriff Brady, along with deputies George Hindman, Billy Mathews, John Long, and George W. Peppin were making their way down the main street of Lincoln from the Murphy store toward the courthouse. Along the route they had to pass an adobe fence that connected with what used to be Tunstall's store. Behind the wall crouched Billy the Kid, Fred Waite, Henry Brown, John Middleton, and two black men—George Washington and Severin Bates.

As the lawmen passed, the Kid rose up and shot at Mathews but missed him. The Kid, in fact, had tried to shoot Mathews several days earlier but was unsuccessful. Waite, Middleton, and Brown fired into the startled group of lawmen. Brady was shot dead on the spot and Hindman was mortally wounded. The rest fled down the street and took shelter behind another wall.

The Kid jumped over the fence and ran toward Brady's body. Weeks earlier, Brady had confiscated a pearl-handled .44 caliber revolver from him and refused to return it. The sheriff was wearing it when he was shot. As the Kid reached down to retrieve his weapon, Billy Mathews fired a rifle from behind the wall where he was hiding. The bullet tore through the Kid's right hip and went on to strike Waite in the leg.

On April 4, the Regulators—this time composed of the Kid, Dick Brewer, John Middleton, Charlie Bowdre, and George and Frank

Coe—stopped at Blazer's Mill at the base of a low mountain called Sierra Blanca near the Rio Tularosa. As the men dined on a meal prepared by Mrs. Godfroy, Andrew "Buckshot" Roberts (no relation to William Henry Roberts) rode up on a mule. Buckshot Roberts had been part of the posse that rode to Tunstall's ranch but was not directly involved in the killing of the rancher. The Regulators had warrants for his arrest.

When Roberts rode up, he noticed the Regulators' rifles stacked against one wall of the dining hall. Brewer spotted him and asked Frank Coe to invite Buckshot to surrender. Roberts refused, so Brewer sent out George Coe, John Middleton, and Charlie Bowdre to arrest him. Roberts was heard to shout "No!" in response. At that moment, Bowdre shot him in the stomach. Firing his own rifle, Roberts managed to make his way to a room a few feet away. One of his bullets shot the trigger finger off of Regulator George Coe's right hand and another struck Bowdre's gunbelt. Once inside the room, Roberts pulled a mattress from the bed and placed it across the doorway. He lay down on it, his rifle aimed at the retreating Regulators.

Brewer ran down the hill toward the creek and positioned himself behind a stack of firewood. From this position he believed he could get a clear shot at Roberts. He rose up from behind the stack and spotted his target in the doorway. He knelt down, checked his revolver, and then rose up for a second time. Just as his head cleared the pile of wood, Roberts fired, striking Brewer in the head and killing him instantly. Leaving Brewer's body where it lay and not wishing to confront Roberts, the rest of the Regulators rode away. Buckshot Roberts died from his stomach wound the next morning.

On April 9, 1878, the Lincoln County Commissioners named John Copeland the new sheriff. Copeland was a McSween sympathizer. A short time later, the Murphy faction used their power and influence to convince Governor Samuel B. Axtell to remove Copeland and appoint George W. Peppin, Brady's former deputy, an enemy of the Regulators, and a fellow Mason.

On July 14, Peppin organized a posse and went in search of the Regulators. As the posse was returning from the fruitless quest, McSween rode into Lincoln with most of the Regulators behind him at the same time the posse returned. Immediately, gunfire broke out between the two factions. McSween and his men went directly to his house and store. In preparation for the confrontation with Peppin and his men,

McSween had the windows barricaded and gun ports carved into the adobe walls of the structures.

For the next two days Peppin's posse and the Regulators exchanged gunfire, succeeding only in striking one horse and one mule. On the third day, one of Peppin's deputies was wounded and carried away. He died one month later. After two more days of fighting, Colonel N. A. M. Dudley arrived from Fort Stanton with a force of black cavalrymen. In a wagon they carried a Gatling gun and other heavy armament. On seeing the arrival of the military, some of the Regulators mounted up and rode away. Others were routed by Dudley's forces and chased away. The remainder, fourteen of them, sought shelter in the McSween house.

After five days of confrontation with occasional shooting, Dudley's troops set the McSween house afire in the hope of driving the occupants into the street. As the fire advanced throughout the mostly wooden structure, the men inside, along with wife Susan McSween, retreated to the kitchen. Just before full dark, the men decided to make a run for it. Harvey Morris, who was studying law with McSween, stepped out of the kitchen door into the backyard. Behind him came Billy the Kid, Jose Chavez y Chavez, McSween, Vicente Romero, and Francisco Zamora.

After a few steps, Morris was shot down. The Kid and Chavez y Chavez made it through the yard and down the bank to the Rio Bonito where they hid in the willows. As he made his escape, the Kid shot and killed Deputy Bob Beckwith. McSween, Zamora, and Romero were driven back into the house. As they made another attempt, they were shot down by deputies John Jones and John Kinney with help from several of Dudley's soldiers.

At this point, the outcome of the short-lived Lincoln County War was inevitable. The few remaining in the McSween house, including the lawyer's wife, surrendered and left the structure just before it collapsed in flames.

SEVEN

◆◆◆

Aftermath

During the Lincoln County War, Pat Garrett was living fifty miles away in Roswell and tending to his businesses and family. President Rutherford B. Hayes expressed dismay at news of the five-day war. He immediately removed Governor Axtell and replaced him with Lew Wallace, a former Civil War general. A short time later, Wallace's acclaimed novel, *Ben Hur*, would be published. In a quandary about who was responsible for the war, who benefitted, and who suffered, Wallace proclaimed amnesty for everyone involved who was, at the time, an official resident of New Mexico.

In February 1879, Billy the Kid and fellow former Regulator Tom O'Folliard met with Jimmy Dolan, Jesse Evans, and a man named Bill Campbell in a Lincoln saloon in an attempt to arrive at a truce. The four of them agreed to stop fighting with each other and shook hands. After leaving the saloon, the Kid spotted Mrs. McSween and her lawyer, Huston Chapman, approach Dolan, Evans, and Campbell, who were standing in the street. An argument broke out between the two parties. Dolan and Campbell pulled out their handguns. Dolan shot Chapman. Allegedly, Dolan poured whiskey over Chapman's dead body and set him on fire. The Kid, aware there were warrants still out for him, left the scene and traveled to San Patricio, about five miles southeast of Lincoln.

One week later, Governor Wallace, curious as to why no arrests had been made in the shooting of Chapman, came to Lincoln. One of his first actions was to suspend Colonel Dudley from his Fort Stanton command and replace him with Colonel Henry Carroll. Apparently having no confidence in the local law enforcement authorities, Wallace instructed Carroll to arrest the shooters of Chapman. Carroll arrested Jesse Evans and Bill Campbell and incarcerated them at Fort Stanton.

It is also believed that Wallace was looking into the cattle contracts controlled by the so-called Santa Fe Ring and which were manipulated by Murphy and attorney Thomas B. Catron.

On learning that Wallace was in Lincoln looking into the Chapman murder, Billy the Kid had a letter drafted to the governor. He informed Wallace that he was an eyewitness to the killing. The Kid proposed a secret meeting with the governor at the home of John B. "Squire" Wilson. The governor agreed. Billy arrived after dark on the evening of March 17 and the two men visited for hours. The Kid explained what he and O'Folliard had seen. Wallace asked him to testify in court. He also invited him to testify against Colonel Dudley in his upcoming court-martial at Fort Stanton.

According to an interview with William Henry Roberts (aka Billy the Kid), Wallace agreed to pardon the outlaw "if I would stand trial on my indictments in the district court in Lincoln. I also agreed to testify against Dudley."

Roberts further related:

> The governor promised that he would send Sheriff [Kimball] down to San Patricio to arrest me, and he allowed me to pick the men who would come with [Kimball] so none of them would be my old enemies. Governor Wallace gave me his promise that he would appoint Judge Leonard, his personal lawyer, to defend me. I had the word of the governor on all these things before I left Squire Wilson's house.

The outlaw and the governor shook hands on the deal and the Kid rode back to San Patricio.

Billy the Kid and Tom O'Folliard surrendered to Sheriff Kimball (sometimes spelled Kimbrel and Kimbrell) on March 21. On April 14, the Kid testified before the grand jury relative to what he had seen during the killing of Chapman. Dolan was subsequently indicted for murder. Dudley and Peppin were indicted for arson.

The prosecuting attorney, William R. Rynerson, moved to have the Kid indicted for the murders of Sheriff William Brady and George Hindman. Rynerson asked for and received a change of venue to the town of Mesilla in Doña Ana County. The judge in Mesilla was Warren Bristol, a Murphy man. It soon became clear to the Kid that the governor was not going to keep his word. The outlaw was returned to the Lincoln County jail until such time as he could be taken to Mesilla.

Dolan later secured a change of venue to a neighboring county. He never served a minute in jail for his crime. Jesse Evans never showed up for any of the trial. He escaped to Fort Davis, Texas, where he was arrested for a robbery, convicted, and sentenced to a term at the Texas state prison in Huntsville. A short time later he escaped and was never seen or heard from again.

The stage was now set for the appearance of Pat Garrett.

EIGHT

❖❖❖

Reenter Garrett

Sheriff Kimball turned out to be a poor choice for sheriff of Lincoln County. He preferred to remain in his office rather than investigate crimes and pursue malefactors. Cattle and horse rustlers were aware of Kimball's reluctance to enforce the law, and as a result cattlemen were suffering more than ever. On April 15, John Chisum wrote a letter to Governor Wallace decrying the conditions. He explained in detail where the rustlers were encamped and how they could best be brought to justice. In the letter, Chisum recommended Pat Garrett as a man who could take charge of a company of men to capture the rustlers.

Pat Garrett, sufficiently removed from the fighting associated with the Lincoln County War, was nevertheless acquainted with a few of the participants, including Billy the Kid. There is no question that Garrett knew the Kid, and it has been suggested that the two even rustled cattle together.

At the onset of the Lincoln County War, a small band of Comanche took a herd of horses from a ranch near Roswell. Garrett and several other men comprised a posse that went in search of them. One week later, the posse returned to Roswell with the horses and evidence that they had killed the Indians. This likely represented the beginnings of Garrett's reputation as a man hunter, a trait often looked for and prized in lawmen of the day.

Roswell resident Captain Joseph C. Lee, along with John Chisum, traveled to Fort Sumner and approached Garrett with a proposition. A meeting was held, and by the time the men parted ways, Garrett had agreed to move to Roswell in time to qualify for the November 2, 1880, election. He was to oppose Kimball in the contest for sheriff.

Both Garrett and Kimball ran on the Democratic ticket, but Kimball was a Republican. In those days such a thing was not unusual. Kimball had previously served in a number of elected positions and was regarded as the favorite, drawing support from many ranchers and the area's Mexican-Americans.

Garrett, on the other hand, had John Chisum as his principal backer. With Chisum came a number of prominent and successful Pecos Valley ranchers, as well as all of those associated with the House of Murphy. The convention named Joseph A. LaRue, a Lincoln businessman, as chairman. In this position he manifested overt support for Garrett.

During the convention's nomination process, James J. Dolan, Will Dowlin (manager of Dolan's store), and David Easton loudly and often denigrated what they regarded as Kimball's incompetence as a lawman. Garrett was labeled a law-and-order candidate and an effective deterrent to outlawry in the region. By the end of the convention, Garrett was nominated.

Between the Democratic nomination and the election, Kimball decided to run for the office of sheriff as an Independent. Some researchers claim he ran as a Republican. The two men each set out on campaigns to entice voters to place them in office. Because Garrett was backed by Chisum, he had an initial problem with Mexicans, who despised the rancher. Some of them alleged that Chisum had taken land from them when he was expanding his already large holdings. Chisum's method of acquiring land was to send out a gang of gunmen to run the Mexicans off of their small farms. Chisum was also a law unto himself, often capturing and punishing rustlers, squatters, and trespassers, many of whom were Mexicans.

For the most part, however, Garrett got along well with the Mexicans and claimed many friends in the Mexican communities. In addition, being married to the former Apolonia Gutiérrez did not hurt him any during the campaign.

By the time the polls closed, Kimball had earned 179 votes to Garrett's 320. Lincoln County had elected a new sheriff, and Pat Garrett's new mission was to rid the area of outlaws.

NINE

❖❖❖

Counterfeit Money

Although Pat Garrett would not take office as sheriff of Lincoln County for two months following the November 2 election, he was appointed as a deputy by the freshly defeated Sheriff Kimball. Kimball was responding to pressure applied by Chisum and his fellow cattlemen to have Garrett installed into the official judicial system and get him busy pursuing cattle and horse rustlers as well as other outlaws that were plaguing the area. Garrett had already demonstrated his ability and willingness to do so, in stark contrast to Kimball.

Around this time, the United States Treasury Department (USTD) was becoming interested in some odd goings-on in Lincoln County. They were aware of the outlawry committed by Billy the Kid and his gang, but were more concerned with the growing number of counterfeit bills that were showing up throughout that part of New Mexico. In response, the USTD sent Secret Service agent Azariah F. Wild to Lincoln to investigate.

Shortly after arriving in Lincoln, Wild met with James J. Dolan, who showed him a hundred-dollar bill he had been paid by Billy Wilson. Wilson was a small-time outlaw who sometimes ran with the Kid. In the days and weeks that followed, more of the counterfeit money began showing up. As a result of his sleuthing, Wild identified the distributors of the bogus hundred-dollar bills as Wilson, Tom Cooper, Sam Dedrick, and W. W. West. Cooper, Dedrick, and West, like Wilson, were small-time and little-known rustlers and thieves. Because of their loose association with the Kid, Wild determined that cracking the case against the counterfeiters would also likely result in a general purging of the entire outlaw element in Lincoln County.

Wild's first step in facilitating the cleanup was to ask United States Marshal John Sherman to arrest the suspects. Sherman declined. Wild concluded that Sherman, along with other area law enforcement authorities, was simply afraid of the outlaws. The Kid and his gang, as well as others, went about their rustling and robbing activities with impunity, knowing well that the authorities lacked the desire to chase them down. Wild considered the elected officials inept and cowardly, and was surprised to find these characteristics manifested in the capital of Santa Fe as well.

Wild decided to recruit a small company of men to go in pursuit of the counterfeiters. In a short time he signed on Pat Garrett, Benjamin Ellis, former sheriff George Kimball, John Hurley, J. C. Lea, and Frank Stewart. This done, Wild contacted Marshal Sherman and requested U.S. deputy marshal commissions for each of them. Sherman complied, and soon Wild commanded an official force.

Wild instructed Kimball and Hurley to drive the outlaws from the town of White Oaks toward the west. Garrett was in charge of coming up from the south and engaging the fleeing criminals, either capturing or killing them. A third group would stand by ready to intercept any who chanced to escape.

Wild was confident that his plan would work, but he was foiled when some of the outlaws held up a stage carrying the United States mail and found Wild's official reports relating to his plot. Aware that his intentions had been discovered, Wild called off everything. With his own life possibly in danger now, he concerned himself with keeping a low profile for a while.

During the time Wild was in hiding, he formulated a new plan. He communicated with J. C. Lea in Roswell and asked him to recommend someone competent and reliable to work undercover in Fort Sumner and observe the activities of the outlaws. Lea recommended Pat Garrett.

On November 20, 1880, Garrett, accompanied by Barney Mason, arrived from Roswell. Mason was an odd choice as Garrett's partner. At the time, Mason and Garrett were good friends, had both been employed by Pete Maxwell for a time, and served as each other's best man at their double wedding. Mason, however, was little more than a small-time outlaw himself, and was noted for his incompetence as well as his inability to tell the truth. Since Mason's past was associated with lawlessness, Garrett believed he would be in a good position to infiltrate the outlaw camp.

Mason informed Wild of a meeting he'd had with Daniel Dedrick, brother of Sam Dedrick. Daniel had been serving time in an Arkansas prison for rustling but had escaped and fled to Lincoln County. At the meeting was a man named Duncan, who, according to Mason, had just arrived from New York and was carrying a suitcase filled with counterfeit money. According to Mason, the two men asked him to take the counterfeit currency to El Paso, purchase a herd of cattle, and deliver the livestock to Dedrick at Bosque Grande.

Wild listened to Mason's report but was unsure whether or not to believe him. He sent Mason back to Bosque Grande to gather more information relative to what the outlaws were plotting. By November 26, Mason had not returned, and Wild was beginning to question his own judgment.

On November 29, Wild was in Roswell. Mason rode there and informed him that Dedrick and a partner named W. W. West decided against the cattle purchase. The counterfeiters, according to Mason, were concerned about the increased presence of lawmen in the region. A short time later, a Garrett-led twenty-man posse including U.S. Deputy Marshal Robert Olinger, Barney Mason, and Wild traveled to Bosque Grande. Intent on capturing the counterfeiters, they also hoped that the Kid might be there so that he and his gang could be apprehended.

With Garrett and all of the available lawmen departing Roswell, the citizens grew concerned that the outlaws, known to be residing in the area, would attack the town. Fear and paranoia was the order of the day as a number of the residents barricaded themselves in the post office, guns at the ready in the event they were forced to make a last stand. Finally, after several hours of nothing happening, they disbanded and returned to their homes.

By now, Garrett's principal charge was related to capturing or killing Billy the Kid and Billy Wilson. Ranchers and businessmen alike were in agreement that if the Kid and his gang were eliminated the rustling would stop. Garrett was feeling the pressure. At dawn on November 30, Garrett led the posse onto Dedrick's ranch. They were disappointed to find no one there save for John J. Webb, who was wanted for murder, and George Davis, who was wanted for horse theft. The two outlaws were handcuffed and forced to ride along with the posse as it went in search of its quarry. They rode toward Fort Sumner.

When Garrett and his band arrived at Fort Sumner, they were told that Billy the Kid and his gang, aware of the pursuit, had ridden away earlier toward the northeast and headed toward Thomas Yearby's ranch at Las Cañaditas. Garrett left four of his men to guard the two prisoners and continued on. Along the way, they spotted Tom

O'Folliard, who they presumed was also headed for Yearby's ranch to join the Kid. Garrett led the posse on what he thought would be a route that would cut off O'Folliard. By the time they traversed arroyos, thickets of cactus and mesquite, and otherwise rough terrain, however, they were still several hundred yards behind the young outlaw. O'Folliard fired his rifle at the pursuing lawman and spurred his mount on toward the ranch.

On arriving at Yearby's place, Garrett urged caution at the approach. When the place appeared deserted, he and several others rode up to the house, dismounted, and burst through the door only to find Charlie Bowdre, his wife, and another woman. During the search of the premises, the lawmen found two mules that had been stolen from a stage station and four horses that had been taken from a neighboring rancher.

On December 5, Garrett and his posse returned to Fort Sumner. Garrett notified Wild in Roswell that their horses were suffering from distemper and requested additional riding stock along with some reinforcements. Wild telegraphed Garrett that he was sending Sheriff Kimball and Deputy Marshal John Hurley.

Without waiting for Hurley, Kimball, or fresh horses, Garrett, operating on the hunch that the Kid and his gang were headed for Los Portales, fifty miles away to the southeast, ordered his trail-weary posse back into the saddle. On arriving, he found the outlaws gone, if they had ever been there in the first place. The posse returned to Fort Sumner.

On the way back to Fort Sumner, the posse stopped for a bite to eat at the Wilcox Ranch. There, Garrett learned that Charlie Bowdre had left a message stating that he wanted to meet. Garrett sent a return note stating a time and a road-fork location just outside of Fort Sumner. During the meeting, Garrett told Bowdre that any of the Kid's gang members who defected and promised to lead an honest life would be granted leniency. Bowdre, who did not trust Garrett, only promised to limit his association with the Kid.

By the time Garrett returned to Fort Sumner, the promised reinforcements had still not arrived. He sent a telegram to San Miguel County Sheriff Don Desiderio Romero requesting that he meet him on the road to Las Vegas so he could turn over the prisoners Davis and Webb. Garrett dismissed the posse except for Mason, and he rented a wagon in which to transport the prisoners.

Romero, on receiving Garrett's message, deputized Francisco Romero, Vidal Ortiz, Doroteo Sandoval, Martin Vigil, and a man named Baker. The deputies rode to Puerto de Luna forty-five miles northwest of Fort Sumner to wait for Garrett. While waiting, they decided to spend their time drinking in the local saloon. By the time Garrett arrived, the deputies were quite drunk. According to Garrett, in his book *The Authentic Life of Billy the Kid*, the deputies approached him, boasting and swaggering.

Garrett turned the prisoners over to Romero, obtained a receipt, and, in the company of Mason, walked over to a nearby store to wash up from the long and dusty travel. While Garrett and Mason were in the store, a man named Juan Silva (some reports say Juanito Maes) approached Garrett in a drunken and blustering manner and told him that he, Silva, was a thief and murderer. He asked Garrett if he wanted to take him prisoner. Garrett told the man he had no warrant for his arrest and therefore had no need to place him in custody.

A few minutes later, again according to Garrett, another local tough named Mariano Leyva, walked into the store and told Garrett that no gringo would ever dare arrest him. Garrett only turned away and ignored him. Leyva walked back out on to the front porch of the store and boasted to the crowd that Garrett could never take him. While he was speaking, Leyva turned to point into the store and received a vicious slap to the head from Garrett, who had come up behind him. Leyva was knocked off the porch and into the dirt of the road. Leyva drew his pistol and fired at Garrett, missing by a wide margin. Garrett drew and fired his revolver and likewise missed, but his second shot struck Leyva in the shoulder.

After Leyva was helped away by his friends, Francisco Romero entered the store and informed Garrett he was under arrest for shooting Leyva. Mason, standing nearby, pointed his rifle at Romero's stomach and asked Garrett for permission to shoot him. Romero turned and left the building.

The above account comes entirely from Pat Garrett and, as was to become a habit with him, may have been filled with exaggerations relative to his description of his own poise and courage. There exists, in fact, evidence that this event may not have happened the way Garrett described it. Researcher and author Maurice G. Fulton once told of receiving a letter from Deputy Romero, who described the incident, and his narrative indicated it was nothing like Garrett said it was.

Romero stated that none of his men had been drinking, nor did they even approach Garrett. He also stated that it was, in fact, Garrett who had gotten drunk in the store and, following the confrontation with Leyva, surrendered his weapons to Romero when instructed to do so. The following day, Garrett stood before the local justice of the peace, who listened to the story and released him. Leyva was fined $80 for attempted murder.

Before leaving Puerto de Luna for Lincoln County, Garrett was approached by prisoner Webb, who stated he feared he would be killed during the trip to Las Vegas. Garrett agreed to ride along to protect him.

TEN

✦✦✦

Tracking the Gang

More manpower was being called in to assist in the tracking and capture of Billy the Kid and his outlaw gang. While Pat Garrett was involved with the drama of dealing with Romero's deputies, the Kid and his gang, after stealing some horses, were hiding out at the Greathouse Ranch. The ranch, which included a trading post, was located forty miles north of White Oaks and was co-owned by "Whiskey Jim" Greathouse and Fred Kuch.

Greathouse had a sketchy past that included rustling, and he was known to be sympathetic to the outlaws. For a time, Greathouse worked for Skelton Glenn on the buffalo range in the Texas Panhandle along with Pat Garrett. He was also among the drunken group of buffalo hunters that pursued the band of raiding Comanche to Yellow House Canyon in 1877 and were badly defeated. Kuch was believed to have been involved in smuggling goods from Mexico. Greathouse later went into another partnership with Kuch, opening a tavern and trading post near Corona, New Mexico, on the well-traveled White Oaks–Las Vegas road.

Azariah Wild reported that, according to his sources, Billy the Kid and six other outlaws rode into White Oaks on the morning of November 20, 1880, and robbed two businesses, taking rifles, blankets, and overcoats. On their way out of town, gunfire was exchanged with a handful of White Oaks citizens.

Two days later, a White Oaks deputy sheriff organized a posse to travel to the Greathouse Ranch with the objective being to arrest the outlaws. Following a brief exchange of gunfire, the somewhat timid and overly cautious posse decided to ride back to town. Before leaving, however, posse members found two of the outlaws sleeping in one of the outbuildings and took them prisoner. One of them was

Moses Dedrick, the brother of the Dedricks who were known to be passing counterfeit bills.

A report of the confrontation with the outlaws reached the desk of someone in authority at Fort Stanton. Fearing that the outlaws might be tempted by the military payroll that stopped at the Greathouse Ranch, a Lieutenant Clark, along with a dozen troopers, was dispatched to meet the pay wagon and escort it. The paymaster arrived at the ranch, conducted business, and departed with no incident. On returning to the post, Clark reported that Billy the Kid, along with seventeen men, was staying at the ranch.

On November 30, the Kid, accompanied by Dave Rudabaugh and Billy Wilson, rode into White Oaks. Spotting Deputy James Redman on the street and recognizing him as the leader of the posse that came to the Greathouse Ranch earlier, they reportedly fired several shots at him but missed. The next morning, James Carlyle, a White Oaks blacksmith and a sometime deputy, organized another posse of twelve men to ride back to the ranch and confront the outlaws.

On arriving at the ranch, Carlyle positioned his posse men around the house to guard against any escape attempt. Carlyle then rode to the front of the house and called out for those inside to surrender. The door opened, someone peered out and took an assessment of what was going on, then retreated inside, slamming the door.

Some time later, Greathouse, who did not care for the notion that his house was under siege by lawmen, suggested that he offer himself to the posse as a hostage while Carlyle came inside the ranch house to talk with the outlaws. Everyone agreed, and as it grew full dark, Carlyle entered the house and Greathouse presented himself to the posse.

The Kid asked Carlyle if he had a warrant. Carlyle replied that he did not, but informed the Kid that he was wanted for the killing of Sheriff Brady. The deputy told the Kid that the badge he was wearing was all he needed to carry out the arrest. Billy the Kid informed Carlyle that surrender was out of the question. Word of the decision was passed to the posse men waiting outside.

At midnight, a note was delivered to the Kid from a posse member stating that if Carlyle were not released in five minutes they would kill Greathouse. After that time passed, a shot was fired outside, and a moment later followed by several more. Carlyle, believing that one of the posse men had shot and killed Greathouse, began to fear for his own life. Panicked, he jumped through the front window, rolled off the porch, and fell into the snow that covered the ground. He was instantly shot down from a fusillade of gunfire.

According to William Henry Roberts's (aka Billy the Kid) recollection of the fight, after Carlyle jumped through the window,

> his own men started firing. They shot him down without any warning. . . . They thought it was me making an escape. . . . Not one of my men fired a shot. Carlyle's own posse killed him. We were going to make Carlyle ride out with us after dark. When the posse saw that Carlyle was dead, they pulled out. We waited until it got dark and then we slipped away from the ranch and got out that night.

The posse rode away without bothering to recover Carlyle's body. Two days later, every building on the Greathouse ranch was set afire and the barns, outbuildings, and corrals were burned to the ground. The arsonists were never identified.

Deputy U.S. Marshal John Hurley, along with Sheriff Kimball, continued their pursuit of Billy the Kid and his gang. By December 4, Hurley sent a report to Wild that they were unable to find the trail of the outlaws and were returning to Lincoln.

By the time the news of Carlyle's death had spread across the country, much of the citizenry grew outraged at the ongoing criminal deeds of Billy the Kid and his gang. The newspapers printed the story that the Kid was responsible for Carlyle's murder, leaving out any mention of the possibility that his own men had killed him.

On December 12, Billy the Kid had another letter drafted to Governor Lew Wallace. He explained what had happened at the Greathouse Ranch and placed the blame on Carlyle's own posse. He also wrote that Garrett had gone to Yearby's ranch and seized two mules that rightfully belonged to him, the Kid. He said Garrett claimed the mules were stolen and that he had a right to confiscate any outlaw property. The Kid also told Wallace that John Chisum was behind the efforts to capture or kill him because of the ongoing cattle rustling. The Kid denied that he was a leader of any gang.

Wallace did not respond to the Kid, but issued a notice that a $500 reward would be paid "for the delivery of Bonney alias 'The Kid' to the sheriff of Lincoln County." The reward attracted the attention of Bill Moore, a foreman on the LX Ranch in Texas. Moore was certain that he had lost dozens of horses to raids by Billy the Kid and his gang. He summoned one of his cowhands, Charles Siringo, and ordered him to take five bold men and go after the Kid. Siringo chose Big Foot Wallace, Jim East, Cal Polk, Lon Chambers, and Lee Hall. By the time Siringo and his men reached Tascosa, he was joined by six more men.

Shortly after arriving in New Mexico, Siringo, who liked to have a good time, sent his posse on to Anton Chico. He then rode to Las Vegas, New Mexico, where he squandered all of the money he had been given to purchase supplies by drinking and playing cards. He was able to acquire a few supplies on credit, and after stocking up rejoined his men, who had moved on to White Oaks.

While Siringo and his men were settling in, U.S Deputy Marshal Frank Stewart, along with a representative of some Texas cattlemen, departed Las Vegas with a posse of ten men intent on catching up with the Kid. When Garrett learned of this, he sent Barney Mason to head off Stewart and directed him and his men to go back to Las Vegas. Stewart rode to Las Vegas, but sent his men on to White Oaks.

During a meeting at White Oaks, it was agreed that the three posses would combine and that Garrett would be in charge. Garrett and Stewart, along with the riders, traveled to White Oaks to inform Siringo of their decision. At White Oaks, Garrett briefed the riders on what they could expect, and warned them that the Kid and his gang had no fear of fighting and were not afraid to fire their weapons at any and all who threatened them. Garrett selected seven men to ride with him: Frank Stewart, Lon Chambers, Lee Hall, Jim East, Tom Emory, Luis Bozeman, and Bob Williams. Siringo, along with the remainder of the riders, decided against riding out in the bitterly cold New Mexico winter and opted to stay in White Oaks drinking and gambling.

Garrett and his team left White Oaks and rode to Puerto de Luna. There, they were joined by four residents: Charles Rudolph, George Wilson, and Juan and Jose Roibal. Remaining in Puerto de Luna, Garrett sent Jose Roibal to Fort Sumner to learn something pertinent on the whereabouts of the Kid. Roibal returned December 18 and informed Garrett that the Kid was at Fort Sumner, along with Tom O'Folliard, Charlie Bowdre, Billy Wilson, Dave Rudabaugh, and Tom Pickett.

Garrett and his band of lawmen rode to the outskirts of Fort Sumner. Leaving the deputies stationed at all of the roads leading out of the town, Garrett and Mason rode in to look for the Kid. They went to the livery where the outlaws normally stabled their horses but it was empty of livestock. Garrett awoke the owner and prodded him for information. He learned that the outlaws left the previous night. Garrett summoned his men and they spent the night at the livery.

The next morning, Garrett noted that his movements were being observed by a man named Juan Gallegos. Suspicious, Garrett arrested him and learned that Gallegos had been paid by the Kid to watch the deputies and report to him on their activities. Gallegos told Garrett that the Kid was aware that he was tracking him and had ridden to the Wilcox Ranch east of town.

Under threat of arrest, Garrett forced another Fort Sumner resident, Jose Valdez, to write a note to the Kid stating that Garrett and the posse had departed Fort Sumner for Roswell. Garrett wanted the Kid to believe that it was safe to return to Fort Sumner.

Garrett learned that on previous visits to Fort Sumner, the Kid and his gang went to the old hospital east of the plaza, where Charlie Bowdre's wife would prepare supper. On the evening of December 19, Garrett and his men occupied the building. Lon Chambers and Lee Hall were left outside to guard the horses and watch for incoming riders. As they waited, Garrett noticed several Mexicans hanging around the plaza. Since it was well below freezing and there were two inches of snow on the ground, he thought this strange. Suspecting they were stationed there to warn the Kid of the presence of the lawmen, he had them all arrested and placed in the jail.

According to Garrett, Chambers burst through the door at 8:00 PM and informed him that riders were approaching. Garrett grabbed his rifle and stationed himself behind a column supporting the porch from which hung a number of harnesses. The rest of the posse positioned themselves at various locations in the darkness to greet the riders with gunfire if necessary.

Riding single-file into town came Billy the Kid and his gang. Bundled up against the cold, they rode low over their horses. Garrett claimed that, desiring a chew of tobacco, the Kid rode to the rear of the file and up to Billy Wilson to borrow one, leaving O'Folliard in the lead. How Garrett would have known such a thing is unclear, and it is quite possible that he made it up. The outlaws rode up to the hospital building suspecting nothing.

Garrett hollered out for the men to stop. O'Folliard reached for his handgun and Garrett and Chambers both fired their rifles. Garrett claimed his slug struck O'Folliard in the chest. Chambers fired at Pickett but missed. The rest of the outlaws wheeled and galloped away.

O'Folliard's horse bucked and faunched at the gunfire, but the mortally wounded man managed to hang on. The animal turned and dashed one hundred fifty yards down the road before O'Folliard could get it under control. He rode back to the hospital begging Garrett not to shoot.

Some of the posse men approached O'Folliard and helped him off the horse. He was carried inside the room and placed on a cot. Someone tore open his shirt, examined the wound, and indicated the outlaw would not live much longer. Less than an hour later, he died.

William Henry Roberts's version differed from Garrett's. Roberts stated that Bowdre and his wife were living at the hospital and that was their first stop. As they rode up to the hospital, Garrett and his men fired at them from inside the building.

> As we rode in, I took another road, thinking they might be watching for us. I scouted around to see if anybody was around town. . . . Tom and the boys rode right up to Bowdre's in the dark and Garrett and his men started shooting at my boys and hit Tom. . . . The others wheeled their horses and rode out of town. They was just a bunch of cowards, hiding out in that house like that and firing away at us. I heard the shooting from where I had ridden and then I rode on in to find the rest of the boys riding out of town as fast as they could go. I caught up with them and they told me Tom was hit and down. We cleared out of town in a blinding snowstorm.

Roberts claimed that he later learned that O'Folliard had begged for a drink of water as he lay dying on the cot, but none of the lawmen would give him one.

ELEVEN

✦✦✦

Stinking Springs

Anxious to be as far away from Garrett and his gunmen as possible, Billy the Kid and his gang galloped out of Fort Sumner toward the ranch of Thomas Wilcox. Before fleeing the town, Dave Rudabaugh's horse was shot. The wounded animal, bleeding heavily, managed to travel another few miles before dropping dead on the road. Rudabaugh rode double with Billy Wilson the rest of the way.

Fearing Garrett would organize pursuit, the outlaws stuffed their saddlebags with canned goods and other items taken from Wilcox's larder. Some of the gang were resistant to continuing their flight in the bitter cold and increasing winds. Billy the Kid suggested the same storm would likely keep Garrett in Fort Sumner and that, for the time being, they would be safe at the ranch. This turned out to be a serious mistake in strategy.

As a precaution, the Kid asked Wilcox's partner, Emanuel Brazil, to ride into town, determine what Garrett was going to do, and report back at the ranch. Unknown to the Kid, Brazil had little sympathy or concern for the plight of the outlaws. Brazil rode into Fort Sumner and located Garrett. He immediately informed the lawman that the gang was hiding out at his ranch and was expecting him back with a report on the activities of the posse. Garrett told Brazil to return to the ranch and act as if everything was normal. If the gang decided to ride away, he was to head back to Fort Sumner and let Garrett know. Around midnight on December 20, Brazil rode back into Fort Sumner and told Garrett that the gang had departed but did not tell him where they were going.

At dawn the following morning, Garrett and his posse rode up to the Wilcox ranch house. The trail of the fleeing outlaws was easily located in the snow-covered ground. Garrett led his men eastward from the Wilcox Ranch and toward Arroyo Taiban.

Earlier, Billy the Kid and his gang arrived at a rock cabin at a location known as Stinking Springs. The cabin served as a sometime residence for area cattle and sheep ranchers when working their stock in this region. The outlaws settled, unaware that Garrett and the posse were on their way to the same location.

Garrett knew of the cabin at Stinking Springs and assumed correctly that that was where the gang would set up a temporary camp. After dark on the night of December 21, Garrett halted the posse about one-half mile from the structure. Gathering his men, he told them that silence was important, that he wanted to station the men around it and surprise their quarry at first light.

After creeping up to about four hundred yards from the structure in the dark, Garrett sent half of the posse, led by Stewart, to one side of the cabin. Following Garrett, the rest of the posse covered the other side. Garrett and one other deputy stationed themselves close to the front entrance, which had no door.

From his position, Garrett noted that three horses were tied to the rafters projecting from the low roof. Since they were trailing five men, he suspected the other two horses were inside. Assuming the five outlaws were still asleep, Garrett passed word along to Stewart that they should slip into the house and capture the gang while they were still sleeping. Stewart was resistant to the plan and argued successfully for waiting until daylight. For the rest of the night, the posse men maintained their positions, wrapped in their blankets or huddled in their overcoats against the severe chill. As they waited, Garrett passed the word to each of them that the primary goal of this mission was to kill Billy the Kid. Once the Kid was dead, he said, the rest of the gang would likely surrender. Though once friends, Garrett, in his quest for success in the office of sheriff and with his eye on greater status, regarded the Kid as expendable.

In his book, Garrett claimed he was the only member of the posse that had ever seen Billy the Kid. He told the men that the Kid could be recognized by the headgear he normally wore—a wide-brimmed Mexican sombrero. Garrett said if such a man was spotted, that he would raise his rifle and that would be the signal to shoot.

As the first light of the sun appeared on the eastern horizon, piercing the fading storm clouds, the posse could hear the sounds of men stirring inside the cabin. A few moments later, one of the outlaws stepped through the doorway. He was wearing a heavy coat with the collar turned up against the cold and a sombrero pulled low over his face.

From several yards away, Garrett raised his rifle and took aim. A second later a fusillade of shots tore through the silence of the early morning, several of them striking the target. At the same time Garrett realized it was not the Kid. Charlie Bowdre, who had been carrying a nosebag of feed for one of the horses, screamed in pain and surprise and staggered back into the cabin.

A few moments passed, and Billy Wilson called out to Garrett. He said that Bowdre was dying and wanted to come out and surrender. Garrett shouted back to let him do so. According to Garrett, just before Bowdre stumbled out of the doorway, the Kid handed him a revolver and told him to shoot as many of the posse men as he could. This is likely another Garrett fantasy.

Bowdre staggered out into the snow, weapon in his hand. He spotted Garrett, managed a few lurching steps toward him, and, as Garrett wrote, collapsed into the arms of the sheriff-elect. Roberts's version of the incident is somewhat less dramatic. He stated that Bowdre fell to the ground just as he stepped outside the doorway.

The outlaws remained in the cabin, refusing to surrender to the posse. From inside, one of them reached out and untied the reins of one of the horses and was slowly leading it into the structure. Garrett reasoned that the outlaws would try to get all of the animals inside the cabin, mount up, and attempt an escape. Just as the horse reached the doorway, Garrett shot it with his rifle, killing the animal instantly. The horse dropped at the entrance, effectively blocking it. Following this, Garrett claimed he then shot through the ropes tethering the remaining mounts. Once freed, he said, they wandered away.

Shooting through the ropes by which the two remaining horses were tethered would take near superhuman marksmanship. We must assume Garrett was, conservatively speaking, at least twenty yards from the rope targets, probably more. We must also assume, with good reason, that the ropes tethering the horses were no thicker than one-quarter to three-eighths of an inch, a standard-size rope for such things. Thus, we have a shooter presumably armed with a rifle (Garrett doesn't say) with the ability to pierce a one-quarter-inch target a significant distance away, ropes connected to horses that we must take for granted were standing absolutely still. How many shots? Garrett doesn't say. And then, Garrett says, the horses simply "walked away." If the horses did indeed just walk away, they were remarkably calm only seconds after having one of their own shot dead and their tethers shot through mere inches from their heads. Garrett is asking a lot of the readers of his version of what happened at Stinking Springs. In William Henry Roberts's account of the siege at Stinking Springs, Garrett's remarkable shooting is not mentioned at all. The truth is, anyone having experience with horse behavior and target shooting would be inclined to think that Garrett was exaggerating this incident. Or lying.

Inside the rock cabin, the Kid mounted his mare and attempted to jump it over the dead horse and escape. His mount shied from the dead animal and refused to budge, so the idea was abandoned.

At some point during the morning siege, Garrett selected a few of the posse men, led them back to the Wilcox Ranch, and prepared a breakfast. On returning to Stinking Springs, he sent the remainder of the posse to get something to eat. Garrett also had extra provisions packed in the event that they were forced to prepare dinner at the site.

Later in the day, according to Garrett, Rudabaugh waved a white bandanna through an open window and invited Garrett to discuss terms of surrender. Garrett invited Rudabaugh outside. After exiting the doorway, Rudabaugh told Garrett that the men inside were willing to give up if they were allowed to live. Garrett agreed, and one by one the outlaws stepped out of the cabin. Garrett had a meal prepared for them from the provisions.

The posse loaded Bowdre's body into a wagon. Following this, the four remaining gang members, their hands and feet tied with ropes, were placed in the wagon, which was driven to Fort Sumner. In Garrett's book, he states that, on reaching the town, he picked up Bowdre's body out of the wagon and carried it to Bowdre's wife. According to Garrett, he instructed the new widow to purchase a fine suit in which to bury her late husband and send the bill to him.

The Kid, Rudabaugh, Billy Wilson, and Tom Pickett were taken to the blacksmith shop, where leg irons were fastened to their ankles and handcuffs applied. The Kid was shackled to Dave Rudabaugh. A short time later, the prisoners were loaded back into the wagon and Garrett led a procession consisting of Barney Mason, Lee Hall, Frank Stewart, James East, and Poker Tom, along with the prisoners, out onto the trail toward Las Vegas, New Mexico.

TWELVE

Prisoner Transfer

The party consisting of Billy the Kid, Dave Rudabaugh, Billy Wilson, and Tom Pickett, along with Pat Garrett and his posse, arrived at Puerto de Luna on Christmas day. Following a meal, the prisoners were herded back into the wagon and the group continued on. During the afternoon of the following day they rode into Las Vegas, New Mexico. Citizens gathered around the wagon on learning the identity of the prisoners. They were curious about Billy the Kid, but had a special interest in Dave Rudabaugh.

In 1879, Rudabaugh had been found guilty of robbing a train and breaking into sacks of U.S. mail. He was tried, convicted, and sentenced to ninety-nine years. On April 2, 1880, Rudabaugh broke out of the Las Vegas jail, killing the jailor in the process. The crowd at the wagon, on recognizing Rudabaugh, demanded he be turned over to them so he could be hanged. Garrett ignored them and delivered his prisoners straight to the jail.

The apprehending of the outlaw Billy the Kid, along with the reappearance of Dave Rudabaugh, attracted the attention of J. H. Koogler, the editor of the *Las Vegas Gazette*, who went to interview the two men. Before long, most of the area citizens were aware that the Kid, along with Dave Rudabaugh, Tom Pickett, and Billy Wilson were in the Las Vegas jail.

Up until that time, most people had heard of Billy the Kid but had no idea what he looked like or anything about his demeanor. The interview, which appeared in the December 28, 1880, issue of the *Las Vegas Gazette*, changed all of that. The Kid was described as being about five feet, eight inches tall and weighing one hundred forty pounds. He was "slightly built and lithe" and looked like a schoolboy with "silky fuzz on his upper lip, clear blue eyes . . . light hair and complexion." The only imperfection, the reporter pointed out, were his "two prominent front teeth, slightly protruding like a squirrel's teeth." This printed description of Billy the Kid would later create strong doubts about Garrett's version of forthcoming events.

The Kid was charming and engaging during his interview. Not so Rudabaugh. The reporter remarked on Rudabaugh's slovenly appearance, his poor and worn clothes and boots, and his general uncleanliness. Those who knew Rudabaugh often commented that he never took a bath and never drank water, preferring hard liquor as his liquid of choice. He was coarse, rude, and ill mannered.

Before arriving in New Mexico, Rudabaugh had had a short career robbing stagecoaches in Kansas, which served to line his pockets with gold and attract the attention of law enforcement authorities. He was eventually captured by lawman Bat Masterson, who offered him a deal: If Rudabaugh would identify the members of his gang that robbed a coach he would be set free. The outlaw agreed to do so. His partners were arrested, tried, convicted, and sent to prison and Rudabaugh sought greener pastures, eventually arriving in New Mexico and falling in with Billy the Kid.

While the Kid was being interviewed, Garrett sent his posse members home, except for Barney Mason and Frank Stewart. He told the two deputies that, having captured the outlaws, all that was left to do was to deliver them to the United States marshal at Santa Fe.

Having rested themselves and their horses, Garrett and Stewart went to pick up the prisoners only to be met with an argument relative to jurisdictional authority. Garrett agreed to transport the Kid, Rudabaugh, and Billy Wilson to Santa Fe and leave Tom Pickett in Las Vegas, explaining that the only reason he arrested Pickett was because he was with the others. A jailer was summoned to retrieve the prisoners. A short time later, only Billy the Kid and Billy Wilson were brought into the front office of the jail. The jailer handed Garrett a paper relating to the transfer of custody and told him to sign it.

Garrett demanded that Rudabaugh be included and an argument ensued. Growing angry, Garrett informed the jailer that he was a deputy United States marshal and held a higher claim to Rudabaugh, who had federal charges pending against him relative to the earlier train robbery in which mail sacks were opened and robbed. This, according to Garrett, made Rudabaugh a federal prisoner and by law, he would have to stand trial in Santa Fe before facing other charges. Garrett's argument prevailed, and a few minutes later he was escorting three chained prisoners toward the train.

On the way to the train, Garrett noticed a crowd was gathering. Because there were shouted threats relative to releasing Rudabaugh to them, Garrett recruited Mike Cosgrove, a local mail carrier, to assist him with moving the prisoners. Amid the shouts and hostility, Garrett managed to secure his prisoners in a private railroad car.

A short time later, the train began to move. Before it got far, a number of armed men climbed onto the engine, held guns on the engineer, and demanded that he pull it to a stop. Garrett grew concerned when he felt the train slow down and then stop altogether. He told Stewart that if the crowd approached the car in which the prisoners were held, they were to fire upon them. Stewart agreed.

Garrett ordered Stewart to cover one end of the car while he guarded the other. Garrett stepped out of the door and onto the iron platform and faced the crowd. Las Vegas Deputy Sheriff Desiderio Romero, followed by five men, approached the platform and started climbing up only to be stopped by Garrett. At this point, the deputy turned to the growing crowd and shouted that they were going to enter the car and seize Rudabaugh.

Garrett pulled his revolver from his holster, pointed it at the deputy, and demanded that he and his followers get off of the train. Romero paused for just a moment, then scurried to the ground. Garrett reentered the railroad car. Rudabaugh was clearly nervous that the crowd was going to have its way and that he would be carried off to the nearest tree to be lynched. Throughout this drama, the Kid remained calm. Garrett claimed that he told him and Rudabaugh that if it came to a gunfight, that he would provide them both with weapons.

Deputy United States Marshal J. F. Morley arrived and asked Garrett if he needed some help. Garrett sent him to the office of A. F. Robinson, the chief engineer for the Santa Fe Railroad, to instruct him to furnish a crew to take over the train and get them to Santa Fe. Robinson refused. Morley stomped out of the engineer's office and strode across the yard to the train. He climbed up into the engine, surveyed all of the dials, switches, and levers, and began manipulating them. A few moments later, he had the train in motion on the way down the track toward Santa Fe. On reaching their destination, the prisoners were signed over to Deputy United States Marshal Charles Conklin.

THIRTEEN

◆◆◆

The Trial

Billy the Kid, who was to play an important role in the life and legacy of Sheriff Pat Garrett, was placed in the jail at Santa Fe. Not content to wait for the unfolding of the legal process, the Kid and Rudabaugh made plans to escape. Using forks, spoons, and whatever other sharp-edged implements they could acquire, the two men undertook to dig a tunnel in order to affect a breakout. Fearing such a thing, the Santa Fe sheriff enlisted another prisoner to keep an eye on the two and report back to him.

On March 1, 1881, the spy reported to the sheriff that a breakout was on the verge of happening. The sheriff and a contingent of law-men entered the cell holding the Kid and Rudabaugh and found a tunnel under one of the beds. The Kid was devastated by the discovery.

Weeks later, Rudabaugh was transferred back to the jail at Las Vegas, where he was to be hanged. On December 3, he dug through the walls of his cell and escaped. Legend has it that Rudabaugh fled to Parral in the Mexican state of Chihuahua. There, he pursued his nefarious ways to the point where the citizens, tiring of his criminal activities and bullying manners, shot him dead, cut off his head, and mounted it on a stick in the middle of town.

For his efforts to escape, Billy the Kid was placed in solitary confine-ment. His cell was constructed of solid rock with no windows. To pass the time, and in an effort to keep from going to trial, the Kid had a letter drafted to New Mexico Governor Lew Wallace. Earlier, Wallace had promised to exonerate the Kid from his crimes if he would assist in the arrest and conviction of Colonel Dudley. The Kid kept his part of the bargain, but Wallace had not.

On March 28, Billy the Kid was transferred from his cell in Santa Fe to Mesilla, New Mexico. Here, he was scheduled to stand trial for the killing of Buckshot Roberts, Morris J. Bernstein (a Mescalero Apache Indian Reservation clerk), and Lincoln County Sheriff William Brady.

For the trial, a Mesilla home was transformed into a courthouse. The presiding judge was Warren Bristol. Billy the Kid, handcuffed, was seated before the judge. Two wooden benches were supplied for spectators. Against the wall sat the twelve jurors.

It was decided to drop the charges for the killing of Roberts and Bernstein. Both of those cases were weak and the prosecution feared the risk of an acquittal. It was determined instead to charge the Kid with the killing of Sheriff Brady and transfer the case to the territorial court.

Initially, Governor Wallace, when negotiating with the Kid, told him he would provide his own lawyer, Ira E. Leonard, to defend him. It was not to happen. The Kid was appointed a lawyer: Colonel Albert Jennings Fountain. On April 8, Fountain told the court that the defendant was ready for trial. It took only two days. In addressing the jury, Judge Bristol provided a choice of only two verdicts: Murder in the first degree, which is punishable by death, or acquittal. Then he told the jury that there existed "no evidence . . . showing that the killing of Brady is murder in any other degree than the first." Fountain objected to the statement and requested a less demanding tone in the judge's directive, but was unsuccessful.

The jury found Billy the Kid guilty of the killing of Sheriff Brady. When invited to speak before the passing of the sentence, the Kid declined. On April 15, Judge Bristol read the order that Billy the Kid was to be delivered to the custody of Lincoln County Sheriff Pat Garrett. On Friday, May 13, 1881, he was to be "hanged by the neck until his body be dead."

FOURTEEN
✦✦✦

Delivery

Sending Billy the Kid to Lincoln County for his execution set in motion the momentum that was to secure for generations the world's perception of Sheriff Pat Garrett. It can be argued that without Billy the Kid, few would even recognize the name Pat Garrett. Garrett's future reputation hinged on this young outlaw, and was to be a by-product of all that had gone before and what would transpire over the next few weeks.

The December 28 issue of the *Santa Fe New Mexican* published a glowing editorial praising "Sheriff Pat Garrett and his posse of brave men." Garrett's image and reputation as a competent lawman was making him a recognizable and popular figure in New Mexico. A vain and ego-driven man, Garrett reveled in the recognition and the subsequent handshaking and congratulations that followed.

Garrett's popularity, however, far exceeded his income and compensation. Lauded as he was, he was still finding it difficult to bring in enough money to feed his family and pay his expenses. He also required funds to pay deputies and informants. According to Garrett biographers, the sheriff was a heavy drinker. He needed money for alcohol for himself and for those whose friendships he cultivated. He was also an inveterate gambler, and it required money to support this habit. Though addicted to cards, dice, and horse races, Garrett apparently lost more often than he won, for he was often in debt to his gambling friends and others who lent him money for those pursuits.

With these things in mind, Garrett, who was in desperate need of funds, anticipated collecting the $500 reward offered by Governor Lew Wallace for the capture of Billy the Kid. This, however, proved to be more difficult than the lawman expected. Queries to the governor's office in Santa Fe were ignored. As it turned out, Wallace, fresh with the success of his first published novel, *Ben Hur*, which was released on November 12, 1880, was enjoying his own fame and was, in fact, on a book tour in the east.

Garrett and Deputy Frank Stewart filed reward claims before acting Governor W. G. Ritch. Ritch responded by stating he had no authority to remove monies from the state treasury for such things. He also questioned the legitimacy of the claims. Ritch told Garrett that the reward was for the capture and delivery of Billy the Kid to the sheriff of Lincoln County. Since Garrett would not legally assume the office of sheriff until January 1, and since he had not delivered the outlaw to the current sheriff George Kimball, he was not eligible for the reward since he had not complied with the specific conditions.

Garrett was surprised at this decision at first, then angered. Newspapers in the area were sympathetic to the lawman, stating that the reward should be paid to him since he had done the state of New Mexico a great service. They presented the case that Garrett was acting as sheriff at the time of the capture and the outlaw was legally in his custody. Public opinion in favor of Garrett began to swell, and a number of individuals began submitting contributions. At least two citizens each gave Garrett $500, and nearly two dozen others provided sums ranging from $5 to $50.

With his newfound wealth, along with his $4 per diem and six and a half cents travel allowance, Garrett suddenly found himself a man of means in the context of the time. He wasted no time in purchasing a small ranch near Eagle Creek, New Mexico. He also invested in a hotel in Lincoln. With whatever was left over, Garrett bought drinks for himself and his hangers-on and returned to gambling.

While Garrett was enjoying his new lifestyle, Billy the Kid was being readied for execution. First, however, he had to be delivered from the Mesilla jail to the courthouse at Lincoln County. Assigned to deliver the outlaw to what was intended to be his final destination were Deputy United States Marshal Robert Olinger and Deputy Sheriff Dave Woods. Accompanying them were five well-armed men: John Kinney, W. A. Lockhart, Billy Mathews, D. M. Reade, and Tom Williams.

Shackled and chained, Billy the Kid made his way from the jail to an ambulance pulled by four horses. He climbed inside and was secured to the back seat. In the driver's seat, Lockhart flicked the reins to get the horses started and the journey was underway. While some wondered at the size of the escort for only one shackled prisoner, the intent was not only to deliver the convicted outlaw to Lincoln, but to assure that no rescue attempt could succeed. Further, they were to discourage the threat of an assassination attempt.

Riding alongside and to the rear of the ambulance were Reade, Williams, and Woods. Inside the ambulance and seated next to the Kid were John Kinney and Billy Mathews. Kinney was a known cattle rustler and murderer, and Mathews was a member of the posse that had killed Tunstall. By comparison, Billy the Kid, sentenced to hang, was no worse a bad man than his guards.

On the opposite side of the ambulance sat Olinger. Olinger, who was not well liked by anyone, including other lawmen, was an obnoxious bully. He had killed men in cold blood, often by shooting them in the back. As he eyed the Kid, he fondled the barrels of his shotgun. On several occasions during the trip to Lincoln, Olinger, patting the weapon, asked the Kid if he wanted to try to make an escape.

The journey to Lincoln was uneventful. On arrival, the Kid was escorted up a set of stairs to the second floor of the Murphy-Dolan Store, which also served as the courthouse and jail for Lincoln. He was led through the sheriff's office, and into a northeast room that once served as Murphy's bedroom. A window faced north onto the main street and another faced east into the yard. On the opposite side of the stairs was another bedroom that served as an armory where rifles and pistols were stored. The outlaw was chained to the floor near a fireplace.

Once the Kid was secured, Garrett dismissed all of the posse members save for Olinger. Garrett assigned the deputy marshal to guard the outlaw while he awaited hanging. Garrett was aware of the animosity between Olinger and Billy the Kid. During the Lincoln County War the two men were on opposite sides. Olinger was convinced the Kid killed his friend Bob Beckwith during the skirmish, and he was probably correct. Olinger also claimed James Carlyle as a friend, and held a grudge against the Kid for his role in the deputy sheriff's death.

Hatred and animosity reigned between the Kid and Olinger. It seemed a confrontation was inevitable. When the animosity reached the point of no return, Garrett was nowhere around. His absence would cause him some embarrassment.

FIFTEEN

◆◆◆

Escape

Billy the Kid was chained to the courthouse floor, handcuffed, and helpless. He was constantly taunted and bullied by Olinger. The deputy told the outlaw that it was going to be a great pleasure to pull the lever to the trap door that would send him through the floor of the gallows to hang by his neck until dead.

Assisting Olinger was Deputy Sheriff J. W. Bell. Bell, unlike Olinger, was quiet and reserved, and got along well with the Kid. From time to time, Bell and the Kid would play cards or checkers.

On the morning of April 28, Olinger was sitting on a bench facing Billy the Kid. As the Kid watched, Olinger broke open his shotgun and inserted an eighteen-grain buckshot shell into each barrel. According to Garrett in his book, *The Authentic Life of Billy the Kid*, Olinger stared into the outlaw's face, chuckled, and stated, "The man who gets one of these loads will feel it." How Garrett would have known what Olinger said is a puzzle, since he was out of town in White Oaks and miles away when the alleged comment was made.

At noon, Bell arrived to guard the Kid and Olinger walked some other prisoners across the street to the Wortley Hotel for lunch. Before leaving, he placed his shotgun in the armory. He closed the door to the gun room but did not lock it.

What follows is shrouded in controversy. For generations following the events of the afternoon of April 28, the only source of information pertaining to what took place in the Murphy-Dolan Store/Lincoln County Courthouse came from the account provided by Pat Garrett in his oft-discredited book, *The Authentic Life of Billy the Kid*. Garrett claimed he got his information from Gottfried. Gauss was a former priest who worked as a handyman around the courthouse.

According to Garrett, Bell, in response to a request from Billy the Kid, escorted the outlaw down the stairs and out of the building into the corral, allegedly to use an outhouse where a pistol may have been hidden for him. Garrett wrote that Bell, on returning, "allowed the Kid to get considerably in advance." When the Kid reached the top of the stairs, said Garrett, he turned to the right, pushed through the door to the armory, and withdrew a "six-shooter." He hurried back to the landing and faced Bell, who was twelve steps below on the stairs. The Kid fired the weapon. Bell was struck under the right arm, the bullet passing through the body and exiting under the left arm. Wounded, the deputy turned and ran down the stairs and out the back door toward the corral. He dropped dead before reaching it.

Garrett claimed that, as a result of examining some marks on the wall of the stairway, "the ball had hit the wall on Bell's right, caromed, passed through his body, and buried itself in an adobe on his left."

There is, frankly, little logic attached to this event the way Garrett described it. The lawman could not possibly have had any knowledge of what transpired in the courthouse since he was not there, nor was anyone else nearby to witness what occurred. It is unlikely that Bell, a veteran and experienced lawman, would have allowed an outlaw as notorious as Billy the Kid to get so far ahead of him on returning from the outhouse. Garrett stated that Bell was "twelve steps below on the stair." And this was *after* the Kid had had time to "step through the door to the armory" and grab a revolver.

This sequence was entirely made up by Garrett. It is inconceivable that Bell, who was given charge of the most notorious outlaw in the American Southwest at the time, would have provided him a head start of that magnitude up the stairs to the second-floor landing.

Garrett's account continues. As Bell staggered down the stairs and out of the building, the Kid stepped up to the south window, where he could see the deputy fall. He slipped his hands out of the cuffs, a skill he mastered as a result of his double-jointed thumbs, and tossed them out the window at the body. Shackled at the ankles, he shuffled over to Garrett's office and seized Olinger's double-barreled shotgun. He then made his way to the east window that looked out over the yard.

Having heard the shot that killed Bell, Olinger, accompanied by Luther M. Clements, left the hotel, crossed the street, and was at the gate when Gauss yelled to him that the Kid had killed Bell. At that moment, according to Garrett, the Kid called to Olinger from the window, saying "Hello, old boy." Olinger looked up and saw the Kid aiming the shotgun at him and responded, "Yes, and he's killed me, too."

With that, the Kid pulled the trigger on the shotgun, sending a load of buckshot into Olinger's right shoulder, breast, and side. Leaving the window, he went back through the guardroom, through Garrett's office, into the hall, and out onto the balcony. From this position he could see the body of Olinger lying on the ground. According to Garrett, he aimed the shotgun once again and fired the other barrel, striking the deputy marshal again in the chest.

The Kid then broke the gun across the wooden balcony railing and threw the pieces at Olinger, allegedly stating, "That's it, damn you, you won't follow me anymore with that gun."

The Kid shuffled and slid along the floor back to the armory and grabbed two revolvers and a rifle. Calling out to Gauss, he told him to bring a file. Gauss found one and tossed it up to the Kid through the window. The Kid instructed the handyman to saddle a horse and bring it to the courthouse. When Gauss left, he proceeded to file away at the chains, eventually separating one of the links.

After some difficulty, Gauss returned with the horse. By this time, the Kid had been alone on the second floor of the courthouse for nearly an hour. Finally, he came out of the building and approached the horse, which broke away and ran toward the nearby Rio Bonito. The Kid then ordered Andrew Nimley, one of the prisoners, to retrieve the horse. This done, the Kid mounted up and rode away to the west on the road that led to Fort Stanton. Four miles out of town, he turned north and rode in the direction of Las Tablas.

How Garrett, or Gauss, seemed to possess knowledge of what took place inside the courthouse, particularly the circumstances surrounding the shooting of Bell, remain unclear. Gauss never entered the building during this time, and Garrett had departed Lincoln the previous day and was miles away in the town of White Oaks.

There is yet another version of what happened in the Lincoln County Courthouse on April 28, 1881. During an interview in 1948, William Henry Roberts, aka Billy the Kid, provided a somewhat different account of the events in the courthouse that led to his escape.

During a 1948 visit to the Lincoln County Courthouse with William V. Morrison, Roberts, who was eighty-eight years old, manifested a deep familiarity with the building as it existed in 1881, sixty-seven

years earlier. Since that time, the structure had been extensively re-
modeled both inside and out and today bears little resemblance to
what it looked like in 1881. According to blueprints that were found
in a 1938 publication, Roberts described it in precise detail, leaving
no doubt that he had been there.

The following is a paraphrasing of Roberts's version of what took
place on that afternoon. As Roberts related the events to Morrison,
tears filled his eyes as he recalled the taunting by Olinger and the fact
that he had been sentenced to hang.

Sam Corbett and his wife visited the Kid on the second floor of the
courthouse. While the deputies were otherwise occupied, Corbett, a
friend of the outlaw, whispered that he had hidden a pistol in the
latrine. The next evening, after making certain Olinger was inside the
Wortley Hotel, the Kid asked Bell to unchain him from the floor so he
could visit the privy located in the corral. At first Bell refused, explaining that he should wait until Olinger returned. Finally relenting, Bell
went to Garrett's office to retrieve the key. While he was gone, the Kid
slipped his right hand from the cuffs. As the deputy opened the lock
that held the leg shackles to the floor, the Kid swung the cuffs, striking
Bell in the back of the head several times. When Bell tumbled to the
floor, the Kid grabbed his gun and pointed it at him.

The Kid told Bell he would not hurt him if he would do as he was
told. He ordered the deputy to unlock the armory door so he could
obtain some weapons and ammunition. Afterward, he said, he would
lock Bell inside while he made his escape. Bell made his way toward
the armory while the Kid shuffled behind, his ankles still shackled
together with a fourteen-inch chain (some accounts claim it was
seventeen inches).

When Bell stepped into the hall, he made a break for the stairway.
The Kid followed as fast as he could, arriving at the landing as Bell
was making his way down the stairs.

In Roberts's words from *Billy the Kid: The Lost Interviews* (2012):

> I had no choice. I had to shoot him before he ran down and warned
> Olinger. . . . When he reached the third or fourth step, I pulled the trigger
> too quickly, and the bullet struck the wall on that side. It must have rico-
> cheted and struck him under the arm, coming out the other side. I saw
> his body jerk then he fell down the steps, dying as he fell. He staggered
> out the back door and dropped. He was dead by the time I got to him.

The Kid scuttled back upstairs, where he picked up Olinger's shotgun "where he stood it against the wall that morning." He hurried over to the window, saw Olinger crossing the street with another man. As Olinger approached the corner of the building, the Kid aimed the shotgun at him and shouted, "Look up, Bob. I want to shoot you in the face with your own buckshot. I don't want to shoot you in the back like you did other men and the Jones boy." With that, he pulled the trigger. Olinger's knees buckled and he fell backward. The Kid fired the second blast into him.

The Kid then ran downstairs and out the side door, where he saw Gauss and another man staring at Bell's body. He instructed Gauss to cut the chain linking the shackles on his ankles. Gauss obtained a saw and tried to separate a link but was unable. The Kid told him to get an ax and chop it in half. Gauss returned in a moment with one. The Kid spread his legs and placed the chain over a rock. Gauss chopped at the chain as the Kid held Bell's .44 on him. When the chain had been severed, the Kid tied each broken end to his belt with a cord so he could ride a horse.

After sending Gauss to fetch a horse, the Kid ran back upstairs and took a Winchester and scabbard along with two .44 single-action Colts, holsters, and a belt of ammunition. He ran back down the stairs and out the front of the jail, where Gauss and a young boy named Gallegos had tied the horse. He jumped into the saddle but slid off the other side. With help from the Gallegos youth, he managed to obtain a secure perch in the saddle. The Kid rode west out of Lincoln and up north into a canyon and the home of a friend, Cipio Salazar, who cut the bolts on the leg irons.

The Kid knew he had to leave New Mexico or face the prospect of being arrested again and brought to the gallows. Before doing so, however, he fled first to Fort Sumner, where he had friends who would hide him out for a time.

SIXTEEN

◆◆◆

Crime Scene Investigation, Lincoln County Courthouse

When one is faced with two widely varying accounts of the same event, a comparison study is in order. For the record, only two men were inside the courthouse during the time Billy the Kid affected his escape—Deputy Bell and the Kid. Bell did not survive to relate his version of the event, but the Kid, in the figure of William Henry Roberts, did. Garrett was miles away from the courthouse during the Kid's escape and he could only reconstruct the event one of two ways: He either relied heavily on Gottfried Gauss's version of what took place, or he made up a sequence of events out of whole cloth. Gauss was able to relate to Garrett what took place outside of the courthouse with some authority, but not inside because he was not present.

No formal investigation was conducted of the escape of Billy the Kid. Such an investigation would have been a normal police procedure. Pat Garrett apparently arrived at an explanation, one that appeared to have been concocted out of thin air, and everyone took him at his word.

It was not until 2004 when a police investigation of Billy the Kid's escape from the Lincoln County Courthouse finally took place. It was a belated investigation, to be sure, but it was, in fact, the only one that was ever conducted.

Two things about Billy the Kid's killing of Deputy Bell bothered Steve Sederwall, a former policeman and criminal investigator for the United States Government who owns and operates his own detective agency. The first was related to the statement made by Sheriff Pat Garrett that Bell was shot twelve steps down from the landing, then turned and staggered out the back door of the courthouse, where he fell dead. The second was related to a statement made by Sophie Poe, the wife of Garrett's deputy John Poe. John and Sophie took up residence in one of the rooms of the courthouse, and during their time there, Sophie complained often of the bloodstains at the *top* of the stairs on the landing.

Just after noon on August 1, 2004, Sederwall, in the company of forensic analyst Dr. Henry Lee, television producer Bill Kurtis, United States Marshal historian Dave Turk, crime scene investigator Cal Ostler, and Lincoln County Sheriff Gary Graves gathered at the Lincoln County Courthouse.

The second-floor hallway had been re-covered some time in the past with newer wooden floorboards. These were removed in order to expose the original floorboards. It was further discovered that the staircase had been replaced years earlier and was not the same one upon which Deputy Bell staggered down after being shot.

Upon the boards of the landing, o-Tolidine, a chemical presumptive test reagent for blood, was applied. Dr. Lee, using a Q-tip, swabbed the chemical reagent into the cracks between the boards. This done, he applied another chemical to the end of the Q-tip, causing it to turn blue. This precise reaction indicated "positive for blood residue."

While examining the underside of the landing at the top of the steps, brown stains from uncountable applications of mop water could be seen. Chemicals were likewise applied to this region to test for the presence of blood. Testing took place over a period of two hours. The tests showed several small areas that reacted positively to the presence of blood, both on the surface of the floorboards and under the stairwell landing where it had been carried by mop water. There is no record of any other event in the courthouse besides the beating and shooting of Deputy Bell that might have provided for an alternate source of the blood found on the landing.

What can be gleaned from the official report of this investigation of a more than century-old crime scene? There are at least two ways to gain some perspective on what transpired here in 1881.

Sederwall, with over thirty years of experience as a lawman and investigator, offers this explanation. Assuming for a moment that the Kid retrieved a handgun that allegedly was hidden by Sam Corbett in the outhouse, then it can also be assumed that he secured it in his waistband under his shirt. After leaving the outhouse, the Kid is marched back into the courthouse by Bell, the Kid leading the way. When the Kid reaches the landing at the top of the stairs, he withdraws the weapon, turns, cocks it, and points it at the deputy, who is a short distance behind him.

It is a fact that Billy the Kid and James Bell were on friendly terms. Sederwall believes the Kid did not intend to kill Bell, but take him prisoner. During an interview with Gottfried Gauss nine years after the event, the handyman stated that the Kid told him, "I'm sorry I had to kill [Bell] but I couldn't help it." John P. Meadows, in his book *Pat Garrett and Billy the Kid as I Knew Them* (2004), wrote that "what the Kid wanted to do was to make both Bell and Olinger prisoners." Author Maurice G. Fulton wrote, "The Kid and Bell had been on friendly terms and only as a last resort, in self-protection, would the Kid have shot him."

Based on investigations, experiences, and analyses of similar events, here is how Sederwall sees the incident unfolding: As the Kid turns on Bell with the handgun, Bell becomes confused, not being able to process this information fast enough. All of Bell's senses are focused on the weapon, the threat. His heart rate jumps from normal to over 140 beats per minute, he develops tunnel vision. All of this happens in the space of a heartbeat. Fight or flight mode takes over. Without making a conscious decision, Bell lunges forward and grabs the weapon held by Billy the Kid with his right hand. As his fingers wrap around the barrel and cylinder of the revolver, the Kid's muscle reaction takes over in the same manner as Bell's did. The Kid jumps backward, but is restricted by the length of chain linking his ankle shackles. He starts to fall, and in so doing, pulls the trigger.

Bell was stuck under the right arm, the ball passing through the body and coming out under the left arm. He still maintains a grip on the weapon and falls to the floor in front of the Kid.

The crime scene investigation indicated that Bell had lost a great deal of blood. This, according to Sederwall, is the blood that was detected on the landing.

There is an alternative to this scenario. William Henry Roberts stated that, after slipping one of his handcuffs, he had severely beaten Bell about the head several times. The scalp is highly vascular, that is, it contains numerous blood vessels. Head wounds, therefore, have the potential to bleed profusely. Roberts then states that Bell stepped into the hall and made a break for the stairs. The physical activity of his flight, along with the associated panic from the beating and the escape attempt, generated a massive release of adrenalin in Bell accompanied by an increased heart rate and blood pressure, causing the blood from his head wounds to flow freely. By the time Bell reached the landing at the top of the stairs, it can be reasonably assumed that blood was dripping from his head. If only for an instant, Bell paused at the landing prior to bounding down the stairs. He either saw, heard, or intuited that Billy the Kid was in pursuit only a few steps behind him, shuffling along the hallway as best as his shackles would permit. Bell paused long enough to allow a significant amount of blood from his wounds to drip onto the landing at this point, the origin of the stains detected by Dr. Henry Lee's crime scene investigation decades later. When Bell's corpse was examined by a physician a short time later in a room adjacent to a corral behind the courthouse, it was noted that he had massive head wounds.

When Garrett returned from White Oaks two days after the escape, he would have seen the head wounds on Deputy Bell, yet he never mentioned them. If he had studied the crime scene carefully, as any competent lawman would, he would have spotted the bloodstains on the landing at the *top* of the stairs, yet he never commented on them. If Sophie Poe had been annoyed by the bloodstains on the landing for two years, they surely would have been obvious to Garrett only two days after the killing. Could it be possible that Garrett neither checked on Bell nor took the time and trouble to examine the scene of the shooting?

In the final analysis, Sederwall's conclusions relative to what occurred in the Lincoln County Courthouse on April 28, 1881, have plausibility. Likewise, there is plausibility associated with the account provided by William Henry Roberts. What does not possess plausibility, however, is the account provided by the man who was the chief investigative officer at the time, Pat Garrett. Not only did Garrett not mention critical evidence at the scene of the crime, he lied about the entire incident.

Information about another post-escape event has come to light that further underscores the duplicity of which Pat Garrett was capable. Garrett was the administrator of Olinger's estate. In a sworn statement filed with the Probate Court of Lincoln County on April 21, 1883, Garrett stated that the deputy died with no money in his pockets. Garrett stated that the county owed Olinger fifty dollars but that Olinger owed him, Garrett, eighty-four dollars. Garrett then made a claim for the money. Garrett further wrote that "there is nothing remaining belonging to said estate so far as I have been able to ascertain."

Regarding Olinger's shotgun, the one the Kid used to kill him, Garrett said that because it was broken, it had no value. Further, Garrett never mentioned the handguns Olinger was wearing when he was shot. Recall that Olinger had just escorted prisoners from the courthouse to the Wortley Hotel for lunch. With all of the shooting and killing that had been taking place in Lincoln County, and with the noted outlaw Billy the Kid locked up in the courthouse, no sane lawman would undertake such a thing without being well armed. Furthermore, Olinger was known to carry two handguns. Texas Ranger J. B. Gillett, who had observed Billy the Kid being guarded by Olinger weeks earlier, had described the deputy as wearing "a brace of pistols." A brace, in this case, is defined as a pair. It was further observed by Bell Hudson in author Mary Hudson Brothers's book (*Billy the Kid: The Most Hated, the Most Loved Outlaw New Mexico Ever Produced*, 2007) that "Big Bob died with his two .45s in his hands, his beloved shotgun in two pieces across his body."

What happened to Olinger's shotgun and pistols? A letter written by Hiram Dow, an attorney with the Hervey, Dow, and Hinkle law firm in Roswell, explains that he was the executor of the estate of J. Smith Lea, who died on August 25, 1933. Dow wrote that one of Lea's possessions was a "Whitleyville ten gauge shotgun serial number 903." This was Olinger's weapon and the one used by the Kid to kill him. Dow further explained that "In 1884, Pat Garrett gave . . . Lea [the weapon] . . . out of gratitude for some favors Mr. Lea had granted Mr. Garrett."

Garrett swore to the probate court that Olinger's weapon had no value. Garrett then took possession of the shotgun. Later, however, Garrett presents the shotgun to Lea "out of gratitude for favors." It appears as though Garrett paid off a debt with the shotgun that had no value. Clearly, Garrett was aware of the historical value of the weapon.

And what of Olinger's pistols? Garrett did not mention them, but they were seen in the deputy's possession when he died. There is a possibility that they were stolen by a person or persons unknown. There is also the possibility, based on the deception pulled by Garrett relating to the shotgun, that the sheriff confiscated the weapons and kept them.

SEVENTEEN

✦✦✦

Enter John W. Poe

For better or worse, lawman John W. Poe became linked with Pat Garrett. Better in some ways, because Poe was regarded as a skilled and competent lawman and proved an invaluable asset to Garrett. On the other hand, Poe's published account of what transpired during the pursuit of Billy the Kid and the shooting of the man in Pete Maxwell's bedroom around midnight on July 14, 1881, differs markedly from Garrett's.

When Pat Garrett received the news of Billy the Kid's escape and the killing of Bell and Olinger, he was thirty miles away in the town of White Oaks. The sheriff returned immediately to Lincoln and organized a number of posses to search throughout the area for the Kid. Search parties even traveled eastward into the Panhandle of Texas, but no sign of the outlaw could be found. Rumors circulated that he had fled to Mexico.

Weeks passed, and Garrett's reputation as an effective and efficient lawman, the sheriff who had captured Billy the Kid, began to fade. When New Mexico residents spoke of the Kid now, they talked about his bravery and daring as manifested during his escape from the Lincoln County jail. The Kid, already well known, was gaining the reputation of a hero among many, the youth who was friend to and admired by the Mexicans and Anglos alike, and who had thwarted the plots and plans of the gringo lawmen.

When area citizens spoke of Garrett, he was now regarded as an individual who had been fortunate to have encountered and captured Billy the Kid, but that it was not likely to happen again. In the minds of many, Garrett was aligned with the state's political and economic power base, a structure that generally ignored the needs of the Mexicans. The Kid, who was clearly an opponent of the power structure, was held in higher regard than the sheriff. In addition to being a favorite of the Mexicans, the Kid was also looked upon with favor by many of the Anglo owners of small ranches who themselves had felt pressure from the elected officials and others who sought to determine how the county was run. Many of these men openly detested Garrett and regarded him as a willing puppet of those in authority, including large ranch owner John Chisum.

As time passed and Garrett and his posses had no success in locating the Kid, citizens interpreted this as a lack of concern by the lawman. Garrett, however, claimed that he was "constantly but quietly at work, seeking information." In spite of his assertions, and regardless of his own opinion of himself, Garrett's concerns grew and his confidence was shaken. He sensed the growing disdain for him and his efforts, and he began to resent those who were slow to align themselves with his attempts at capturing the Kid. By the first week of June, Garrett threatened to resign his post unless citizens rallied around and supported him in the execution of his duties.

Assistance came from an unexpected source. Texas Panhandle ranchers had long been plagued by cattle rustlers, and Billy the Kid was known to be part of a gang that had caused them a great deal of trouble in the past. Led by Charles Goodnight, the Texas ranchmen took up a collection to help fund the search for the Kid. They also enlisted the services of John W. Poe to assist Garrett in his efforts. Oliver Goodnight, who had charge of the monies oriented toward their effort, told Poe he could count on the cattlemen's association for whatever financial assistance he deemed necessary.

Poe had been a deputy sheriff in Wheeler County in the Panhandle of Texas and held a commission as a deputy United States marshal. Poe had also been a buffalo hunter, the marshal at Fort Griffin, Texas, and a deputy United States marshal. He was generally regarded as competent, honest, and fair. Poe traveled to White Oaks and established a headquarters. He was introduced to Garrett there in March 1881.

While Billy the Kid was in jail at Mesilla, Poe was investigating ways in which to eliminate livestock rustling operations in the area. In order to facilitate this goal, he requested a special commission from Garrett. Since the Texas cattlemen were providing the funds for this task, Garrett saw no reason not to go along. When the Kid escaped from the Lincoln County jail on April 28, Garrett gave Poe the responsibility to locate the Kid and submit a report.

A few weeks later, New Mexico governor Lew Wallace, who had returned from his book tour, posted a new reward, a five hundred dollar one for anyone who captured the Kid and delivered him to any sheriff in New Mexico. Some have regarded this offer as a slap in the face to Garrett and his futile efforts to find the outlaw. In spite of the reward, New Mexico lawmen appeared less than enthusiastic about finding the Kid, preferring to believe that he had fled to Mexico.

The truth, however, was that Billy the Kid had returned to Fort Sumner and was living on Pete Maxwell's ranch. This decision on the part of the outlaw was to set the stage for a final confrontation with Pat Garrett, a confrontation that was to forever cement the image of the lawman in the minds of the American populace. As it turned out, it was an image based on a lie.

EIGHTEEN

◆◆◆

The Shooting

Fort Sumner was the last place Garrett, or anybody else, expected Billy the Kid to be hiding out. Since he was on the run following his escape from the Lincoln County jail and the killings of Bell and Olinger, most were convinced he would be far away by now. Long a friend to the two hundred or so Mexicans who lived there, the Kid could rely on them to keep his whereabouts secret. On the other hand, his infatuation with Paulita Maxwell, the sixteen-year-old sister of Pete Maxwell, was to prove to be his undoing.

So upset was rancher Maxwell with this relationship that he sent one of his workers to White Oaks to tell John Poe that the Kid was hiding out at the ranch. As fast as he was able, Poe alerted Garrett, who at first was disbelieving. It was only after Poe's ongoing encouragement that Garrett agreed to investigate. In order to keep a problem between Maxwell and the Mexican population at his ranch from developing, Garrett and Poe made up a story that the deputy learned of the Kid's whereabouts by overhearing a conversation at White Oaks.

Garrett and Poe traveled to Roswell, where they enlisted Thomas L. McKinney. McKinney, nicknamed "Tip" or "Kip," according to various writers, found the claim of the Kid hiding out at Fort Sumner unbelievable, but agreed to go along anyway. McKinney was a cattle rancher at Seven Rivers, Texas, and a deputy U.S. marshal. On the evening of July 13, the three men set up camp at the mouth of Taiban Arroyo five miles south of Fort Sumner. The next morning, Poe, who was not known in the community, agreed to ride into town and see what he could find out.

Around 10:00 AM, Poe found himself moving about the settlement trying to learn whether or not the Kid was there. As one of only a half-dozen Anglos in the area, Poe stood out among the natives. His questions were met with suspicion, answers were vague and misleading, and he learned little. Following his visit to Fort Sumner, Poe rode seven miles north of town to the ranch of Milnor Rudolph near the small community of Sunnyside. Milnor told Poe that he had heard the Kid was in Fort Sumner but that he did not believe it. He said that the Kid was too smart to be hanging about the place when he knew lawmen were searching for him and there was a reward for his capture or killing.

When Poe rendezvoused with Garrett and McKinney that evening at the prearranged location of Punta de la Glorieta, four miles north of Fort Sumner, he related his experience to the sheriff. Garrett was inclined to abandon the search, but Poe's strong conviction that the Kid was nearby caused him to agree to pursue the original objective. It was decided that they would maintain a watch on the home of Celsa Gutiér-rez, another of the Kid's girlfriends. Celsa lived with her husband in a small apartment that was once part of the post quartermaster's store.

Garrett decided to ride into the tiny community and visit with Pete Maxwell. If anyone knew the whereabouts of the Kid, reasoned Garrett, it would be the rancher. According to Garrett, the three lawmen had ridden to a point close to Maxwell's residence when they came upon a campsite and a man named Jacobs. Here, they unsaddled, shared some coffee, and proceeded on foot to a nearby orchard.

In his book, Garrett stated that the orchard ran from the campsite "down to a row of old buildings . . . not more than sixty yards from Maxwell's house." As Garrett, Poe, and McKinney approached the houses, Garrett said they "heard the sound of voices conversing in Spanish," though they were too far away to hear words distinctly. As they watched from hiding, "a man rose from the ground, in full view, but too far away to recognize. He wore a broad-brimmed hat, a dark vest and pants, and was in his shirt sleeves." This man, claimed Garrett, was Billy the Kid. Taking a different route, the three lawmen walked to Maxwell's house.

John Poe's version of what took place differs markedly from Garrett's. Poe never mentioned Jacobs or pausing at a campsite for coffee. Poe further states that they entered the peach orchard and stationed themselves in the "gloom of the shadow of the peach trees." From this point they watched the buildings for two hours. Finally, according to Poe, Garrett stated that he felt like they weren't accomplishing anything and proposed they leave town.

In Poe's account, there is no mention of hearing voices or of observing the man Garrett claimed was Billy the Kid, or anyone else for that matter. The latter would seem to be an important point if, indeed, it ever happened. Poe also wrote that he suggested that instead of leaving town, they go to Maxwell's residence and determine what sort of pertinent information the rancher might have relative to the Kid's whereabouts. Here we have two widely varying versions of the same event by two men who claimed to have experienced it together.

Garrett stated he then led the two deputies along an alternate path and arrived at Maxwell's house from the opposite direction. The one-story structure had a porch extending across the front on the northeast side. After leaving the orchard, Garrett, Poe, and McKinney traveled a southeastern-oriented path that passed to the rear of Maxwell's house, then turned northeasterly along the side of the structure, and arrived at the porch. The premises were enclosed by a "paling fence, one side of which ran parallel to and along the edge of the street up to and across the end of the porch to the corner of the building." Leaving Poe and McKinney "at the end of the porch, about twenty feet from the door of Pete's room," Garrett entered Maxwell's room through a door left open on account of the extremely warm weather. Poe stated that he "sat on the edge of the porch in the small open gateway leading from the street onto the porch" while McKinney squatted on the outside of the fence. Poe would have been no more than twenty feet from Maxwell's open window

It is worth noting here that Poe had never seen Billy the Kid, or Pete Maxwell for that matter. Some claim that McKinney had never seen the Kid either, though others maintain that the two had known one another.

After entering Maxwell's room and finding the rancher in bed, Garrett stated that he walked to the head of it and sat down on it near the pillow and next to the rancher. Maxwell told the sheriff that the Kid had been around but he didn't know whether or not he had departed.

Thirty seconds after Garrett entered Maxwell's room, Poe stated he spotted a "man approaching me on the inside of and along the fence, some forty or fifty steps away." The man, said Poe, was bareheaded, wore only socks on his feet, and was fastening his trousers as he approached at a brisk pace. Poe initially thought the newcomer was Maxwell or some guest who was staying at the residence. According to Poe, the man was an arm's length away before he saw the deputy.

On spotting Poe, who was still seated, the newcomer allegedly pointed his six-shooter at the deputy, jumped onto the porch, and asked, "*Quien es?*" (Who is it?) Before he could answer, Poe claims, the man backed away from him toward the door of Maxwell's room.

McKinney, who had taken a seat on the edge of the porch, rose to his feet. As he did so, one of his spurs caught under the porch boards and he nearly fell. The newcomer laughed at this, then repeated "*Quien es?*" several times. Poe then stood up and took a step toward the newcomer, telling him not to be alarmed. With another step forward from Poe, the man, according to the deputy's account, "backed up into the doorway of Maxwell's room."

Poe's statement is in error. Given the layout of the Maxwell residence, the newcomer, while talking with Poe, could only have backed into the doorway that opened into the main hallway of the building. The doorway to Maxwell's room was still ten feet away on the left. Given that Poe claimed to have entered the room in which the newcomer was shot and killed, he would have had to pass through the one doorway, walk three to four steps down the hall, and then pass through a second doorway into the rancher's room. Yet his description of what happened could not possibly have happened that way. Poe was describing a situation that could not occur.

At this point, according to Poe, the man "halted for a moment, his body concealed by the thick adobe wall at the side of the doorway, from where he put his head out and asked in Spanish for the fourth or fifth time, "*Quien es?*" Poe was within a few feet of the man when he disappeared into the room.

In contrast with Poe's description of the arrival of the Kid, Garrett claimed the outlaw "sprang quickly into the door, looking back" and calling out "*Quien es?*" twice.

When no one replied, wrote Garrett, the man entered the room. Garrett said the newcomer held a revolver in his right hand and a butcher knife in his left. Poe had made no mention of a knife.

Garrett:

The Kid came towards me. Before he reached the bed, I whispered, "Who is it, Pete?" but received no reply. . . . The intruder came close to me, leaned both hands on the bed, his right hand almost touching my knee, and asked in a low tone: "Who are they, Pete?" At that same instant Maxwell whispered to me, "That's him!" Simultaneously the Kid must have seen or felt the presence of a third person at the head of the bed. He raised quickly his pistol, a self cocker, within a foot of my breast. Retreating rapidly across the room he cried: "*Quien es? Quien es?*" All this occurred in a moment. Quickly as possible I drew my revolver and fired, threw my body aside, and fired again. The second shot was useless: The Kid fell dead.

It should be pointed out that in this room Garrett was able to see the newcomer enter the door twenty feet away from where he was seated on the bed, but the man could not see Garrett, even when he was only a step away from the bed upon which the lawman was seated. This is a troubling inconsistency.

In his letter to the governor, written on July 15, wherein he informed him of the shooting, Garrett stated, "It was my desire to have been able to take him alive, but his coming upon me so suddenly and unexpectedly led me to believe that he had seen me enter the room, or had been informed by some one of the fact, and that he came there armed with pistol and knife expressly to kill me if he could." More on this statement later.

Garrett stated Maxwell dove over the foot of the bed, dragging the bedclothes with him. "I went to the door," said the sheriff, "and met Poe and McKinney there." Poe wrote that Garrett "came out, brushing against me as he passed." Maxwell then ran out of the room. Surprised, Poe and McKinney pointed their handguns at him and Maxwell cried, "Don't shoot! Don't shoot!"

Poe wrote that Garrett leaned against the wall at the side of the door and said, "That was the Kid that came in there onto me, and I think I have got him." Poe replied, "Pat, the Kid would not come to this place; you have shot the wrong man." On making this statement, Garrett appeared to be in doubt himself, but then recovered and said he was confident that the man he shot was Billy the Kid.

At this point, according to Garrett's narrative, the three lawmen entered the room and examined the body. But Deputy Poe offered a different version. He stated that the darkness within the room was such "that we were unable to see what the conditions were on the inside or what the result of the shooting had been." Following what he referred to as "forceful persuasion," Poe stated that he convinced Maxwell to bring a tallow candle. Maxwell placed the candle on the windowsill outside the room, the dim light being just enough to allow then to see a man lying stretched out on his back and clearly dead. Convinced the man on the floor was no longer a threat, the three lawmen then entered the room.

NINETEEN

+ + +

Discrepancies

To many, Garrett's problems with Billy the Kid had come to an end. The truth, however, was that they were just beginning. The subsequent inquests served only to generate doubt as to whom it was that Garrett actually shot and killed that night. And the dramatic differences between the accounts of Garrett and Poe were to further cause the curious to wonder who was telling the truth and who was lying. The closer one examines the details of this event as reported by Garrett, the more convinced one grows that he was untruthful.

To compound all of these problems with obvious contradictions and inconsistencies, there is yet a third version of what took place in Fort Sumner on July 14, 1881. William Henry Roberts, aka Billy the Kid, tells a different story.

According to Roberts, he and a friend named Barlow rode up to Jesus Silva's Fort Sumner house in the dark. Barlow was a sometime employee at Maxwell's ranch, had been described as being half-Mexican, was the same height and weight as Billy the Kid, but was dark complected and had a beard.

Earlier, the Kid had been staying at the Yerby ranch and heard from Saval Gutiérrez that Garrett was chasing him. He and Barlow hid their horses in a nearby barn and entered Silva's house through the back door. Roberts told Silva they were hungry. Silva responded that he had some beans but no meat, but informed his guests that Maxwell had killed a steer earlier and the beef was hanging on his back porch. Barlow wanted meat with his meal and Silva told him to cut some off of Maxwell's beef.

Several minutes after Barlow left, Roberts and Silva heard shooting coming from the direction of Maxwell's house. Roberts grabbed one of his revolvers and ran out but could see little in the darkness. He ran toward Maxwell's porch when he heard another gunshot and was struck in the jaw. He stumbled but kept running, a broken tooth rolling around inside his mouth. He fired his weapon where he had last seen a muzzle flash. He spotted a body lying on the back porch and knew immediately that it was Barlow.

Roberts ran toward the porch but was met by more gunfire. He was struck in the shoulder and a bullet grazed the top of his skull, rendering him semiconscious. His mouth and shoulder were bleeding and he became disoriented. He only knew he had to get away from the Maxwell house before he was killed. He stumbled down an alley. When he ran past an adobe house, he spied a door slightly open and allowing a bit of lantern light to spill out into the alley. When he reached the door, an old Mexican woman pulled him inside, closed the door, and helped him to a chair. As she wiped the blood from his face and shoulder and treated his wounds with tallow, Roberts passed out.

While Roberts was being treated by the Mexican woman, a number of Fort Sumner residents were gathering around Pete Maxwell's bedroom, some of them, according to Poe, bewailing the death of their friend, Billy the Kid. According to Poe, "Several women pleaded for permission to take charge of the body, which we allowed them to do. They carried it . . . to a carpenter shop, where it was laid out on a workbench."

Two hours before dawn, Roberts regained consciousness. While the old woman was inspecting his wounds, he noticed another woman in the room. When his vision cleared, he recognized Celsa Gutiérrez. Celsa informed him that Garrett and his men were still inside Maxwell's house and were afraid to come out in the dark, convinced that the Kid's friends would shoot them.

Celsa confirmed what the Kid had already guessed: Garrett and his posse had been lying in wait for him at Maxwell's. She also told him she sent for his friend, Frank Lobato, who was bringing two saddled horses into the alley so they could escape.

Celsa also told Roberts that Garrett was telling everyone that the Kid was dead. She said Barlow had been shot outside the house and the lawmen dragged the body into the bedroom and were telling everyone that it was that of Billy the Kid. She also stated that several men were sent by Garrett to the nearby Fort Sumner cemetery to dig a grave. She told him that she and Deluvina Maxwell cried and carried on about the Kid's death for show, but all knew that Garrett had killed the wrong man. She said Garrett would bury the body first thing in the morning.

By this time, Lobato had arrived with the horses and the two men mounted up and rode away.

TWENTY

◆◆◆

Contradictions

When Deputy John Poe visited earlier with Milnor Rudolph at his ranch, he was unaware that his host was a friend to Billy the Kid. Poe reported that Rudoph appeared nervous, and it is likely that he was so because he knew exactly where the Kid was hiding and was likely intent on protecting him. Though Poe presumed Rudolph was withholding information, writer Alfred Adler suggests, "Rudolph and the natives cannot be dissociated from the other inhabitants of Fort Sumner who were . . . eager to hide the Kid."

Garrett unilaterally decided that the man he had killed was Billy the Kid. What a wonderful opportunity, continued Adler, for the coroner's jury to continue the ruse, and to continue to protect their friend Billy by making his death official.

The truth is, the only surviving witnesses to the shooting of the man in Pete Maxwell's bedroom were Garrett and Maxwell. Deputies Poe and McKinney were within a few feet of the room but were participants only in the events that followed. At the time, Maxwell contributed very little relative to explaining what happened in his bedroom. McKinney likewise remained silent about the events of that night for most of his life, but years later made comments that cast doubt on the versions of what happened that had been offered by Garrett and Poe.

Ultimately, all that is known, or at least what has been repeated over and over again by historians, is what was written by Garrett in *Authentic Life* and by Poe in *The Death of Billy the Kid*. Even a cursory examination of the accounts presented in these two publications, however, reveals some contradictions above and beyond those already discussed.

Garrett writes that shortly after arriving at Maxwell's estate, he and the deputies spotted a man in the orchard that he claims was Billy the Kid. He never explains, however, how he knew it to be so. Garrett then writes, "The Kid by me unrecognized." Did Garrett recognize the Kid or not? He contradicts himself. It is easy for one to suspect that Garrett, whose veracity by this time is easily questioned, was making an attempt to portray the danger as being a bit greater than it actually was. Could it be that the incident never happened? Could it be that Garrett made it up? It would seem so.

Deputy Poe, on the other hand, never mentioned this incident, one that any investigator would consider important if, in fact, it happened at all. If Garrett's account was true, then such a dramatic moment would have been recalled and noted by Poe. It is more likely that it never happened.

Garrett based his "recognition" on the mode of apparel worn by the subject, but the young man who entered Maxwell's bedroom a short time later was clothed in completely different garb.

There are several more bothersome elements to these two different versions of what allegedly took place.

First, Garrett's statement that he stepped into Maxwell's room through the open door, "left open on account of the extremely warm weather," deserves comment. Fort Sumner, located in east-central New Mexico, would indeed be warm in the middle of July. However, anyone who had acquired any experience living in such a place, would never leave his or her door open in the middle of the night. This region of Fort Sumner is populated with skunks and rattlesnakes—both nocturnal animals—that would and could easily enter the open door of a domicile. Other potentially harmful creatures that populate this area that might be kept at bay with a closed door include scorpions and centipedes. In the days before air-conditioning, people who lived in environments such as this would leave their windows open to catch a breeze, but never a door. Garrett's mention of the open door is suspicious.

Second, in his book Garrett claimed the newcomer arrived at Maxwell's house in his stocking feet. To get to the house, the man was forced to traverse bare ground littered with gravel, thorns, thistles, burrs, stickers, and other piercing objects, not to mention the aforementioned rattlesnakes and scorpions that dwelled there. No sane man would do such a thing. Furthermore, socks were considered a kind of a luxury in those days; many a cowhand went without them. It is hard to believe that one would risk the wear and tear on a pair of socks, as well as on his own feet, by walking across such nasty ground.

These two contentions by Garrett carry with them no logic whatsoever. Experience and analysis provide for no other conclusion than that they could not have happened the way he described them, if, in fact, they happened at all.

Garrett claimed that the newcomer entered Maxwell's bedroom "and came close to me, leaned both hands on the bed, his right hand almost touching my knee," then he asked Maxwell who those men were outside. Garrett said Maxwell "whispered to me, 'That's him!'" The Kid apparently could not see Garrett on the bed with Maxwell, but Garrett said he could see the Kid as he "came towards me." Why is it that one man could see in the room and the other could not?

The account Garrett presented in his book differs from what he reported to the governor in his letter of July 15, a portion of which was quoted in the previous chapter. In his letter, Garrett stated that he believed the Kid had seen him enter Maxwell's bedroom, or had been informed that the sheriff was there, and that the Kid came "armed with pistol and knife expressly to kill me."

If what Garrett wrote had any element of truth to it, that the Kid arrived at Maxwell's room "expressly" to kill him, why then would the Kid, who was aware that Garrett and his deputies were searching for him and would have been on the alert for the sheriff or any other lawmen, stumble into the dark bedroom asking Maxwell who was outside? Garrett, in fact, contradicts himself. Did Garrett lie about the encounter with the intruder in the bedroom or about the notion that the Kid arrived to kill him? Or did he lie about both?

Garrett then stated that he drew his "revolver and fired, threw my body aside, and fired again." This statement represents additional troubling inconsistencies. Given the proximity of Maxwell's open bedroom window to the front porch, the two men seated on the bed were likely no more than twenty feet away from where Poe, McKinney, and the newcomer were speaking outside the open window. Garrett must have heard them for he even said "McKinney, who was seated, rose to his feet. As he did so, one of his spurs caught under the porch and he nearly fell." The newcomer laughed at this and then said "*Quien es?*" several times. Poe then stepped up and told the newcomer not to be alarmed.

It is inconceivable that Garrett could not have heard the three men talking as well as the commotion, however slight, of McKinney tripping, his spurs surely jingling as he did so. Hearing the arrival of the newcomer, Garrett, suspecting Billy the Kid was in the neighborhood and wanted to kill him, would not have waited for the newcomer to enter the room, place his hands on the bed, and ask Maxwell a question before pulling his revolver. An experienced lawman would never allow such a thing to happen. Garrett lied about this episode.

Garrett also lied when he wrote that he drew his revolver and fired, "threw my body aside, and fired again." In order for this statement to be true, Garrett, in throwing his body aside, would have had to have made a giant leap from the bed to the opposite side of the room, a distance of no less than fifteen feet, for his second bullet perforated the washstand at an angle that indicated he was on his knees in the far corner of the room when he fired. Garrett wrote that he, Poe, and McKinney "searched long and faithfully—found both my bullet marks and none other." Where could he have found them? If he found the bullet holes in the washstand, he surely would not have admitted it came from his gun, for it proved his initial explanation of what happened was untrue. And where was the second "mark?" Did Garrett suggest the bullet that struck the newcomer in the chest passed through his body and punctured the wall behind him?

It is important to analyze Garrett's shooting of the newcomer and subsequent behavior in greater detail and from the standpoint of an expert experienced with such things. David A. Brewer, a Homeland Security and senior law enforcement specialist for the Federal Law Enforcement Training Center in Artesia, New Mexico, is well qualified to assess such behavior.

According to Brewer, stressful situations such as a shooting generate increases in heart rates to levels exceeding 140 beats per minute. In response, the brain tells the muscles of the body to reduce blood flow to the fine motor skills groups and increase it to the large motor skills groups. This enables the individual to engage the "fight or flight" mode.

In many cases, other involuntary responses occur, including perceptual narrowing, loss of peripheral vision, senses appearing in black and white, auditory occlusion, involuntary tracking of threats, increased blood pressure, loss of fine motor skills, and loss of one's ability to think clearly.

A second area of research indicates that the body reacts to certain stimuli that can cause it to flinch or react involuntarily. The three common stimuli are fear or sudden surprise, push-pull reflex, and imbalance. An example of fear or sudden surprise reflex would be a police officer pursuing a suspect in a dark building and having the suspect suddenly jump out from a hiding place causing a startle effect. If the officer had his weapon in single-action mode (cocked trigger), he would more than likely discharge his weapon by jerking the trigger out of a reflex action.

An example of imbalance occurs when a police officer is pursuing a suspect with his weapon in hand and suddenly loses balance. A reflex action occurs in the gun hand that increases the pressure on the trigger finger, thus causing the accidental discharge of the weapon.

It is clear that Brewer's descriptions fit the sequence of events in which Pat Garrett was involved as depicted in the prologue to this book. Garrett, who is already on edge as a result of attempting to arrest or kill the outlaw Billy the Kid around midnight at one of the Kid's known haunts, is in a stressful situation. Garrett is then startled by the newcomer entering Maxwell's bedroom, which further causes an increase in heart rate and blood pressure, thus engaging the fight or flight mode.

Garrett responded and reacted to the newcomer as a result of the fear Brewer described, fear that caused the lawman to raise his revolver and shoot the intruder, a reflex action. Garrett then states he "threw my body aside and fired again." Referring again to the sequence of events in the prologue to this book, Garrett not only threw his body aside, but also scrambled around in an attempt to flee from the room. From a panicked, and unbalanced, position on the floor, he fired his second shot. Because he was still blinded by the flash of the first shot and unable to perceive clearly where he was in the room or what he was shooting at, he hit the washstand. (See appendix II.)

After Poe suggested to Garrett that he might have killed the wrong man, the sheriff replied that he did not err and that he "knew the Kid's voice too well to be mistaken." According to Garrett, however, the man who entered Maxwell's bedroom was whispering or speaking in low tones. When Garrett claimed he knew the Kid's voice, did he mean his whisper? In spite of Garrett's claimed intimacy with the Kid's voice, he still had to ask Maxwell who the newcomer was. On the subject of the Kid's voice, Garrett once again contradicts himself and erodes his credibility even further.

Garrett stated that just before the shooting, "a man sprang quickly into the door" to Maxwell's room. By contrast, Poe wrote that the stranger "backed into the doorway . . . halted for a moment . . . put out his head and asked in Spanish for the fourth or fifth time who I was. I was within a few feet of him when he disappeared into the room." Here we have two remarkably different versions of the same event from two men who allegedly witnessed it together.

Maxwell's bedroom was not very large—twenty feet by twenty feet—and the porch on which the newcomer was standing was just outside the door to the building. The two men inside the room—Garrett and Maxwell—one or both of them nervous and alert would certainly have been aware of the arrival of a stranger as a result of the conversation taking place between him and Deputy Poe only a few feet away. It remains difficult to believe that Garrett and Maxwell were not aware of the arrival of the newcomer who was, at the time, speaking to Poe and backing into the doorway. Yet, Garrett insisted that the man "sprang quickly" into the room. Which was it: Did he back in, or did he spring? These actions cannot be confused with each other. And into which doorway? The one that led directly into Maxwell's room or the one that opened into the building? It remains unclear.

Furthermore, why would a man who manifested nervousness at the presence of the two deputies outside spring into a dark room without knowing who was inside? There is no sense or logic associated with the reaction, or with Garrett's explanation. Either Garrett or Poe, or both, must be mistaken.

Garrett stated that it was so dark in Maxwell' bedroom that the intruder came within inches, close enough to touch, yet the sheriff could not see him. In spite of that, Garrett claimed that, only a moment earlier, he could see a butcher knife and a pistol in the newcomer's hands. On the other hand, Maxwell's night vision was apparently keen enough, according to Garrett, to identify the newcomer as the Kid to the sheriff. Records show that on that night in 1881, the sky was clear and the waning moon was at 87 percent of full, bathing the landscape outside in a brightness sufficient to identify objects several yards away. Assuming Maxwell had his windows open, it would be easy to assume a level of brightness was also available to the room. In *Billy the Kid: A Handbook* (1989), author Jon Tuska refers to this entire sequence as a Garrett fantasy.

No one can seem to agree on how light or dark the room was. According to Garrett's narrative, the three lawman, after a moment, entered Maxwell's room together and examined the body. Yet Poe stated that the darkness within the room was such that "we were unable to see what the conditions were on the inside or what the result of the shooting had been." Another contradiction.

There were other significant discrepancies and contradictions in the published writings of Garrett and Poe. In *Authentic Life*, Garrett states that he learned that the Kid was in the area as a result of a letter that had been written to him by a rancher named Brazel, who claimed to be hiding from the outlaw. In his book, Poe writes that it was *he* who learned about the Kid's whereabouts from a Texas man and that he, Poe, communicated that information to Garrett, who was reluctant to believe him. Once again, two entirely different versions of the same event exist. Somebody is lying.

Even the similarities in the accounts of the two men are troublesome. For instance, in *Authentic Life*, Garrett states that he had not blundered, that he "knew the Kid's voice too well to be mistaken." This is an odd statement coming only moments after the sheriff had to ask Maxwell who the newcomer was. In *The Death of Billy the Kid* published thirty-eight years later, Poe, after telling Garrett that he shot the wrong man, quotes the sheriff as responding, "I'm sure that was him, for I know his voice too well to be mistaken."

Poe's manuscript on the death of the Kid, originally published in *Wide World Magazine* and coming nearly four decades after the shooting, seemed quite precise regarding Garrett's statement from that long-ago night. Was Poe's memory so keen that he remembered the sheriff's exact words? Or is it more likely that his recollections of that night were influenced by his own reading of Garrett's account?

And why, after disagreeing with Garrett that night on who was actually killed, did Poe finally come around to supporting the sheriff's version? The answer may lie in the fact that both men were Masons and were committed to a fraternal bond relative to collaborating their stories. This explanation has been provided by a number of Masons.

Yet another troubling aspect of the shooting as described by Garrett relates to the two deputies who were standing nearby as the action was taking place. As close to Maxwell's room as they were, Poe and McKinney could not have helped but hear the two shots fired by Garrett. They were no more than twenty feet away and probably much closer. It can also be assumed that from the time of Garrett's first shot followed by his subsequent fumbling and panicked search for the door until he finally raced out of the building, a total of about thirty seconds had elapsed. While this was going on, what could the two deputies have been doing? Steve Sederwall, as well as others with professional law enforcement experience, have explained that at the sound of the first shot the two deputies would have pulled their weapons and started for the room. They would *not* have left their boss alone with and at the mercy of the presumably armed desperado. Instead, Poe and McKinney, according to Garrett's version of the event, merely stood outside of the building apparently waiting for the sheriff to emerge. Every law enforcement officer to whom this situation was described insisted the entire sequence as described by Garrett was a lie.

There are even more inconsistencies to be found when Poe's published account is compared with those of others. According to Poe, when he peered into Maxwell's room, he "saw a man lying on his back, dead, in the middle of the room." Yet Jesus Silva tells Miguel Antonio Otero in *The Real Billy the Kid: With New Light on the Lincoln County War* that when he entered Maxwell's bedroom moments after the shooting, the dead man was "stretched out, face down." Silva claimed that after entering the room, "we turned him over."

Poe also claims that the body was removed from the room a "short time after the shooting" and carried "across the yard to a carpenter shop, where it was laid out on a workbench, the women placing lighted candles around it according to their ideas of properly conducting a wake for the dead."

In stark contradiction to Poe is Charles Frederick Rudulph, in his book *Los Billitos: The Story of Billy the Kid and His Gang* (1980), who writes that Milnor Rudolph conducted the proceedings of the coroner's jury on the morning of July 15 in Pete Maxwell's bedroom with the body still lying on the floor. In *Billy the Kid: A Short and Violent Life*, author Utley also writes that the body was removed the day following the killing and after the Rudolph-conducted inquest. Once again, radically different versions of the same event. Did all of these people have different experiences, or was somebody, or everybody, lying, or at the very least misrepresenting what actually happened?

Many years later, Pete Maxwell became acquainted with Roswell-area rancher Bud Avants. Maxwell told Avants that he wanted to tell him something but made him promise not to repeat it as long as he, Maxwell, was alive. Maxwell told Avants, "You can put it in the Bible if you want to, because it's the truth."

Maxwell told Avants that Pat Garrett did not kill Billy the Kid. He explained that there was little light in the bedroom and that he and

Garrett were in the dark when the intruder stepped through the door. Maxwell said the newcomer sensed someone else was in the room and asked, *"Quien es?"* In stark contrast to Garrett's version of what happened, Maxwell said the sheriff simply raised his revolver and fired, killing the man with a shot through the chest. Later, when a match was struck and the body examined, they "saw that it was not the Kid."

Maxwell went on to say that Garrett was "pretty well shook up, as he didn't want it said that he had killed the wrong man." The man who was killed, said Maxwell, was a Mexican. Maxwell agreed to keep quiet about the mistake.

Then there is the question of the gun. Both Garrett and Poe claimed that the man who entered Maxwell's bedroom carried a .41 caliber pistol in his right hand and a butcher knife in his left. According to author Donald Cline, Poe later claimed the pistol was a .38 Colt double-action and he never saw it until Garrett brought it from the room of Celsa Gutiérrez. If the stranger were the Kid, why was he carrying a caliber of pistol he was never known to use? When the Kid escaped from the Lincoln County jail, he took two .44s from the armory, his favored handguns.

Did the man Garrett claimed to be the Kid carry a gun at all? In *Violence in Lincoln County* (1957), author William H. Keleher writes that the person who walked into Maxwell's bedroom had only a knife. Utley writes that a "belief persists that Billy was armed only with a butcher knife" and that "Garrett and Poe had reason to want the world to believe that Billy carried a pistol." In *History of the Lincoln County War* (1968), Maurice G. Fulton states that the man carried only a butcher knife. Former New Mexico governor Miguel Otero, who interviewed Fort Sumner residents Francisco Lobato, Jesus Silva, and Deluvina Maxwell, learned that the man shot by Garrett did not have a pistol in his possession when he was killed.

Was a pistol placed in the right hand of the dead man after the shooting to make it appear he was armed? Garrett, who had high political ambitions, must have realized that shooting an unarmed man would not look good. If indeed a pistol were provided, a so-called drop weapon, whoever did so made the mistake and gave the dead man a gun Billy the Kid never used.

There is more. There is no agreement on whether two shots were fired or three, and there is disagreement on whether the body of the slain man was inside or outside the room. Author Frederick Nolan contends that *Authentic Life* was written to make Garrett look good, that it was necessary to "exaggerate the Kid's recklessness, his gun fighting skills, his murderous nature," all designed to "present Garrett as a courageous lawman."

Odelia Bernice Finley Johnson, great-granddaughter of Lucien B. Maxwell, once related an account by Deluvina Maxwell, who was one of Pete Maxwell's workers, that conflicts with the positions taken by Garrett and Poe. According to Johnson, Garrett and the two deputies were afraid to enter the room after the shooting, believing that the stranger was only wounded and lying in wait for them. After roundly cursing Garrett, Deluvina grabbed a candle and walked into the bedroom—perhaps the first to do so—to render aid to the victim.

The question *"Quien es?"* asked of Poe, McKinney, and Maxwell by the stranger provides another provocative element. William Henry Roberts maintained that the man who went into Maxwell's room was a friend who went by the name Billy Barlow. Author C. L. Sonnichsen learned from Roberts that Barlow was half-Mexican. If Billy the Kid, an Anglo, had encountered Poe and McKinney, two Anglo lawmen, outside of Maxwell's building, would he not have addressed them in English? On entering Maxwell's bedroom and encountering the rancher who could speak English, why would he pose a question in Spanish? It is more likely that a person of Mexican heritage would be more inclined to speak Spanish than English.

More important, if the man who approached Maxwell's room that night was the Kid, living on the run, sentenced to hang, and hiding out because of the posted reward for his capture or death, he would hardly have paused long enough to ask Poe and McKinney a question. The Kid had been informed that a posse was on his trail and that several citizens of Fort Sumner had alerted him to the presence of Garrett. The Kid would surely have been more careful than to have simply blundered up to Maxwell's house on a night that he knew there were lawmen looking for him. To believe otherwise defies common sense. Even Poe told Garrett, "The Kid would not come to this place."

The fugitive, having already killed Olinger and Bell, would most likely have avoided the confrontation. If confrontation were inevitable, the Kid would have been more inclined to shoot the two deputies than ask them questions. According to Poe, there was a full moon (actually 87 percent of full), light enough for anyone to see that the two men hanging around outside of Maxwell's bedroom were not Fort Sumner residents. Strangers were certainly enough to arouse the suspicion of a man wanted for killing law enforcement officers who knew he was being pursued; unless, of course, the man who went to Maxwell's room was not Billy the Kid.

If Billy the Kid had approached the house that night, as Garrett claimed, McKinney might have recognized him because there is evidence that the two men were acquainted. In the light of the nearly full moon, McKinney could see that the newcomer was not the Kid so he simply let him pass. Why, then, didn't McKinney say anything when Garrett was intent on identifying the dead man as the outlaw? McKinney, relatively young and inexperienced, worked for Garrett. Perhaps he only did what he was told to do.

There exists still another version of the shooting. In *Alias Billy the Kid*, Sonnichsen provides the following account, taken from an April 15, 1944, interview with Jack Fountain, a son of Colonel Albert J. Fountain. Jack Fountain rode with Garrett for weeks at a time, and on one occasion the now-former sheriff of Lincoln County told him what he called "the straight of Billy's death." It took some time for Garrett to come to the point, but he finally said he would tell the true story.

When Billy the Kid got away after killing Bell and Olinger, Garrett explained, the county commissioners assigned him to bring in the young outlaw. Garrett learned that the Kid was in Fort Sumner. By the time Garrett and his deputies arrived at Maxwell's and tied their horses, the Kid had just come in off the range and was looking for something to eat. He was told Maxwell had just killed a steer. According to Fountain, Garrett said the beef was hanging in a little outer room from one of the vigas. "There was a candle and materials for making a light in the niche in the wall. He made a light and held it up while he cut. I was in Pete's room talking. Billy heard something and asked who was there. Pete said, 'Nobody.' I looked out at a perfect target—Billy lighting himself up with the candle. At first I was just going to wing him. Then I thought if he ever got to his gun it was him or me. My conscience bothers me about it now."

If Fountain's account is true it explains the presence of a body outside of the room as some have reported. Is Fountain credible? There is no reason to suspect he is any less credible than Pat Garrett.

Given the evidence available for determining what happened in Maxwell's bedroom that night, it is obvious there is no consensus and there is little to support the notion that Garrett was telling the truth about anything. Garrett's "recital of circumstances surrounding the Kid's death on the night of July 14, 1881," according to Nolan, "may have been the biggest lie of all."

The published historical accounts of the shooting appear rife with inconsistencies and contradictions and, according to Nolan, "lies." Rather than clearing up the problem, they simply add to the confusion. How could so many people have so many different versions of what occurred that night, with most of them differing from Garrett's? None of the so-called facts related to the death of Billy the Kid at the hands of Pat Garrett have ever been supported by logical and defensible evidence. By contrast, the account provided by William Henry Roberts of what occurred that night is more consistent and makes as much sense as Garrett's or more. While Garrett's version of the events is fraught with contradiction and inconsistencies, Roberts has never been proven wrong.

The truth is, there is very little corroborative, logical evidence on which to base the claim that Billy the Kid was shot and killed by Sheriff Pat Garrett on the night of July 14, 1881. The fact that Garrett contradicts himself and is contradicted by others again and again relative to the event leaves numerous questions about what happened that night.

There is more to ponder. For a number of reasons, it was in the best interest of Pat Garrett to maintain that the man he killed was Billy the Kid. If he were able to get away with it, he would avoid being charged with a serious mistake—killing an innocent man. If Garrett could claim that the Kid died at his hands, he would garner prestige for bringing an end to the Southwest's most famous outlaw. In addition, he would receive a significant amount of reward money.

Desperate, Garrett may have presumed that the Kid, knowing there was a price on his head and that he was destined to hang if captured, would leave the country for good. That is precisely what Roberts did.

Some have suggested that there might have been a conspiracy. Could there have been collusion between Garrett and Poe to fabricate a story about the death of an armed and dangerous Billy the Kid? Given the fraternal allegiance between the two men, as well as being fellow lawmen, the possibility cannot be ruled out. It is a documented fact that lawmen lie all the time to protect one another.

Or, could Garrett and Poe have sincerely believed that the man that was killed that night was the Kid when the victim may actually have been Barlow? Poe had never seen the Kid, so he would have agreed to anything Garrett told him.

According to Roberts, he and Barlow once worked together on a ranch near Muleshoe, Texas. He doubted that Barlow was his real name. He said his friend was slightly younger, about the same size, had dark hair and a beard. Barlow was a heavy drinker and had been imbibing on the night of July 14.

In 1948, an old man named Manuel Taylor related a Billy the Kid incident to L. S. Cardwell of Las Cruces, New Mexico. Taylor claimed that he knew the Kid well during the time the two were in Silver City from 1868 to 1871. Taylor maintained that the man shot by Garrett was not the Kid but a young cattle detective from somewhere in the east. Taylor also claimed that he ran into the Kid in Guadalajara, Mexico, in 1914, where they both recognized one another. According to Sonnichsen, Taylor was well known in his hometown of Hillsboro, New Mexico, and was reported to be "truthful and trustworthy."

And what of Deputy McKinney? If there were a plot to convince others that the Kid was shot and killed by Garrett, did McKinney go along with it? Tacitly, he did so by remaining quiet for a long time. McKinney, however, was not silent forever.

In a letter to William Waters, dated June 29, 1955, paralegal investigator William V. Morrison provides some insight into McKinney's subsequent role in the events. In later years, according to a McKinney cousin, the lawman stated to relatives that he, McKinney, killed the man in Maxwell's bedroom "by mistake and the Kid got away."

In the same letter, Morrison also relates a portion of a telephone conversation he had with a grandson of McKinney. The grandson stated that the deputy "contended the man was killed on the outside and the Kid got away." This bit of information, if true, supports Roberts's version of the event and his mention of seeing a body lying on the porch.

Another incident related in the same letter dealt with a telephone call received by Ted Andress, the president of the law firm that Morrison represented at the time of Roberts's appeal for a pardon in 1949. Andress stated that the call came from a man who said that he was willing to testify that "McKinney had reminded Garrett in a saloon in Uvalde, Texas, that Garrett should know that he had not killed anyone on that night."

The numerous accounts of the shooting in Maxwell's bedroom on July 14, 1881, are not consistent, not even the ones from those who were present and involved. Analysis of all of the accounts leads to the conclusion that at least one person, and probably more, is lying. Garrett's words bear the unmistakable mark of fabrication.

Even Leon Metz, an avowed Garrett apologist, has written that almost "from the moment that Garrett's pistol cracked in Pete Maxwell's
bedroom and Billy toppled to the floor, controversy has surrounded
the killing." And in a surprise statement, on being confronted with
the ponderous evidence of contradiction and lying, author Metz even
acknowledged that "There is enough evidence, indeed, to make one
wonder whether Garrett actually killed [Billy the Kid] at all."

Given a complete and in-depth, logical analysis of all of the available evidence related to the shooting in Maxwell's bedroom, it is impossible to embrace the status quo version. In truth, the only inescapable conclusions are:

1. While it is clear that someone was shot and killed that night,
   there exists not a shred of evidence to prove that it was the outlaw
   Billy the Kid. All one has for this is Garrett's word.
2. Pat Garrett lied about the entire incident.

TWENTY-ONE

❖❖❖

The Mystery of the Inquests

As if Pat Garrett's actions and interpretations of the alleged shooting and killing of the outlaw Billy the Kid were not confusing enough, his role with regard to the subsequent inquests can be considered even more bizarre. There was not one single inquest, as is common with a death, but three.

While it was still dark following the shooting of the man who entered Maxwell's bedroom, A. P. Anaya and a friend "were called as members of the coroner's jury the night the Kid was killed, and this jury wrote out a verdict stating simply that the Kid had come to his death as a result of a wound from a gun at the hands of Pat Garrett, officer." Anaya, who went on to become a member of the New Mexico state legislature, made the comment to George Fitzpatrick, the editor of *New Mexico* magazine. Whether Anaya and the friend were the only members of the jury is not clear. Nor is it clear that they actually saw the body of the slain man. Anaya then claimed that this verdict was lost and that Pat Garrett and Manuel Abreau, his brother-in-law, drafted a second one, a "more flowery one for filing."

According to published history, Garrett sent Justice of the Peace Alejandro Segura to summon Milnor Rudolph and give him the responsibility of assembling a coroner's jury and assume the role of foreman. Rudolph rode into Fort Sumner on the morning of July 15, a few hours following the deliberations of the first coroner's jury. He found the citizens excited, confused, and angry. He found Garrett, Poe, and McKinney barricaded in Maxwell's bedroom, concerned they would be attacked by the angry mob of Billy the Kid sympathizers that had gathered outside of the house.

Rudolph recruited five men and arranged a meeting in Maxwell's bedroom where, according to Charles Frederick Rudulph, a descendant of Minor's but who spelled the name differently, the body still lay on the floor. In his book, Garrett claimed that the body had been taken to a nearby carpenter shop for a wake shortly after the shooting. It is improbable that the body was reclaimed from the wake and repositioned on the floor. What is probable is that Garrett was not telling the truth about this event.

It was reported that Rudolph and the jurymen listened to versions of the shooting by Garrett and Maxwell. Rudolph then wrote out the report and the jurors signed it or made their mark. The jury concluded that "William Bonney was killed by a shot on the left breast in the region of the heart, fired from a pistol in the hand of Patrick F. Garrett, and our verdict is that the act of the said Garrett was justifiable homicide, and we are unanimous in the opinion that the gratitude of the whole community is due to the said Garrett and that he deserves to be rewarded."

For reasons never explained, this coroner's jury report was never entered into the official records of San Miguel County. In fact, Justice Segura never made an entry regarding the report in his own books. Even more perplexing, and stunning, is the fact that the signers of the second report either misspelled their names, or Rudolph misspelled them. Furthermore, the members of the second coroner's jury were different from those who served on the first. The signers of the second report (original spelling included here) were M. Rudolph, President, Anton Sabedra [sic], Pedro Anto [sic] Lucero, Jose X Silba [sic], Sabal X Gutiérrez, and Lorenzo X Jaramillo.

Could it be that the second coroner's report was coerced, or a forgery, one arranged for and perhaps dictated by Garrett himself? To further compound the growing confusion surrounding the dead man and the role of Garrett, E. B. Mann, in his book *Guns and Gunfighters*, reported that only three of the witnesses on the second jury identified the body and that one of them later stated that it was not Billy the Kid but another person. Whether anyone associated with the second coroner's report ever actually saw the body remains uncertain.

And then the second report, like the first, went missing. To this day no one knows what happened to either of them. Anaya stated the first was lost. Garrett claimed he filed the second with the district attorney of the First Judicial District in Las Vegas, the San Miguel County seat. Billy the Kid researcher Donald R. Lavash maintains that "the coroner's report is properly considered a death certificate and is on file at the New Mexico State Records Center and Archives in Santa Fe." Why Lavash would make such a statement is unclear when no such

document was ever located there and no one has ever been able to find
it anywhere. On November 21, 1949, Alicia Romero, New Mexico's
Secretary of State, responded to an inquiry from William V. Morrison,
stating that there "is no record in this office of any coroner's verdict
in the purported death of William H. Bonny [*sic*]."

According to an August 14, 1951, letter to Morrison from Fourth
Judicial District attorney Jose E. Armijo, the coroner's report "is not
now, and never has been, among the records in this office." That same
month, however, the *El Paso Times* reported that writer and self-
proclaimed Lincoln County historian Maurice G. Fulton claimed he
had in his possession "a photostatic copy" of the coroner's report,
though he never mentioned whether it was the first or the second.
Fulton discovered the report, he said, "while searching the file dealing
with the reward for the killing of Billy the Kid . . . among the records
of the office of the Secretary of the Territory of New Mexico." The
existence of the document was immediately challenged and, to date,
has never been verified as authentic.

In other words, the death of Billy the Kid was never officially recorded in the state of New Mexico, or anywhere else for that matter.
Nowhere does there exist, in fact, any legal proof of the death of Billy
the Kid.

Another pertinent question is: Why was a coroner's report never
filed among Lincoln County records? According to William A. Keleher,
author of *Violence in Lincoln County*, the second coroner's report was
written in Spanish and attached to a cover letter penned by Garrett.
Keleher claims that a copy of the document was found during the
1930s in the Office of the Commissioner of Public Lands in the capitol
building at Santa Fe, a claim that has never been substantiated. To
date, no one has ever seen the document.

In the copy of the verdict mentioned by Keleher, the words spoken
by the man who entered Maxwell's bedroom were in English, not
Spanish as stated by Garrett and Poe, thus providing for more inconsistency and contradiction.

The sequence of events that ultimately yielded two inquests is
unusual, and the related contradictions and inconsistencies invite
suspicion, particularly of the individual responsible for overseeing the
proceedings—Pat Garrett.

Like the shooting, the inquest of the man Garrett claimed was Billy
the Kid has been shrouded in confusion and mystery. The uncommon
speed with which the inquest was handled was peculiar and suspect.

According to writer Frank Richard Prassell in *The Great American Outlaw*, "Lawmen of the era normally went to considerable effort to verify the deaths of fugitives for two good reasons: To foreclose a later charge of killing an innocent party, and to facilitate the collection of rewards."

It is possible that Garrett knew he was guilty of killing an innocent man and therefore wanted the process to move quickly so that the victim could be buried before the mistake was discovered. It is also odd that the Rudolph report states that Garrett "deserves to be rewarded." Such an opinion is beyond the duties and obligations of a coroner's jury that leads many to suspect that the line, if not the entire report, was dictated by Garrett himself.

Another curious fact that bothers competent researchers of western outlaw and lawman history is related to the fact that Garrett did not have the body of one of the Southwest's, perhaps America's, most famous bad men placed on public display, a common practice during that time. Furthermore, Garrett did not take the time to pose for a photograph with the body, another common and accepted practice of the day.

According to some versions of the incident, Garrett had the body locked in Maxwell's room overnight and allowed only a few to see it. Could Garrett, knowing the man he shot was not Billy the Kid, not have wanted the corpse placed on display or photographed because people would know that it was not that of the outlaw?

Pat Garrett never collected the five hundred dollar reward offered by New Mexico governor Lew Wallace for the apprehension of Billy the Kid. Garrett petitioned for the reward money on July 20, 1881. The reward was denied by acting-governor W. G. Ritch. According to writer Tuska, some questions were raised relative to whether Garrett had really killed Billy the Kid. A few Garrett supporters and apologists suggest that the request for the reward was denied because the application was not submitted in proper legal form. This is an absurd contention. Garrett was a professional lawman with significant experience. He would have known what the "proper legal form" was for such a document.

Others refer to the problem generated by the purported death certificate, which was never found. Tuska suggests that after Garrett was turned down, Charlie Green, editor of the *Santa Fe New Mexican* and a Garrett crony, recommended to the sheriff that he have yet another coroner's report drafted. The document was written, the third one, by Manuel Abreau, Garrett's brother-in-law. It contained signatures of men "who had not been present at the original hearing and it contains obviously slanted statements which indicate for what use it was intended." Is this the sort of thing that would be undertaken and/or condoned by an honest lawman?

It is crystal clear that Garrett was not beyond being duplicitous and self-serving at the expense of the truth. If Garrett had killed the right man in Maxwell's bedroom, none of the subsequent ploys would have been necessary, and there would have been no need for all of the confusion and contradiction relative what had actually taken place. With Garrett in charge, the entire episode was a disaster, a succession of lies and contradictions. Garrett hurried along not one but two inquests, refused to place the body on display, refused to have his photograph made with the corpse, had the body buried posthaste, and then almost a week later initiated a third coroner's report! And for what reason? There can be only one logical explanation: The dead man was *not* Billy the Kid.

Author Jon Tuska states that it is "quite possible that the original document mentioned that the Kid was unarmed and was therefore suppressed." Tuska also raised the question of whether the coroner's jury, made up of men largely sympathetic to the Kid, would have concluded by recommending the reward not being paid to Garrett. Perhaps that is the reason why the original became "lost." Since Garrett was the official in charge, he bears responsibility for losing it and orchestrating the second report, the one that was more favorable to him.

In spite of the fact that Garrett was never given the reward for "apprehending" the Kid, crony James J. Dolan raised $1,150 and presented it to the sheriff. According to an article in the *Las Vegas Optic*, rancher John Chisum gave the sheriff another $1,000. An article appearing in an August 5, 1951, *El Paso Times* stated that a total of an additional $2,300 was collected for Garrett from citizens in Santa Fe, Las Vegas, Silver City, Las Cruces, and Mesilla.

On February 18, 1882, after Garrett purchased approximately $500 worth of drinks for members of the New Mexico Territorial Legislature, the constituents voted to pass an act providing the reward money for "the arrest of Billy the Kid." According to Sonnichsen, the legislature at the time was "heavily loaded" with Garrett's henchmen. Apparently none of the legislators were aware, or cared, that Garrett never arrested anyone and that the identity of the man he killed was in dispute even then. This act, written by the legislators, credits Garrett with killing Billy the Kid "on or about the month of August, 1881." They couldn't even get the date correct.

Given the facts related to the events following the shooting of the man in Pete Maxwell's bedroom, the various inquests, the contradictions, the lies, the subsequent complications related to the burial of the dead man (chapter 22), the strange behavior of the sheriff, and more, the conclusion that the dead man was Billy the Kid is, without doubt, questionable. Garrett, and Garrett cronies, circumvented the truth of what happened.

TWENTY-TWO

---◆◆◆---

Burial

The events related to the interment of the man Garrett shot and killed and claimed was Billy the Kid underscores the duplicity associated with what many regard as one of the most important and eventful episodes in western outlaw and lawman history. Colorful though these characters are, very little of what people think they know about the relationship between Pat Garrett and Billy the Kid and the events that occurred in Fort Sumner on July 14 and 15, 1881, are true. If anything, they further cast Pat Garrett in the role of prevaricator.

The burial of the dead man, like the shooting and the inquests, is fraught with inconsistency and contradiction and has not escaped criticism, controversy, and questions. A number of researchers have written that the body was prepared and dressed for burial immediately following the second inquest. On the afternoon of July 15, less than sixteen hours after he was killed, the dead man was placed in a wooden coffin that had been quickly nailed together from scrap lumber and lowered into a hole in the nearby Fort Sumner military cemetery next to the graves of Tom O'Folliard and Charlie Bowdre, friends of Billy the Kid. Even as this was being done, residents of Fort Sumner were already discussing among themselves that it was not the Kid who was killed but another man. The interment proceeded at an astonishing and unheard of pace. Garrett apparently could not get the body of the man he killed into the ground fast enough.

Though difficult to verify, there is a possibility that only a handful of people other than Garrett, Poe, and McKinney ever saw the body of the dead man on the floor of Maxwell's bedroom, and most of them said it was not Billy the Kid who had been killed.

Leon Metz, author of *Pat Garrett: The Story of a Western Lawman*, brings up the possibility that passing off any body as that of Billy the Kid could easily have been done "since neither Poe nor Tip McKinney recognized the Kid, and both would be inclined to accept almost any body that Garrett claimed was Billy's." Garrett could then petition for the reward, says Metz, as well as the honor and prestige that went with killing the Southwest's most noted outlaw.

On July 28, an article appeared in a Silver City newspaper, the *Grant County Herald*, regarding the shooting and subsequent burial of "Billy the Kid." Titled "Exit 'The Kid'" and written by editor S. M. Ashenfelter, the article stated, in part, "Since his escape from the Lincoln County jail," the outlaw Billy the Kid "has allowed his beard to grow, and he has stained his skin brown to look like a Mexican."

The description of the body fits not that of Billy the Kid but rather Billy Barlow, the man William Henry Roberts insisted was killed. Pertinent to this, Sonnichsen related some secondhand information about a man named Arthur Hyde. During a 1914 interview, Hyde, who lived in Fort Sumner at the time of the shooting, stated that it was a young Mexican who was shot, one who looked a lot like Billy the Kid, and that he was set up by Pat Garrett.

Only six-and-a-half months prior to the shooting in Fort Sumner, J. H. Koogler, editor of the *Las Vegas Gazette*, interviewed Billy the Kid while he was in town awaiting transportation to Mesilla for trial. In describing the outlaw, Koogler wrote, "There was nothing very mannish about him in appearance, for he looked and acted a mere boy. He is about five feet eight or nine inches tall, lightly built and lithe, weighing about 140; a frank open countenance, looking like a school boy, with the traditional silky fuzz on his upper lip; clear blue eyes, with a roguish snap about them; light hair and complexion."

The body of the dead man that was placed in the casket was described by newspaperman Ashenfelter as having dark skin and a beard. The Kid was never known to have dark skin or dark hair, and given that his facial hair had been earlier described as "silky fuzz," any beard he might have grown would have been insignificant. Furthermore, it can be assumed that if the body of the dead man had been stained "in order to look like a Mexican," it is unlikely that such stain could be found in Fort Sumner. If it were, it would have been washed off during the preparation of the body. No one has adequately provided an explanation for why one would perceive a need to stain one's skin.

According to Dr. J. M. Tanner in *Growth at Adolescence*, sexual maturity ratings (SMRs) are developmental stages not necessarily related to chronological age. SMRs 1 and 2 are associated with early adolescence in males ten to fifteen years of age. During SMR 2 in males, facial hair may appear, and is often of a fine and silky texture. Middle adolescence (SMRs 3 and 4) typically begins between years twelve and fifteen. Late adolescence (SMR 5) is generally reached between the fourteenth and sixteenth years, although it may not appear until much later.

During SMR 5, which according to Tanner can occur "as late as the early twenties in some individuals," secondary sex characteristics begin to develop. In the male, facial hair spreads to the chin and chest. Tanner points out that the length of time between SMR 2, associated with silky fuzz, and SMR 5, associated with a beard, can be as long as three years.

Thus, if Billy the Kid, at age twenty-one, was still exhibiting "silky fuzz on his upper lip" as described by Koogler, this indicates he was experiencing delayed sexual maturity. Based on Tanner's research, it is improbable to impossible that, given the chronology of the SMR sequences, the Kid could have gone from "light hair and complexion" and "silky fuzz" to dark skin and a beard in only six and a half months.

Based on the descriptions provided by Ashenfelter and Koogler, the body in the casket could *not* have been Billy the Kid. The biological processes associated with such dramatic endochronological changes do not exist such that they would cause a light-complected lad with silky fuzz to evolve to a dark-skinned man with a beard in such a short time. It is inconceivable that Pat Garrett was unaware that the man placed in the coffin was *not* Billy the Kid.

In a March 1980 article that appeared in *Frontier Times* magazine, writer Ben W. Kemp shares some pertinent information told to him by his uncle, John Graham, a Fort Sumner resident who knew Billy the Kid. On the morning following the shooting, Graham and a Mexican were sent to dig the grave for Garrett's victim. Graham stated that when the wagon carrying the casket arrived, it was accompanied by an armed guard "with strict orders to see that no one opened it to see what was inside." The word used was *what*, not *who*.

According to Kemp, Graham agreed with John Poe that the body of the dead man was removed from Maxwell's bedroom a short time after the shooting and not the following morning, as stated by others. Kemp quotes Graham, however, as saying that an acquaintance told him that the man killed by Garrett was one of Maxwell's hired hands.

The late Verna Reed, a Carlsbad, New Mexico, resident, said that her great-grandfather, Joseph Wood, helped with the burial. All of his life, Wood insisted that the coffin contained a side of beef, the one that hung outside of Maxwell's room.

So, who, or what, was buried on July 15, 1881, in the Fort Sumner cemetery? There is not a scintilla of verifiable evidence that it was the man known as the outlaw Billy the Kid. Conversely, there exists more compelling evidence that suggests the body was that of Billy Barlow, thus corroborating the version of events provided by William Henry Roberts.

No one today knows where the original "grave" of Billy the Kid was located. The wooden marker that had been placed at the head of the plot was often used by drunks for target practice and was eventually reduced to splinters. A short time later, not even Fort Sumner residents were able to identify the precise spot, according to an interview with Carolina Baca that was published in the book *They Knew Billy the Kid* (1987).

In 1906, twenty-two bodies, believed to be those of soldiers, were disinterred from the cemetery and reburied in the Santa Fe National Cemetery. Supporting evidence is lacking that the remains of the man Garrett wanted the world to believe was Billy the Kid were among them.

On a number of occasions during the past one hundred thirty years, the nearby Pecos River flooded, inflicting damage to the cemetery that was located near the adjacent floodplain. High-velocity floodwaters were observed and recorded carrying away headstones and markers along with coffins and their contents. By the 1930s, as a result of flood damage, there was little left of the cemetery that was recognizable.

In 1937, the four pallbearers who carried the casket alleged to contain the remains of the man shot by Garrett from the wagon to the grave were still alive and living in Fort Sumner. Vicente Otero, Yginio Salazar, Jesus Silva, and Charlie Foor were assembled at the old cemetery and asked to agree on the original location. They were unable to do so, each man selecting a different site. Finally, they agreed to compromise by placing a marker at the approximate center of the four different choices. According to George E. Kaiser, a resident of Artesia, New Mexico, there was a major flood in 1943, which washed away the newer marker as well as the few other graves that had managed to survive earlier floods.

The current gravesite of the man Garrett identified as Billy the Kid is an important tourist attraction for the town of Fort Sumner. The location, situated next to an establishment that caters to tourists and peddles souvenirs and postcards, is a long way from the original burial site. There is no proof that Billy the Kid, or anyone else, for that matter, is buried under the marker.

An attempt by investigator and researcher Steve Sederwall to examine the space beneath the stone in order to learn the truth was rejected by the Fort Sumner city council. Clearly, they did not want to take the chance of the result indicating there was nothing there. In this case, tourism dollars were more important than the truth.

A police-action situation such as the shooting of a presumed outlaw by Garrett should be cut and dried, and typically it undergoes a post-event investigation and analysis. This was never conducted. Such situations occur regularly in the world of law enforcement. Likewise, the subsequent inquests and burial, in normal circumstances, would be straightforward with little debate. They should be free of controversy and contradiction, mystery and duplicity. None of that occurred in this case. The information that leaked out relative to the shooting, inquests, and burial manifested dramatic differences, even among those who were present and involved. In addition, much of it was contradictory and clearly false. To the most casual observer, the entire sequence of events comes across as an embarrassing disaster and smacks of a botched attempt at a cover-up. The man responsible for the entire sequence of events was Pat Garrett.

TWENTY-THREE

---◆◆◆---

The Book

In the weeks following the killing of the man in Pete Maxwell's bedroom Pat Garrett's renown for allegedly ending the life of the Southwest's most notorious bad man grew, and during this time he began taking notice of certain books. In particular, he was growing aware of the dime novels produced by eastern writers that were enjoying booming sales. Intimate with this phenomenon, Garrett was more than ready when his friend Charles W. Green, the editor of the *Santa Fe New Mexican*, visited with him and encouraged him to write his own book, a factual one, about the outlaw Billy the Kid and the final so-called confrontation in Fort Sumner.

With some coaxing, Garrett agreed to the proposition. Greene said he would publish the book if Garrett could find someone to write it. Greene must have known, or suspected, at the time that Garrett was incapable of penning the manuscript himself. Garrett then turned to a friend, Ashmon Upson, called Ash, and invited him onto the project.

Upson was not without personality and color. Originally from South Carolina (some sources say Connecticut), Upson was in his fifties when he and Garrett became acquainted. Following the Civil War, Upson, a newspaperman who had experience with the *New York Tribune*, journeyed west. He visited and lived in such places as Ohio, Kansas, Colorado, Utah, Missouri, and Indian Territory. A short time after landing in New Mexico, he established the *Albuquerque Press* in 1867. He did not remain long, and he wound up with a variety of newspaper jobs throughout the state, including Central City, Fort Stanton, Mesilla, Las Vegas, and elsewhere.

In 1876, Upson was living in Roswell, where he served at various times as a justice of the peace, real estate salesman, notary public, and postmaster. When not otherwise gainfully employed, Upson worked in the general store of Captain J. C. Lea. Upson was known as a drinking man, and most characterizations of him involve this propensity and his inability to properly cope with his alcoholism.

Upson and Garrett most likely met in the town of Roswell. They had much in common: In addition to drinking, they enjoyed horse racing, loose women, and gambling. Upson moved in with the Garrett family in August 1881 and lived with them for a time.

With Upson's considerable assistance, Garrett pursued the challenge of authoring a book. It was released with the ponderous title, *The Authentic Life of Billy the Kid, the Noted Desperado of the Southwest, Whose Deeds of Daring Have Made His Name a Terror on New Mexico, Arizona, and Northern Mexico*. Although Garrett is listed as the sole author, it is obvious that he was assisted in large measure, if not entirely, by Upson. Upson, in an interview years later that was published in James D. Shinkle's *Reminiscences of Roswell Pioneers*, claimed that he wrote every word of it and was ultimately swindled out of his contract to serve as Garrett's ghostwriter.

Most of the details regarding the early life of Billy the Kid came from Upson, who claimed he knew the outlaw as a young boy while living in Silver City. Whether Upson actually knew the Kid is debatable. The truth is that most of the so-called details of the Kid's life were fabricated. Credible historians who have studied *The Authentic Life* have not been kind to either Upson or Garrett. Author Metz insists that Garrett was responsible for most, if not all, of the last half of the book, and, to no one's surprise, he credits the lawman for providing accurate information. Even a casual examination of *The Authentic Life* proves Metz was mistaken.

The Authentic Life was the first of what would eventually amount to over one thousand nonfiction and fiction books written about the famous outlaw. In addition, there exist an uncountable number of newspaper articles, magazine articles, screenplays, musical performances, songs, essays, and even academic dissertations about Billy the Kid. Though the Garrett/Upson book was fraught with error, it is, unfortunately, the one that is most often referred to for information about the famous outlaw.

Writer Frederick Nolan, who, like Metz, clings to the historical status quo regarding the Kid and Pat Garrett, has even referred to *The Authentic Life* as "a fanciful account," filled with "untruths committed by the man whose name it bears as author," "responsible for every single one of the myths about Billy the Kid," "a farrago of nonsense," "unreliable."

It would take almost an entire separate book to identify and discuss the myriad exaggerations, misstatements, and lies packed into *The Authentic Life*. One particularly telling falsehood is related to the Kid's date of birth. Upson ascribes the date as November 23, 1859. An interesting choice, to be sure, as this is precisely when Upson himself was born.

Much of the book is oriented toward emphasizing the Kid's fearlessness and violent outlaw nature, as well as his alleged gun-fighting talents, all exaggerated. This was a calculated move to make Garrett appear heroic, brave, and determined. The book clearly built a "good-versus-evil" scenario where, in the end, the tall, glamorous, and daring lawman vanquishes the evildoer. Such is the stuff of fiction, which, as it turns out, is what most of *The Authentic Life* tends to be.

The Authentic Life sold very few copies, and none of those involved—Greene, Garrett, and Upson—made any money. Upson stated that Greene "bungled in the publication." He also seemed irked that Garrett was listed as the sole author because he, Upson, "wrote every word of it." Even in New Mexico, sales of the book were disappointing, and some suspect that Garrett's personality had much to do with this failure. Author A. M. Gibson wrote, "Curiously, the maudlin sentimentality of many New Mexicans for Billy the Kid had made his killer, Pat Garrett, one of the most hated men in the territory." From all appearances, the Garrett/Upson relationship grew strained in the weeks following publication, with Upson eventually fading from the scene for a time.

The Authentic Life, largely ignored by the reading public in general and the New Mexico population in particular, did not catapult Garrett's status any higher. With the passage of time and occasional close analysis by historians and others, the book ultimately did little to enhance Garrett's credibility. In fact, it accomplished quite the opposite. Many now regarded Garrett's published claims to be largely exaggerated by Upson, if not made up altogether. The fact remains, however, that Garrett allowed his name to be attached to the book as author and was therefore ultimately responsible for every word in the text. If he had problems with what has since been described many times as "falsehoods," "nonsense," and "unreliable," he would have had the opportunity to correct them, but he apparently did not. Then again, one wonders if Garrett even read the book before it was sent to the publisher.

In the meantime, Garrett cast about for other activities with which to become involved. As usual, he needed money, and the job of sheriff did not pay enough for him to pursue his vices to the degree he found necessary.

TWENTY-FOUR

◆◆◆

Transition

Once *The Authentic Life* went into print, Garrett decided he would not be a candidate for sheriff during the 1882 elections. Over the years, some have wondered at this decision, for the likelihood that he would have won was great. It has been guessed that Garrett presumed that he would be able to live comfortably on the royalties from his book, but that was not to happen.

In any event, Garrett decided to back James J. Dolan, a crony and fellow Mason. While at first excited about the notion of being sheriff of Lincoln County, Dolan's interest faded in a short time. John W. Poe, Garrett's able deputy, was substituted and he won the election easily.

According to author Metz, Poe proved to be "incredibly efficient," in stark contrast to Garrett, who was described as "thoroughly inept" when it came to maintaining the office.

Garrett began to direct his attention beyond local politics to area and state issues and his potential role in any of them. A short time earlier, the United States Congress had ordered New Mexico to reapportion, a process whereby the determination of the number of members in the U.S. House of Representatives is based on the population of the state relative to the total United States population. This task fell to the New Mexico Territorial Legislature, but they ignored it and finally adjourned on March 2, 1882, with no decision being made. The job then fell to the recently elected New Mexico governor, Lionel A. Sheldon, along with the president of the Territorial Council and the speaker of the House of Representatives. When all was said and done, Pat Garrett wound up being a resident of the Ninth Council District that included Doña Ana, Grant, and Lincoln Counties. Preparations were undertaken to elect two councilmen.

Doña Ana County's newspaper, the *Rio Grande Republican*, touted John A. Miller of Grant County and David G. Easton of Lincoln

County. Both Miller and Easton supported Garrett during his earlier run for sheriff, but the now former lawman appeared lukewarm regarding these two men. Garrett, in fact, organized a special convention in Lincoln County for the purpose of nominating a so-called People's Ticket of officers. The convention was held on August 22. The *Rio Grande Republican* reported the affair but mentioned only that Miller and Easton had been nominated for councilmen and chose to ignore any others. The article appeared oriented in large part toward attacking the editor of the *White Oaks Golden Era*, a man named Sligh, charging him with an attempt to "stampede and capture the organization." Sligh was a supporter of Pat Garrett.

The article did not mention Garrett at all, but a separate one in the same issue of the *Rio Grande Republican* attacked the former sheriff. It mentioned that Garrett had been nominated as a candidate for councilman and was opposing Miller and Easton. The piece referred to Garrett as "illiterate" and "lacking in gratitude."

The same newspaper published a letter a few weeks later, one written in the same vein as the aforementioned article. It has been suggested that the letter, signed "X," was likely penned by the editor. The writer stated that anyone serving in the legislature should be educated, and that Garrett did not satisfy this requirement. The article further stated that Garrett was "egotistic to a superlative degree." The newspaper piece charged Garrett with collusion with Albert J. Fountain and Captain Lea, both of whom, according to the writer, were using Garrett's popularity to further their own schemes.

Garrett fought back. In a quite literate letter to the *Rio Grande Republican* printed on September 23, Garrett wrote that he did, in fact, appreciate the support of Easton and others during his campaign for sheriff, but because these same people had once helped him did not mean that he was indebted to them forever. Garrett stated he held no animosity toward Easton, but was opposing him in the election for councilman because he was opposed to the tactics and philosophies of "X" and others like him.

Garrett wrote that he had no control over what others claimed was his "illiteracy" and stated it was not "very generous of 'X'" to blame him for such. He also reacted to the charge that the newspaper coverage he had received "for killing the Kid," as "X" claimed, had "turned my head and clouded my better judgment," stating, "I think I know my mind as well as 'X' does, and if there is a higher court than Judge 'X's, I beg to appeal to his decision."

Some might argue that Garrett's reaction to "X's" letter was overly defensive. It is true that Garrett, as Metz writes, "was a proud and bitter man." Garrett was determined to find out who wrote the letter, and suspected W. M. Roberts, a Lincoln attorney. Garrett approached Roberts in a Lincoln store on September 19. According to an article in the *Rio Grande Republican*, by now a staunch Garrett antagonist, Garrett asked Roberts if he wrote the letter. Roberts said he did not. As the two men left the store and walked into the street, Garrett kept probing, eventually coming straight out and accusing Roberts of authoring the letter. Roberts responded by calling Garrett a "goddamned liar." Garrett, already in a rage, pulled his Colt .45 from the holster and whipped Roberts across the head, leaving him bleeding and lying unconscious in the dirt of the street.

By the time the polls closed, Garrett lost by only a few votes. He carried only Lincoln County, where he was well known, but lost heavily in Doña Ana and Grant Counties. He received little to no support from newspapers.

Garrett survived the loss with equanimity. He kept his foot in politics by occasionally serving Lincoln County as a delegate to the capitol at Santa Fe over the next several years as he continued to cast about for other opportunities.

TWENTY-FIVE

✦✦✦

The Pat Garrett Rangers

It wasn't long before Pat Garrett was back on the trail chasing rule breakers. His opportunity came in the form of Texas's Panhandle Cattlemen's Association, the same group that, four years earlier, wearied of the rustling perpetrated by Billy the Kid and his gang. They were also the group that selected Frank Stewart and several others to assist Garrett in pursuing the Kid.

Since the Kid was no longer a threat, the cattlemen now devoted their attention to a number of growing concerns in their local area. Specifically, they were examining ways to deal with small ranchers who were competing for the available water supply. But an even more pressing concern arose when Panhandle cowboys were on the verge of striking for higher wages and seeking a growing economic independence.

Regarding water, the cattlemen with large holdings began fencing off waterholes and even posting guards against the possibility that the smaller ranchers would water their cattle there. Controlling the water was akin to controlling any land that surrounded it. As the smaller ranchers, both Anglo and Mexican, found it more and more difficult to obtain water, they sold out to the ever-expanding larger ranchers. At the same time, the ranchers, perceiving themselves as an elite class, regarded their employees, the cowhands, as little more than common laborers, paying them on the average of $25–$30 per month, and they were generally paid only after a roundup or trail drive.

Cowhands worked from dawn to dark and beyond, were provided two meals per day, and often suffered injury and death in the process of doing their jobs. In addition, most of the cowhands were in debt to their employers as a result of the fact that many items—saddles, blankets, and personal effects—were supplied by the ranchers. The hired hands signed a promissory note for them, an amount that was deducted from their forthcoming paycheck.

In order to earn a little extra money, cowhands occasionally took to mavericking. The term, named after a Texas rancher named Samuel A. Maverick, involved applying a brand to a stray animal that was as yet unmarked. Dozens of men rounded up and branded hundreds, if not thousands, of stray and wild cattle that roamed throughout Texas following the Civil War. The practice was generally regarded as legitimate and was even tolerated by the large ranch owners. In fact, a number of prominent ranchers could credit their start in the cattle business as a result of this common practice.

In the Texas Panhandle some of the ranchers began accusing cowhands of separating unbranded calves from their mothers and burning their own mark on them. Unlike mavericking wild cattle, this was considered another type of rustling.

The cattlemen's association ordered a complete stop to any and all unauthorized or private branding on land controlled by the member ranchers. This move slowed the pace of mavericking, but did not stop it. Further, it placed a hardship on the honest mavericker who was just trying to start his own herd from wild or stray cattle. The order to halt the practice, however, had another effect, one with troublesome consequences.

Since the opportunity to earn extra money via mavericking was halted, and since pay for cowhands was abysmally low, the hired help reacted by demanding higher wages. During the first part of 1883, twenty-five cowhands drafted and signed a document that was circulated throughout the region and stated that they would "not work for less than $50 a month" and that "good cooks shall also receive $50 a month." A third consideration stated that "anyone running an outfit shall not work for less than $75 a month." The final line in the document was tinged with threat: "Anyone violating the above obligations shall suffer the consequences."

Almost immediately, the head of the LIT Ranch presented a compromise by offering to pay cowhands $35 per month and range bosses $65 per month. The offers were turned down. Soon afterward, the LS Ranch management made an offer of $40 per month with bosses receiving proportionately more based on experience.

Strike leader Tom Harris, who was also employed as a wagon boss of the LS Ranch, entered into talks with ranch manager J. E. McAllister and W. M. D. Lee, one of the owners. By the end of the discussions, the LS Ranch offered Harris $100 per month as wagon boss and agreed to pay a salary of $50 for "each cowboy that Harris designated as a top hand."

Harris, well aware that a number of the cowhands were not worth $50 per month and that there would thus be a disparity of wages that would likely cause conflict, turned the offer down. At that point, McAllister fired Harris. The striking cowboys, amounting to almost one hundred men, had nowhere to go and nothing to do until the strike was resolved. They decided to retreat to the nearest town—Tascosa—while they waited out the negotiations.

At the time, Tascosa, located in Oldham County, served as a kind of service center for the area ranches. Its buildings were one-story affairs of adobe and recycled lumber. Tascosa was well known throughout the region as a hub for rustlers, the occasional murder, gambling, and prostitution. The southern edge of Tascosa, known as Hogtown, was replete with brothels and bars.

The temptation of cheap liquor and loose women proved to be too much for most of the cowhands. In a matter of three weeks, they ran out of what little money they had in their pockets and were more than willing to return to work, regardless of the pay. The strike was effectively ended at that point.

Little did the striking cowhands know, their troubles were only beginning. In a short time, W. M. D. Lee published the names of all of them throughout the Panhandle with the warning that they were not to be hired by anyone. Most ranchers, who had deep and extensive needs for cowhands, refused to employ any man whose name appeared on the list. As a result, most of the able-bodied workers left the area. A number of them, angry and vengeance-minded, journeyed into New Mexico, taking with them hundreds of head of cattle they rustled from their former employers. Mavericking evolved into rustling, pure and simple.

A large percentage of the cattle that had been stolen and herded into New Mexico from the Texas Panhandle had counterfeit bills of sale. Some of these were attached to another sheet representing a power of attorney that authorized the bearer to accept cattle bearing a specific brand and drive them across the border. In this manner, hundreds of rustled cattle made their way into the territory.

Problems arose with the Lincoln County ranchers when it was discovered that the newly arrived cattle carried Texas fever. Texas fever was caused by ticks, and a seriously infected cow would sicken and die in a short time. On November 15, 1884, a resolution was passed by the Lincoln County Stock Growers Association stating that the herds of Texas cattle grazing in eastern New Mexico represented a threat in the form of competition for grazing lands and water as well as being carriers of Texas fever.

Judge Warren Bristol, the man who sentenced Billy the Kid to hang for the murder of Sheriff William Brady, ruled that while New Mexico grasslands were public domain, the water holes were to be regarded as private property. Subsequently, by law no cattle could be turned loose on the rangelands until water rights were legally secured.

Meanwhile, over in the Panhandle the cattlemen had grown tired and frustrated with the rustling of their cattle. Following some brief discussion, they located Pat Garrett and invited him to head a company of rangers to put a stop to the outlawry.

The company was called the Home Rangers. In a short time, however, they were referred to as the Pat Garrett Rangers by the small ranchers and squatters. Some writers have claimed that Garrett was awarded a commission from Texas governor John Ireland, but no such document has ever been found. The possibility exists that Ireland granted permission, or perhaps acquiescence, either orally or via a personal letter.

Garrett wasted no time in assembling a group of men to facilitate meeting the goals of the stockmen. In addition to Garrett, the rangers consisted of Bill Anderson, Lon Chambers, G. H. Dobbs, George Jones, Ed King, John Land, Barney Mason, Albert Perry, and Charlie Reason. Anderson, Chambers, Dobbs, King, Land, Perry, and Reason had all been employed by the LS Ranch. Reason was a hopeless drunk; it was said he was never sober the entire time he served with the rangers. Chambers was with Garrett at the confrontation with Billy the Kid and his gang at Stinking Springs. Garrett named Perry First Sergeant. The rangers were paid $60 per month, and Garrett was promised a salary of $5,000 a year. LS Ranch manager J. E. McAllister sold Garrett some prime cattle at one-fourth their value with the promise of buying them back at the going rate when the job was finished.

Jim East, at the time the sheriff of Oldham County, stated he would have nothing to do with the rangers and was surprised at many of the men selected by Garrett. East described them as heavy drinkers and vindictive. It may have been that Garrett was forced to appoint what men were available at the time. The list of rangers, in truth, represented only those men who expressed an interest in the job.

By the time the rangers were assembled, the Panhandle stockmen convinced Governor Ireland to issue a proclamation against carrying handguns. This done, the LS Ranch owners provided $25,000 in the form of a loan to construct a courthouse in Tascosa. As it turned out, the courthouse was necessary in order to provide warrants so that Garrett and his rangers could make arrests. A courthouse was also a requirement for a grand jury. During the first session of the grand jury, a total of 159 warrants were issued, almost all of them for theft of cattle. Thus, Garrett forged ahead, armed with the necessary legal documents to make arrests.

During the days that followed, Garrett and his rangers rode throughout the Panhandle making arrests, mostly ones associated with violating the handgun law. It soon became clear that the intent of the arrest warrants and the handgun stricture was to frighten out of the area those men the big ranchers declared undesirable. In a short time, the Pat Garrett Rangers alienated the majority of the Panhandle's residents. A number of them aggressively opposed the rangers to the point of taking up arms against them. What author Metz calls "private wars" occasionally broke out between Garrett's men and area cowhands.

In February 1885, Garrett arrested Bill Gatlin, Charlie Thompson, and Wade Woods. Thompson had been one of the leaders of the cowboy strikers, and all three men were known to be handy with a running iron and were able to modify almost any brand in the area.

After enlisting the assistance of the heretofore reluctant Sheriff Jim East, Garrett and the rangers rode out at night and in a raging snowstorm, their destination a rock house on the bank of the Canadian River. As a result of the successful employment of a similar tactic against Billy the Kid, Garrett was convinced that the best time to track outlaws was during such a storm. No one expected anybody to be out in such dreadful weather.

One of Garrett's rangers—Dobbs—was familiar with that part of the country and served as guide. After stopping at the small community of Trujillo at 2:00 AM to feed and water their horses and consume a hot meal, they rode on toward the Canadian River. On arriving, Garrett saw that approaching the house from the road could be dangerous since they would be in full view of the occupants, Instead, he directed the rangers about two miles upstream and rode toward the cabin from better concealment. Fifty yards from the house, the rangers dismounted. Garrett ordered his men to different positions around the house in order to prevent escape. In the process, they were spotted by one of the occupants, Bob Bassett, who was gathering firewood. Bassett dropped his load of kindling and raced toward the house yelling a warning.

A moment later, Tom Harris stepped out of the cabin. Angry, he inquired of the rangers why they wanted him. Garrett explained they were there to arrest Billy Gatlin, Charlie Thompson, and Wade Woods. Following a brief discussion, nine men exited the cabin with their hands in the air. They said they wanted no part in any kind of gunplay, and explained that Woods had ridden away earlier, but that Gatlin and Thompson remained inside the house.

A few minutes later, Thompson, in shirtsleeves, stepped outside the doorway and spoke with Garrett. Seeing that the man was shivering violently from the cold, Garrett told him to retrieve his coat. After stepping back inside the cabin, however, Thompson slammed the door shut and screamed that he and Gatlin decided to shoot it out with the rangers.

At this point, Jim East approached the cabin and spoke with Thompson, encouraging him to give himself up and stand trial, that he had a chance to be judged innocent of the cattle rustling charges. Moments later, Thompson, hands in the air, exited the cabin and surrendered to Garrett.

Garrett called for Gatlin to come out, but he refused. Garrett promised him he would be treated the same as Thompson. The two men shouted back and forth for most of the day. Finally, tiring of the ordeal, Garrett told rangers King and Reason to "strip the poles from the lean-to type roof." This done, they would be able to fire their weapons into the cabin if Gatlin continued to refuse to surrender. Once the roof had been opened up, Gatlin called out that he wanted to negotiate only with East, and insisted the sheriff enter the cabin to talk.

East conferred with Garrett, explaining that he and Gatlin had once worked on the same ranch and did not think the man would harm him. Leaving Garrett, East, somewhat nervous, crept toward the partially open door. Spotting Gatlin just inside holding a revolver, East told him to put it down, and then he stepped inside. Gatlin agreed to the surrender and East escorted him to where the posse waited.

Following a quick meal of bacon and coffee, Gatlin and Thompson were transported to Tascosa, where they were shackled and placed in the jail. That night, the two prisoners somehow obtained a file, removed their chains, and escaped, never to be seen again.

Garrett's passion for his job as leader of the rangers was waning. Metz, along with writer Emerson Hough, suggests he was disillusioned by the suspicion that his employers were more interested in having their enemies killed or run out of the country than in bringing them to trial. Garrett disbanded the rangers in the spring of 1885 and decided to have another try at the cattle business.

TWENTY-SIX

Real Estate Agent

It was becoming increasingly clear that Garrett was not cut out to be a rancher. While he possessed knowledge and competencies that could have seen him achieving successes at such an enterprise, Garrett was more inclined toward other pursuits: drinking, gambling, and whoring. In addition, his ever-growing ego demanded he remain in the public eye. His return to ranching turned out to be another failure. He was desperately in need of making a living and in time an opportunity arose.

While visiting in Tascosa, Garrett met a man named Captain Brandon Kirby. Kirby identified himself as an agent who represented Scotsmen who were interested in establishing ranches in the American West. During this time, a number of Europeans—British and Irish as well as Scots—were investing in western cattle ranches.

Kirby told Garrett that he was funded by a Scotsman named James Cree and his job was to seek out some choice ranch lands in south-eastern New Mexico. Garrett in fact, was to be a subagent for Kirby in what was essentially a grand real estate deal. Garrett invited Kirby to Lincoln County and showed him a number of prime properties, all suited to the establishment of large ranches. In August 1885, Garrett assisted Kirby in the purchase of a large ranch near Fort Stanton.

During the ensuing months, Garrett helped Kirby close on a number of other ranch properties, including those of John Poe. Garrett even sold his own holdings.

In time, James Cree himself moved to his large ranch in New Mexico. Soon afterward, Cree appointed Kirby as his ranch manager, with Pat Garrett providing timely assistance. In Scotland, the Crees were a wealthy family, proud of their lineage, and used to being looked up to and respected. In New Mexico they expected the same treatment from the residents and were somewhat disappointed when they did not receive it.

James Cree treated his cowhands much the same way he treated his employees in Scotland—as members of the peasant class. Before long, Kirby noticed that there were very few newborn calves and suspected that they were being rustled. As it turned out, Kirby was correct. In this case, however, the rustling was the result of the neighbors' as well as the cowhands' resentment of the way they were treated by the imperial Crees.

In response to the rustling, Cree imported one hundred fifty Black Angus bulls from Scotland. Cree was convinced that the new bulls would improve the beef quality and production. He also predicted that the calves would be black and thus immediately identifiable as Cree property.

In theory, the plan seemed workable, but it was doomed to failure. On determining Cree's intentions, some of his employees, assisted by neighboring ranchers, castrated most of the bulls. Learning of the neutering, Kirby discharged most of the ranch's cowhands. Concerned about potential violence erupting between the hands and Cree, Garrett formulated a rule that no one was to carry handguns on Cree property. More and more foreign currency was coming into that part of New Mexico, and the owners of smaller ranches, desperate for money, sold out. Already precarious, the relationships between Cree and residents of the area continued to deteriorate.

Not only did Cree have to deal with angry and conspiring cowhands, he was soon to have more than his share of problems with the weather. One of the worst droughts in the history of the region descended on Lincoln County in 1886 and the waterholes on Cree's ranch dried up. As a result, the Angus cattle died from thirst. Ever hopeful, Cree remained long enough to try to survive all of his difficulties. It was not to be. In time, the family returned to Scotland.

With the Cree connection severed, Garrett was once again out of work and began casting around for the next opportunity. It eventually came about as a result of the drought, and Garrett cast his lot with a grand irrigation scheme.

TWENTY-SEVEN

◆◆◆

Pecos Valley Irrigation Venture

Following the winding down of the cowboy strike and the real estate venture, Pat Garrett returned to another of his holdings, an
eighteen-hundred-acre farm and ranch east of Roswell in the Pecos
River Valley, where he lived in relative peace. In addition to a herd of
cattle, Garrett raised pecans, apples, peaches, grapes, and alfalfa. On
the surface, it appeared Garrett had it made and could easily settle
into the life of a prosperous rancher/farmer.

The truth was, however, Garrett was anything but prosperous. Ill-
suited to the farming and ranching life, his crops often went neglected
and his profits, if they existed at all, were marginal. Further, Garrett's
vices used up much of what money he made from his ranching enterprises. Once again, he began to cast about for an opportunity that
might make him some money.

Author Metz referred to Garrett as a visionary, and that he longed
to see the Pecos Valley "flourish with crops, with businesses, with
schools." He envisioned, wrote Metz, "room for both the lion and the
lamb to lie down together." In order for the sand hills empire to flourish, the normally arid region must have water. That meant irrigation:
systems of ditches and canals distributing water throughout the area.
Irrigation cost money, and Garrett, as usual, had none.

The geographic area Garrett had in mind was called the Middle
Basin, a portion of the Pecos River located between Las Vegas, New
Mexico, and the Panhandle of Texas and ranging south to Roswell.
The principal streams flowing through this area included the Spring
River, Salt Creek, Rio Hondo, Rio Feliz, Rio Peñasco, Seven Rivers,
Black River, and Delaware River. Geographers classify this region as
arid to semi-arid. In fact, during drought years, water was scarce to
nonexistent in the aforementioned streams. Without irrigation, agri-
culture would be marginal to impossible.

Following the Civil War, newcomers to the region purchased the cheap land and set about developing crude irrigation systems. The federal government passed the Desert Land Act in 1866 that granted rights-of-way for canals on public lands to those who held legal water rights. Land was offered at $1.25 per acre for 640 acres per person if the purchaser would provide irrigation to the property within three years.

The settlers borrowed money to construct canals and ditches, but most of their efforts ended in failure, much of the land was abandoned, and very little of this money was ever paid back.

In an attempt to lure more settlers to the region, New Mexico passed legislation in 1887 providing opportunities for people to form companies oriented toward the construction and maintenance of reservoirs and canals, as well as ditches or pipelines, for the purpose of irrigation, mining, and/or manufacturing. The legislation encouraged these companies to raise money via the sale of stock. After being apprised of this legislation, Garrett viewed it as an opportunity for him to make some money.

On January 15, 1887, Garrett agreed to purchase one-third of a company called the Texas Irrigation Ditch. The company was owned by Roswell businessman William L. Holloman. By August 15, the company was renamed the Holloman and Garrett Ditch Company. The water was to come, it was decided, from the North Spring River, which was located on Garrett's ranch. According to the deed records, the capital stock equaled $5,000 divided into fifty shares of $100 each.

It is unlikely that any actual money was involved and likely that the finances existed entirely as paperwork. No records of this company have ever been found, and within a short time the company simply disappeared.

With the passage of a few weeks, Garrett purchased a one-sixteenth interest in the Pioneer Ditch Company (PDC) from Thomas B. Zumwalt, another Roswell businessman. Since Garrett had no money, the "purchase" may have been an in-kind agreement. Like the previous venture, the PDC dissolved a short time later, having accomplished nothing.

Despite the setbacks, Garrett was intent on starting up his own irrigation company. Based on what he learned from the previous ventures, he determined it would be feasible to construct a dam a mile-and-a-half below the junction of the Rio Hondo and Berrendo Creek and form a dependable reservoir from the flow of the two streams. Once the reservoir was filled, the water would then be distributed throughout the area via canals. With the potential of a consistent water supply, the normally dry sand hills could be offered for sale. Garrett envisioned income not only from the sale of the land, but also from the sale of water rights.

Garrett's scheme was grand, but to facilitate its development he needed money. He approached Charles B. Eddy, a successful New Mexico cattle rancher. Eddy expressed interest, and though he knew less than Garrett about irrigation, he became excited about the prospect of making more money.

Little time had passed when Charles Greene, the Santa Fe publisher of Garrett's unsuccessful book, entered the picture and expressed an interest in joining the project. On July 18, 1885, Garrett, Eddy, and Greene formed the Pecos Valley Irrigation and Investment Company (PVI&IC). It was agreed that Garrett and Eddy would take care of promotion and granting ditch rights and Greene would be the general manager. Garrett and Greene even traveled to Chicago, where they attempted to solicit investors.

By 1888, following numerous trips to Chicago and other major cities, along with endless meetings with real and potential investors, the necessary backing was gradually acquired. The company incorporated on September 15. In addition to Garrett, Eddy, and Greene, by this time, the major stockholders included Luther P. Bradley, Charles A. Gregory, David L. Hough, and James R. McKay. The company claimed assets of six hundred thousand dollars divided into six thousand shares of one hundred dollars each. The PVI&IC bought out another ditch company and obtained control of an important canal.

The channel became known as the Northern Canal. It stretched over forty miles and a number of other waterways and pipelines were connected to it. Canals and ditches were incised into the Middle Basin terrain by huge plows and scrapers pulled by large teams of mules and horses. For the time and place, it was a massive construction project. Newspapers reported on the venture and people traveled for miles just to observe it.

The project took much longer than predicted, and the costs for the system had been dramatically underestimated by the company. As a result, payroll and equipment expenses grew. By late 1889, it was clear that the company was about to run out of money before the project could be completed.

Charles Eddy made a trip to Colorado Springs, Colorado, to invite Robert Weems Tansill to invest enough money in the PVI&IC to see the project through completion. Tansill was the owner of the Punch Cigar

Company and agreed to invest in the company. He also agreed to convince fellow businessman and neighbor James John Hagerman to assume control of the irrigation company. Hagerman, who had achieved considerable success in constructing railroads, agreed to the arrangement. With the arrival of Hagerman, however, a problem arose. The businessman did not care at all for Pat Garrett. Hagerman did not consider Garrett a social peer, and regarded him as "half-educated."

After traveling to Roswell and inspecting the irrigation project in the Middle Basin, Hagerman bailed out the company with a check for $40,000. Hagerman then reorganized the PVI&IC and gave it a new name—the Pecos Valley Irrigation and Improvement Company. Garrett was not included in the reorganization. Once again, he was out in the cold, and broke.

Following Garrett's departure, the Northern Canal was completed and renamed the Hagerman Canal. Attracted by the availability of water, settlers came to the Middle Basin to purchase land for farms and ranches. In spite of the success of the new company, Hagerman and Eddy found themselves at odds over policy and management decisions. Not long afterward, tensions ran high and Eddy left the company.

A depression struck the area in 1893 and money was difficult to obtain. Banks were unable to lend money or to finance irrigation plans. During October of that year, the Pecos River flooded and the resulting surge of water broke through several dams of the PVI&IC, rendering them useless. With no irrigation water, farmers and ranchers filed for bankruptcy and many fled the area. Hagerman funded dam reconstruction to the tune of $150,000, but it only delayed the inevitable. In 1908, the PVI&IC went into receivership.

Garrett returned to his farm. After six years as an investor/promoter in a variety of Middle Basin irrigation schemes, he was no better off financially than when he started. He pondered which direction to turn next. He needed a way to earn an income, but more importantly, he needed a means to continue to be Pat Garrett, the man and the image he believed he had become.

TWENTY-EIGHT
◆ ◆ ◆

Uvalde

With opportunities limited, Garrett turned toward a path that had long held an attraction for him: politics. His opportunity came when momentum gathered relative to dividing Lincoln County into two separate political entities.

Residents of the town of Roswell, which lay sixty miles east of Lincoln and its courthouse, had been generating momentum toward establishing a new county along with its own courthouse wherein they could more easily conduct business. Whenever a Roswell resident had county business to conduct, such as registering a deed, securing a marriage license, or serving on a jury, they were forced to travel to Lincoln. The trip—over a poor road by horseback or wagon—was a necessary but undesirable part of life. Further, Roswell citizens had little in common with Lincoln residents environmentally, culturally, or economically. The large cattle ranches, all owned and operated by Anglos, were scattered around the Roswell area. Lincoln, a foothills environment nestled in the Capitan Mountains, was populated largely by Mexicans.

As it turned out, there was little opposition to dividing the county in two. The only disagreement encountered was related to the proposed name for the new county. The Mexicans who had been elected to the New Mexico Territorial Legislature wanted the new county to be named after Colonel J. Francisco Chavez. Chavez had been a respected landowner and rancher in the area, descended from the original Spanish settlers who came to this region. Chavez had once served as president of the territorial counsel.

Roswell citizens balked at the county being named after a nonwhite. A strange compromise was arrived at: The name was accepted but the spelling was changed from Chavez to Chaves, the name by which it is known today.

The first Chaves County officials were appointed by the legislature, and Republicans were in the majority. Elections were scheduled for 1890. Area Democrats, seeking to become more involved with the county's government, began laying the groundwork for campaigns. Foremost among them was Pat Garrett, who was convinced he had a lock on being Chaves County's first elected sheriff. He was unprepared for any opposition, and it came as a surprise and a bit of a shock when it arrived in the form of his former deputy, John W. Poe.

Poe had earlier resigned from his position as sheriff of Lincoln County and moved to the Pecos Valley and the new county. Poe successfully backed friend and fellow rancher Campbell Fountain as the Democratic nominee for sheriff. Foiled and angered by this turn of events, Garrett decided to run for the office as an independent, but was soundly defeated.

Garrett was livid and bitter. He could see that the tide of public opinion had shifted and he was no longer the hero he believed himself to be. He decided it was time to leave New Mexico. In a short time, he disposed of his holdings and made plans to set out for Uvalde, Texas, about one hundred miles west of San Antonio. There, he was determined to renew his plans for needed irrigation projects. In April 1891, Garrett, along with his family, now numbering eight children, along with Ash Upson, made the long journey to the dry south Texas community. In spite of Upson's comments relative to the notion that Garrett did not write any part of the book that bore his name, this on-again, off-again relationship was back on. Upson was living with the Garretts at the time the decision was made to move to Uvalde.

Uvalde was a relatively peaceful environment, and life for Pat Garrett settled into a calm. Without the assistance of successful businessmen such as those who were involved in his earlier scheme, the irrigation projects Garrett proposed for the area never got off the ground, and Garrett spent most of his time drinking with Upson, gambling, and racing horses.

Because life's pace was less hectic in Uvalde than before, Garrett was able to spend more time with his family. He particularly doted on daughter Elizabeth, who was blind. Speculation surrounded the cause of Elizabeth's blindness, and the subsequent rumors were not kind to Garrett. One story that made the rounds held Garrett responsible for his daughter's handicap as a result of attacking her during a drunken rage and gouging out her eyes. Another tale, one less horrible, related to the notion that Elizabeth's blindness was caused as a result of the wrong medicine being administered to her when she was a baby. The truth is no evidence exists relative to verifying either of these versions.

The most commonly held explanation of the child's blindness again identifies Garrett as the cause. It was claimed that Elizabeth was born blind as a result of her father being infected with syphilis. It was common knowledge that Garrett indulged himself with prostitutes and other women, and it was long suspected that he carried a venereal disease. This story, however, is similar to the others in that it is supported by no evidence whatsoever. The ultimate truth is that Garrett proved to be a loving father to the child until the day he was killed.

While living in Uvalde, Garrett encountered former deputy Kip McKinney, who, along with John Poe, was with the former sheriff on the night of the shooting in Maxwell's bedroom. El Paso attorney Ted Andress once related a story about a telephone call he received concerning a Garrett-McKinney episode. The call was from a man who said he was willing to testify to the particulars of a conversation between Garrett and McKinney who chanced upon one another in an Uvalde saloon. During the conversation, according to the caller, the subject of Billy the Kid came up. The former deputy reminded Garrett that he had not killed anyone that night in 1881 in Maxwell's bedroom.

Garrett became a regular at the racetrack located just west of Uvalde. His successes were sufficient to encourage him to race his horses at locations throughout that part of Texas as well as in Louisiana. After three years of racing and betting on his horses, however, Garrett had to come to grips with the fact that he and his family were just barely getting by. He was beginning to have thoughts of leaving Uvalde and trying to make his mark elsewhere.

On October 6, 1894, Garrett's longtime friend Ash Upson died. Though the two men had their differences, Upson, by and large, had remained loyal. Perhaps some of Upson's loyalty was related to the fact that Pat Garrett supported him during lean times.

Garrett paid for the funeral and had him buried in the Uvalde cemetery. Following Upson's death. Garrett spent the next fifteen months trying to decide what he wanted to do and where he wanted to go. He knew he had to move to realize his dreams, but where? The answer came in February 1896.

Colonel Albert J. Fountain, a prominent New Mexico attorney, newspaper owner, and politician, and the man who served as Billy the Kid's defense lawyer at the Mesilla trial, disappeared along with his nine-year-old son under mysterious circumstances in New Mexico's White Sands desert. Pat Garrett was summoned to assume a leading role in the investigation.

TWENTY-NINE

◆◆◆

The Fountain Case

The year 1896 rolled around and Pat Garrett was soon to be involved as an investigator in one of America's most baffling mysteries. On February 1 of that year, lawyer, newspaper publisher, and politician Colonel Albert Jennings Fountain and his nine-year-old son Henry vanished somewhere along a road that wound through a portion of New Mexico's White Sands and were never seen again. The mystery captured the nation's attention and remained the most often talked-about disappearance until aviatrix Amelia Earhart vanished somewhere in the Pacific in 1937 to take some of the country's attention away from it.

Albert Jennings Fountain was born on Staten Island, New York, on October 23, 1838. He was born Albert Jennings but later took on the surname Fountain, which was derived from his mother's relatives named de la Fontaine. Fountain arrived in California during the early 1850s and eventually secured a job as a reporter for the *Sacramento Union*. While a resident of California, Fountain worked for a time as a law clerk and eventually passed the California state bar exam.

During the advent of the Civil War, Fountain enlisted in Company E of the First California Infantry Volunteers. Thirteen months later on October 27, 1862, while stationed in New Mexico, Fountain married Mariana Lopez. The union eventually produced ten children.

When his time was up, Fountain reenlisted and spent much of his remaining commitment to the army pursuing the uprising Navajo Indians. During one engagement he was wounded and sent to El Paso, Texas, to recover. Fountain decided he liked the city and moved his family there. While in El Paso, he set up a law practice and joined the Masonic Lodge. In 1869, he was elected to the Texas State Senate.

In 1873, Fountain and his family moved to Mesilla, New Mexico, and into Mariana's former home. Here, Fountain built another law practice. In 1881, Fountain was appointed by the court to defend the outlaw Billy the Kid, a case he lost. Fountain was soon named an assistant United States District Attorney. Further, he was a member of the Mesilla Scouts, a local militia that had the responsibility of defending the town against Indian raids and cattle rustling. In 1883, Fountain attained the rank of colonel in the militia.

In 1887, Fountain established the *Mesilla Independent*, an unapologetically Republican-oriented newspaper. He wrote scathing columns that alternately condemned others and praised himself. Like politicians everywhere, Fountain was blessed (or burdened) with a lofty ego.

The year 1887 also saw the arrival of Albert Bacon Fall in New Mexico. A native Kentuckian, Fall spent some time in Texas prior to moving to New Mexico. Shortly after his moving to the area, he set up his own law practice and served as an attorney for the Democratic Party.

The two Alberts—both strong-willed, temperamental, ruthless, and egocentric—were destined to collide, and before long each man was dedicated to the notion of bringing down the other.

Albert Fall had Southern roots and Fountain was a Yankee from Staten Island. Since the Civil War had only been over for a bit over two decades, feelings still ran high and there was little mixing of the two political and cultural camps. Fountain, by virtue of his age and experience, had achieved a number of successes and was regarded as a political power. Fall, on the other hand, was young, filled with energy, and longed for the prestige and power manifested by the likes of Fountain. Fall saw Fountain as his adversary. Fountain, seeing this in his new rival, was determined to maintain his position.

It must be further noted that Fountain garnered a significant percentage of his votes from the Mexican communities, likely because he was married to a Mexican woman. As a result, many Anglos were convinced they were not being adequately represented by him and sought help from outside the Republican Party. Fall recognized this and was quick to step in. Fall moved to Las Cruces and founded a newspaper, the *Independent Democrat*. Before long, the two men were clashing via editorials in their respective newspapers.

Both men ran for a seat in the New Mexico House of Representatives. The race was a close one and Fountain won by the barest of margins. Soon afterward, Fountain departed for the capitol in Santa Fe, where he was named Speaker of the House.

Albert Fall was disappointed and embarrassed by the defeat, but he attributed it to the fact that Fountain had been in the area longer and was more widely known. With the election barely over, Fall began studying ways in which his next campaign would be more effective. During this time he met Oliver Lee.

Oliver M. Lee was a rancher who owned a huge parcel of land near the Sacramento Mountain's Dog Canyon. Though never proven at that time, Lee was believed to have acquired much of his cattle herd by rustling stock from his neighbors. He was also handy with a gun and possessed a violent streak. From time to time, Lee had need of a lawyer, and he saw something he liked in the young Albert Fall.

Lee was invited to assist with Fall's political ambitions. During the 1892 elections, Democrat Fall manifested so much momentum and success that the Republicans grew frightened and summoned the state militia to guard the polls. Fall responded by sending Oliver Lee and his men, including his three most trusted gunmen—Bill McNew, Jim Gilliland, and Todd Bailey—to handle the problem. During the night, Lee's men arrived in Las Cruces and took up positions on rooftops, guns at the ready. The following morning, the militia, led by W. H. H. Llewellyn and Captain Thomas Brannigan, made their way down the street. Fall stepped out to confront them. He ordered Llewellyn to turn the militia around and leave town or they would all be killed. He pointed to the armed men on the rooftops. Confused and unprepared for the confrontation, Llewellyn and his men milled about for a few minutes and then departed.

When the votes were tallied, the Democrats had won the election. The Republicans challenged the outcome, but soon decided to live with the results. Only a few months would pass before Lee, Gilliland, McNew, and Bailey would return to play a larger role in the life of Albert J. Fountain. And Pat Garrett.

Politics provided a slight distraction from the problems with which the residents of that part of New Mexico had to contend. Because of the arid landscape and the frequent droughts, water and grazing rights remained vital. Legal challenges to waterhole and stream rights often filled the courts. Water equaled money and livelihood. Other challenges, those involving desperate men and gunfire, were not unusual occurrences throughout the Mesilla and Tularosa Valleys, often resulting in the death of one or more of the participants.

Oliver Lee and his band of gunmen were ubiquitous during these times. Accusations involving rustling and killing were leveled against Lee on numerous occasions.

Lee had started out as a small rancher. In time, his holdings expanded and his herd grew, taking up much of the Tularosa Valley. Now, in an ironic turnabout, Lee himself became targeted by cattle thieves. His ranch hands, all competent gunmen, had orders to kill rustlers on sight. During the winter of 1893, Lee spotted Matt Coffelt and Charles Rhodius stealing cattle from a portion of his ranch. He killed them both, entering a plea of self-defense.

A short distance up Dog Canyon and several miles from Lee's ranch house lived a recluse named François Jean Rochas, known as "Frenchy." Rochas maintained an orchard and held the rights to the abundant clear water that emanated from a spring farther up the canyon. On December 26, 1894, three men rode onto Rochas's property and gunned him down. Lee was immediately suspected as one of the killers, but no action against him was ever taken. A few years later, Lee took possession of Rochas's land and installed a pipeline to direct the water to his holdings in the valley below.

In March 1894, twenty-one New Mexico cattle ranchers, all seeking ways to put a halt to the rustling epidemic, met in Las Cruces to form the Southeastern New Mexico Livestock Association. Lee became a member. Colonel Albert J. Fountain was named the association's lawyer, and lost no time in prosecuting rustlers. Several lawbreakers were given prison terms, but most of those captured were invited to leave the area. Despite the efforts of Fountain and the association, rustling continued unabated.

Unknown to Oliver Lee at the time, Fountain regarded him as a prime candidate for arrest for cattle theft. He gradually accumulated evidence and testimony from his neighbors who claimed Lee had rustled anywhere from a single cow to an entire herd. The neighbors were too frightened to accost Lee because the rancher, known to be a hardened killer, was always in the company of his own gunmen, including Gilliland, McNew, and Bailey. They felt they had little recourse except to rely on the livestock association.

The fact that Lee's lawyer, Albert Fall, was Fountain's hated enemy added an element of revenge to the colonel's efforts. Fountain hoped to end rustling in this part of New Mexico as well as dampen Fall's rising political career.

While reports and evidence accumulated, actual proof of Lee's rustling activities was not forthcoming. According to Pinkerton documents, Lee was suspected of having stolen and sold or butchered hundreds of head of cattle. A cowboy detective named Les Dow was hired to gather information on Lee. Dow took a job with one of the large ranches and participated in a group roundup near the Sacramento Mountains. He had an informer on his payroll who told him that there was a "blotched" steer in the Lee-McNew herd. At one point during the roundup, Dow noticed Bill McNew cut out a steer with a suspicious brand. Dow approached McNew and asked him if he owned the animal. McNew said he did and Dow offered to purchase it for twenty dollars. McNew agreed and took the money.

When the opportunity arose, Dow drove the steer to an isolated area, killed, and skinned it. On the inside of the flesh he discovered that the original brand had been altered to match Lee's. Dow reported the discovery to Fountain, and the lawyer decided to charge Lee with rustling.

Fountain's desire to bring down Lee, as well as Albert Fall, likely clouded his logic. The truth was that Lee and Fall, along with their cadre of gunmen and politicos, were determined, vengeful, deadly, and not shy about taking what they wanted. It was well known that they got where they were by killing men. Fountain was aware of these dangers, but he was determined to prosecute Lee and humiliate Fall.

On January 12, 1896, Fountain hitched up a buckboard and prepared to depart Mesilla for the courthouse at Lincoln in order to obtain the necessary indictments against Lee. His wife Mariana sensed Fountain's concern that an attempt might be made on his life, so she insisted he take along their nine-year-old son, Henry. Her thinking was that no one would do anything to harm a child.

Some accounts have Fountain driving, instead of a buckboard, a wagon or a buggy. Most authoritative accounts have identified the vehicle as a buckboard, a light, four-wheeled, horse-drawn carriage of simple construction. The front and rear axles are connected to a platform consisting of one or more boards providing for a small amount of space for transporting cargo behind the driver's seat. The "buckboard" is the front-most board of the wagon upon which the driver rests his feet. A buckboard is generally pulled by a single horse.

It was a cold morning. Fountain and Henry were bundled in blankets against the cold and wind. The two traveled through San Augustine Pass, past Chalk Hill near White Sands, Pellman's Well, La Luz,

Tularosa, and finally arrived at Lincoln. There, detective Les Dow displayed the cow skin showing the brand that had been altered in Lee's favor. Ranchers who had been invited to the hearing provided testimony and supplied evidence against Lee and others. By the end of the session, thirty-two indictments were handed down. Two of them were Case No. 1489, *Territory of New Mexico v. William McNew and Oliver Lee*, a charge of cattle theft, and Case No. 1890, *Territory of New Mexico v. William McNew and Oliver Lee*, a charge of defacing brands. As Fountain was gathering his papers and preparing to leave, a man he had never seen before handed him a note. It read, "If you drop this case we will be your friends. If you go on with it, you will never reach home alive."

On the afternoon of Thursday, January 30, Fountain and Henry traveled eighteen miles out of Lincoln and arrived at the home of Dr. J. H. Blazer near Mescalero. The two spent the night as guests of Blazer, and during the visit, Fountain expressed concern for his safety to his host. Shortly after dawn the next morning, however, Fountain guided the horse-drawn vehicle back onto the road. Almost immediately, he noticed two men following him at a distance such that he could not see their faces. Fountain lashed the horse and tried to place some distance between him and the men. By the end of the day, they arrived in La Luz, a few miles south of Tularosa.

On Saturday, February 1, Fountain and his son departed La Luz and headed for home. As they approached Chalk Hill near the White Sands, Fountain glanced behind him and spotted three men following at a distance. Around noon, Fountain stopped the buckboard to visit with Santos Alvarado, who carried mail from Las Cruces to Tularosa. During their conversation, Fountain told Alvarado that he was concerned about the trio on the road behind him. After a short conversation, Fountain continued on toward Pellman's Well. The location was an opportunity to water the horse before undertaking the final push through Chalk Hill and San Augustine Pass.

Minutes after Fountain left the well, he encountered a second mail carrier, Saturnino Barela. Barela noticed the three men following Fountain and implored the lawyer to ride with him to Luna's Well, spend the night, and travel to Mesilla the next morning. Fountain pondered the offer, but told Barela that Henry was getting a cold and he wanted to get him home. The two men bade good-bye to each other and rode their separate ways. It was the last time anyone except the killers saw Albert Fountain and his son Henry.

Portrait of Sheriff Pat Garrett in 1881. James N. Furlong, Courtesy Palace of the Governors Photo Archives (NMHM/DCA), 105080

The only authenticated photograph of the outlaw, Billy the Kid, as a young man. Jay Robert Nash Collection

This illustration shows Pat Garrett (on white horse) bringing in Billy the Kid, chained in a wagon, to Santa Fe, New Mexico, in 1881 after a two-day shoot-out at Stinking Springs. Jay Robert Nash Collection

Maxwell House, Fort Sumner, New Mexico, where Pat Garrett shot and killed a man he claimed was Billy the Kid. Courtesy Palace of the Governors Photo Archives (NMHM/DCA), 045559

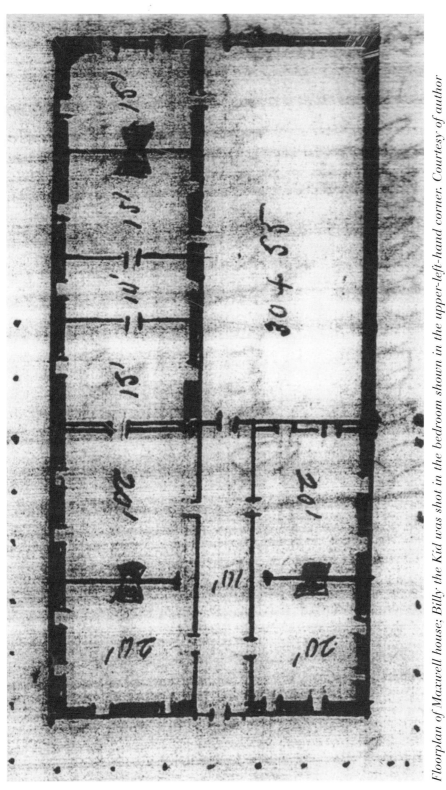

Floorplan of Maxwell house; Billy the Kid was shot in the bedroom shown in the upper-left-hand corner. Courtesy of author

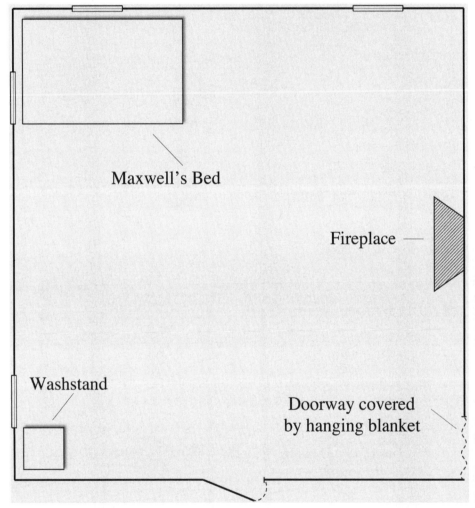

Maxwell's Bed

Fireplace —

Washstand

Doorway covered
by hanging blanket

Bedroom where Billy the Kid was shot; note the two entrances, one of which was covered by a hanging blanket. Courtesy of author

The cover of Pat Garrett's book,
An Authentic Life of Billy the Kid:
The Noted Desperado of the Southwest,
which was published in 1882. Courtesy
Library of Congress [LC-USZ62-87581]

Col. Theodore Roosevelt of the "Rough Riders"—after his return from
Cuba circa 1898. Courtesy Library of Congress [LC-DIG-ppmsca-35734]

Albert B. Fall in around 1912, when he represented New Mexico in the Senate. Courtesy Library of Congress [LC-USZ62-137609]

*Lewis "Lew" Wallace, during
the Civil War when he served
as a general for the Union side.
Courtesy Library of Congress
[LC-DIG-stereo-1s02866]*

*Last Photo of Pat Garrett. Courtesy
Palace of the Governors Photo
Archives (NMHM/DCA), 047632*

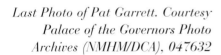

Todd Bailey, the slayer of Pat Garrett. Courtesy Bailey estate

THIRTY

❖ ❖ ❖

Return to New Mexico

In Uvalde, Texas, Pat Garrett read newspaper accounts of the Fountain disappearance. Rumors also reached him that suggested some in New Mexico regarded him as the principal choice to lead an investigation into the matter.

Reasons for suggesting Garrett as the best man to head the pursuit of those responsible for the disappearance and perhaps murder of Colonel Fountain were in large part related to the impotency of the Doña Ana sheriff's department. The current sheriff was Guadalupe Ascarate. According to Metz, Ascarate was "a tool of the politicians, and his deputies were often hired gunmen, on hand if necessary to bully the opposition into submission." When a serious case arose, such as the Fountain disappearance, the sheriff was incompetent to handle such a situation because of his lack of experience and the prevailing politics.

Garrett pondered reentering law enforcement. The truth was, he missed the days when he was looked upon as the hero who put an end to the Lincoln County difficulties. It is likely that Garrett missed the thrill of the chase. But Garrett was a practical man in some respects. According to documentation in the possession of his son, Jarvis Garrett, the former sheriff estimated the job of tracking down the Fountain kidnappers to be worth at least $15,000.

Both Albert Fountain and Albert Fall regarded the office of sheriff of Doña Ana County as an important one, since the man who held that office was often in a position to protect and assist politicians, being one himself. During the election of 1894, Fall supported the candidacy of Ascarate. Fountain backed the opposition Republican candidate, Numa Reymond.

At noon on election day the polls closed one hour for lunch. Eighty-eight votes had been cast. Sometime after lunch as the afternoon voting was underway, someone discovered the morning ballot box was

missing. Later, it was found at the post office. The ballots were still in the box but had clearly been tampered with. Every one of them was marked Democrat.

Oddly, no one moved to void the election. They decided to go ahead with the afternoon voting and deal with the controversy later. When the afternoon votes were counted at the end of the day, the majority of them had been cast for Numa Reymond. In order to determine whether or not the morning votes should be counted, the commissioner's court went into session. As the discussion got underway, Oliver Lee, sporting a revolver and a United States deputy marshal's badge, entered the room and observed the proceedings. Some researchers have suggested that Lee's presence intimidated the voters into accepting the controversial morning ballots. By the time the meeting was adjourned, Ascarate was declared the winner. Fountain, incensed, filed an appeal, one that was still pending when he disappeared.

When Colonel Fountain and his son Henry did not arrive in Mesilla at the expected time, his wife Mariana and the rest of the family grew concerned, even fearful, for they were aware of the lawyer's anxiety regarding a possible threat to his life. Presently, they heard the arrival of a wagon outside and went to investigate. Mariana stepped out on to the porch expecting to find her husband but instead found mail carrier Barela, who dropped by to see if the colonel had arrived.

At his question, Mariana, fearing the worst, dropped to the floor in a faint. Her children carried her into the house, where she heard Barela's account of visiting with her husband the previous day. He also told her that on his way back to Mesilla he followed the tracks of the colonel's buggy and spotted where it had turned sharply off the road and stopped. He saw the tracks of several horses that apparently approached the buckboard. Beyond that, Barela could discern little else.

Albert Fountain Jr. quickly assembled a posse composed of nearby neighbors. Though the weather was quite cold and rain threatened, they rode out back up the trail. In their haste, the posse members had little time to pack supplies. The authorities were also alerted, and Major W. H. H. Llewellyn headed another search party hastening toward the site described by Barela. By the time the two posses arrived in the area it was dark, windy, and frigid. With little leadership or organization, the searchers scattered throughout the sand hills in search of the location described by Barela. Shortly after dawn broke the next morning, February 3, they found what they had been looking for.

The site where Fountain's buckboard had stopped after leaving, or being forced off the road, was one hundred yards from the main route. In the light of day, the posse members saw the tracks of arriving horsemen. Nearby were found horse droppings and cigarette butts, indicating that significant time was spent at that location.

Closer to the road and behind a slight rise topped by a small cluster of brush, the searchers found two spent cartridges. Foot and knee imprints in the sand suggested a shooter had lurked at that location and had fired at least two shots, presumably at Fountain. What could not be discerned was whether or not they were warning shots or shots intended to kill. No blood was found anywhere along the route the buckboard traveled after it left the road. A subsequent search of the spot where the vehicle had stopped, however, identified what must have been a large pool of blood on the ground that had been partially hidden by some low bushes.

After spending more time in the search area, the posses then decided to follow the trail left by the buckboard, which wound through a roadless and rugged landscape.

On the afternoon of February 3, the posses found the buckboard about twelve miles from Chalk Hill. In the buckboard they found a shawl that belonged to Fountain, the note of threat he had received in Lincoln, and his cartridge belt. They also found a hat that belonged to Henry. Missing was Fountain's wooden travel case in which he was transporting the court papers. Though things looked grim, the posse members discerned no indication at that time that the Fountains had been killed.

It was decided to follow the prints of three horses that clearly rode away from the wagon and toward the Jarilla Mountains, some twenty miles west of the Sacramento Mountains. Ahead, the trail passed near Wildy Well. A few miles northeast of Wildy Well was Oliver Lee's Dog Canyon ranch house.

Despite lack of provisions and adequate protection from the cold and wind, the posse pushed on, following the tracks of the three riders. As they approached the Jarilla Mountains, the tracks separated. One man had ridden toward Wildy Well and the other two continued in the direction of the Sacramentos. Major Llewellyn and five men followed the tracks of the two riders, while Carl Clauson and Luis Herrera followed the lone rider. Clausen was Colonel Fountain's son-in-law. The remaining posse members returned to the buckboard and delivered it to Mesilla.

By the time Llewellyn and his party were within two miles of the Lee ranch house, they reined up to discuss what sort of questions they would pose to the rancher regarding the disappearance of Fountain. While they were in a circle debating the process, two of Lee's ranch hands drove a herd of cattle across the trail the posse was following, the one that led to the ranch house, and completely obliterated it. Between being discouraged by the elimination of the trail and more than likely intimidated by the prospect of meeting up with Oliver Lee, Llewellyn turned the posse around and returned to Las Cruces.

Clausen and Herrera followed the tracks of the lone horseman for several miles and eventually arrived at the tiny cabin at Wildy Well. When they approached the shack they were surprised to find Oliver Lee there with four cowhands. When Clausen invited Lee to participate in the search for the Fountains, the cattleman indicated that he could not have cared less about the fate of the colonel and excused himself, claiming he had ranch business to tend to. After Lee rode away, Clausen studied the prints of his horse and determined they were the same ones that they had been following. Clausen decided to ride back to Mesilla and report his discovery.

Weeks passed, and no information on the fate or whereabouts of Colonel Fountain and son Henry was forthcoming. Speculation relative to what had happened to the colonel ran wild. Many assumed he had been murdered, others offered the opinion that he had simply run away.

Albert Fall contributed to the rumors via his *Independent Democrat.* He published reports that Fountain had been spotted in San Francisco, Chicago, and St. Louis, often in the company of a young woman. Other area newspapers ran stories of a more mature and intelligent nature, many decrying the absence of law and order in New Mexico and the negative impact such would have on its petition for statehood.

New Mexico Governor William T. Thornton was deeply troubled by the Fountain mystery. He sponsored a $2,000 reward to anyone who could furnish evidence pertinent to the arrest and conviction of those involved. If one of the perpetrators came forth to claim the payment, according to Thornton, he would be granted a "full and complete pardon." The commissioners of Doña Ana County added $500 to the fund. A few days later the Masonic Lodge of New Mexico upped the reward ante by another $10,000. In addition, a number of Las Cruces and Mesilla businessmen contributed to the reward fund, and in time it exceeded $12,000. This amount of money—a staggering sum for the time—captured the notice of Pat Garrett.

Governor Thornton invited Garrett to meet with him on February 20 in El Paso. Garrett was in town to watch the heavyweight title fight between Bob Fitzsimmons and Peter Maher. The fight was postponed and Thornton and Garrett got together in the governor's hotel room. Following a long discussion on a variety of topics related to statehood, the Doña Ana County sheriff's office, and the Fountain case, the meeting ended and Thornton returned to New Mexico. A short time later the governor filed a recommendation that Garrett be appointed chief deputy, given total jurisdiction in the Fountain case, and receive a salary of $500 per month.

Sheriff Ascarate was not receptive to this recommendation at all. He stated that he resented the intrusion into the operations of his office, and he was not inclined to allow others to determine who his deputies would be. Reymond stepped up and told the Democrats that if Ascarate would resign and allow Pat Garrett to be appointed sheriff, he would see that the appeal and associated lawsuit be withdrawn. Fall objected to the proposal.

On February 24, Garrett was invited to a meeting in El Paso with, according to the *Rio Grande Republican*, some of "the most prominent men in New Mexico" and headed by Governor Thornton. Garrett was invited to pursue the Fountain case as a private detective. He would be paid $8,000 if he succeeded in obtaining an arrest and conviction plus $150 per month for expenses. He was also promised an opportunity to be considered for the office of sheriff.

Garrett accepted the offer. It was timely, for Garrett was broke. Between his gambling debts and the failures associated with his horse racing enterprises, along with his drinking and whoring habits, Garrett had once again depleted his entire resources. Garrett's motivation for accepting the job was fulfilling to his ego, but also an important financial decision.

Later, Garrett moved his family into a rental house in Las Cruces. In 1900 he sold his Uvalde farm to future vice presidential candidate John Nance Garner, a close acquaintance. As far as is known, Garrett never returned to Uvalde. In Las Cruces, he focused on his new mission—to solve the Fountain case. He was also eager to return to politics.

THIRTY-ONE

◆◆◆

Arrests

Pat Garrett was not long in Doña Ana County when he began to grow frustrated at being placed in a position of not being able to make decisions pertinent to the Fountain investigation. He had learned, on arriving, that he was not in charge, as he was led to believe he would be, and he had neither authority to make arrests nor power or influence relative to enlisting the help of citizens. Garrett was not used to being subordinated and thwarted.

Garrett chafed at the fact that he was not appointed sheriff immediately, as he claimed he had been promised. Further, Garrett was embarrassed because it seemed like everyone in New Mexico—the governor, the newspapers, and the citizenry—were watching him and waiting for his next move.

Garrett was unprepared for the criticism that followed his appointment. Elfego Baca, the colorful lawman in Socorro, loudly proclaimed that Governor Thornton had selected the wrong man to lead the investigation. Baca, in fact, boasted that he knew more about the abduction and presumed murder of the Fountains than anyone else in the state and was eminently capable of arresting the killers. It has long been assumed that jealousy no doubt played a role in Baca's stance. The governor's response to the boisterous Baca was to ignore him. Garrett also chose to disregard Baca and feigned a lack of concern about the matter, but it was clear he was bothered by the criticism. Turning his attention toward the case at hand, Garrett received advice from many who were convinced Oliver Lee was behind the killing of the Fountains and insisted on his immediate arrest. Others suggested that the Fountains were still alive and that no crime had been committed.

Though Governor Thornton hired Garrett and promised him that he would eventually occupy the office of sheriff, he was not entirely convinced that the lawman, on his own, would experience any success relative to the Fountain case. What Garrett had going for him was his lingering reputation as a fearless lawman, the man who had been credited for killing the outlaw Billy the Kid. On the strength of that reputation, Garrett could still garner some notice. Politicians of the day, such as Thornton, desired to be the subject of, or close to those who reaped, headlines. In spite of what Thornton regarded as a shrewd political move to have Garrett involved in the investigation, he was likely aware of the former lawman's character issues. As a result, presumably, Thornton contacted, requested, and eventually received assistance from the Pinkerton Detective Agency.

The Pinkertons had been around for nearly a half-century. The agency was founded by Alan Pinkerton, who once served as a bodyguard to President Abraham Lincoln. Pinkerton also founded the United States Secret Service and served as its chief officer. Following the Civil War the agency, headquartered in Chicago, had become famous for its activities related to assisting in the solutions to labor disputes. They also served as strikebreakers, even resorting to violence in the form of beatings and shootings.

Governor Thornton contacted Pinkerton agent James McParland, who headed the Denver office. McParland assigned agent J. C. Fraser to apply his detective skills to assisting in the Fountain investigation. Fraser arrived in Las Cruces on March 10, 1896.

Garrett did not care for what he perceived as the intrusion of the Pinkertons into what he thought was his case alone. As a result, he developed an immediate dislike for Fraser. The Pinkerton man, however, was a highly trained detective who, by all accounts, got along well with coworkers. Garrett was untrained, undisciplined, and his ego balked at what he considered an invasion into his realm as chief investigator. Further, it did not set well with Garrett that the governor requested progress reports from Fraser and not from him.

Though detective Fraser tried hard to get along with Garrett and seek a solution to the Fountain mystery, the tall man remained close-mouthed, refusing to share information with his fellow investigator. In his reports, Fraser never wrote anything negative about Garrett, but it was growing clear that he was becoming frustrated by his style and his unwillingness to cooperate.

Fraser recommended indictments be initiated for the arrests of Oliver Lee, James Gilliland, William McNew, and Bill Carr. Fraser also wanted to arrest Albert Fall as an accomplice but eventually realized that it would be difficult to prove complicity against the elusive and scheming politician.

Garrett told Fraser that arresting the suspects was a bad idea because of the political landscape of the time and place. He stated that arrests should wait until he was named sheriff. He also told Fraser that he believed they required more evidence. Fraser argued that he had developed a strong case for the arrest and prosecution of the aforementioned suspects and that all it needed was for Garrett to obtain statements from them. Fraser's opinion was that all Garrett knew of the case was what he had learned from Fountain supporters, and told him so. Garrett did not care for the rebuke.

Garrett explained to Fraser that it would be difficult to arrest Lee and his men, that they would be hard to find, and that they were dangerous. He also insisted that anything they might say would not be the truth anyway, that they could not expect Lee to admit to killing the Fountains. Garrett argued for constructing a case against Lee and his men slowly and carefully. He suggested they try to identify someone close to Lee who might be willing to provide evidence. Garrett was convinced that either Gilliland or McNew would be prime candidates to turn on their boss. Several attempts were made to gather incriminating information on McNew, but none were successful.

Around this time, the politically motivated Albert Fall decided that Garrett might, in time, be useful to him. Fall was convinced Garrett would eventually be named the sheriff of Doña Ana County and wanted to make certain that the lawman believed Fall was on his side and could be supportive. Though they each represented two different political parties, Fall decided to make friends with Garrett, or at least give the appearance of such.

On March 15, Fraser called on Garrett at his hotel room to discuss some matters and found him in conference with Fall. In a subsequent report, Fraser wrote that Garrett told him that Fall wanted him to be named deputy sheriff and that he, Fall, would be available for any assistance he might find necessary. Fall promised Garrett he would travel to the capital at Santa Fe and lobby for his appointment.

Later, Garrett confessed to Fraser that if Fall was unsuccessful in getting him appointed to the position of sheriff or deputy sheriff that he would likely resign and remove himself from the investigation altogether. Fraser was concerned, for if Garrett was gone from the case, there would be no one left who could initiate the necessary warrants against Lee and others. Garrett undoubtedly was aware of this and was using it as leverage for his position. Fraser was certain that those remaining in the office of sheriff would be unwilling to make the necessary arrests out of fear.

Fraser reported this predicament to Thornton and also solicited assistance from a number of prominent Doña Ana County businessmen and politicos. His efforts yielded success. On March 19, District Judge Gideon Bantz weighed in and declared Numa Reymond the winner of the disputed election. The following day Ascarate moved out of the office and Reymond moved in.

Garrett wasted no time in arranging for a meeting with Reymond. Getting right to the point, Garrett asked the new sheriff when he was going to appoint him chief deputy and the date when the entire office of the sheriff would be turned over to him. Reymond informed Garrett that he had no plans whatsoever of appointing him chief deputy or of giving up his newly attained position. Reymond told Garrett that he had already appointed a man named Oscar Lohman to the position of chief deputy. He further explained to Garrett that the best offer he could make was to hire him as a regular deputy in charge of the Fountain case. In a rage, Garrett stomped out of the office and reported the results of the meeting to Fraser.

Fraser agreed that Reymond's stance was not helpful to the Fountain investigation. If Garrett were to agree to accept a job as a regular deputy he would then be in a position of having to report to Reymond and Lohman. Further, if Reymond should vacate the office, Lohman, who was well-connected politically, was already in a prime position to be named sheriff.

Fraser called upon Major Llewellyn for help. According to Metz, Llewellyn applied his influence to a number of Las Cruces businessmen and raised $1,000 that were used to bribe Reymond and Lohman. Shortly after receiving his payoff, Lohman announced that he did not want to be named chief deputy. Within days, Garrett was appointed to the position. Though there is no evidence of such, it is believed by some that even more money was raised and passed along to Reymond. Whatever the circumstances, the reigning sheriff essentially resigned his position during the last week of April and Garrett was named the new sheriff of Doña Ana County.

With Garrett's yearning for the sheriff's office and all of the political dealings going on, the result was that there was precious little investigation being undertaken relative to the Fountain disappearance save for the determined efforts of Fraser. Being politically minded, Garrett took stock of the situation. For all of his life he had been a Democrat, an affiliation he was proud of. Because Garrett owed his present position of power to the Republicans, he was now in the position of either changing sides or suffering a future defeat at the polls. For Garrett, loyalty took a back seat to practicality, pride, and ego. He was also savvy enough to determine who might best feather his nest. He soon decided to abandon the Democrats. At the next election for sheriff, he ran as an Independent. After being named the winner, he announced his new affiliation with the Republican Party.

During his efforts at gathering information on the Fountain case, Fraser located a man named Slick Miller, who possessed some insight into the murders. Miller was serving time in a New Mexico prison for rustling. He had, in fact, been sentenced by Fountain. On being questioned by another Pinkerton agent named S. B. Sayers, Miller revealed plans made in 1884 by Oliver Lee, William McNew, and Bill Carr to kill Colonel Fountain. Miller claimed the man in charge of the plot was Ed Brown, a small-time cattle rustler from Socorro. Before the plot could be carried out, Fountain's efforts at breaking up the area rustling had succeeded in inhibiting Brown's plans. Miller told Sayers that the men who eventually killed Fountain were the same men that were behind the establishment of the cattlemen's association. Sayers decided to approach Brown with an offer of immunity if he would provide information leading to the arrests and convictions of the Fountain murderers. But first he wanted to frighten the rustler.

Brown was arrested and charged with rustling. Sayers, along with local law enforcement authorities, intimidated Brown into believing that if he did not give up relevant information pertaining to the Fountain case that he could expect to spend a long stretch in prison. Brown turned out to be more determined than the investigators. He denied having any knowledge whatsoever of a plot to kill Fountain. He refused to talk, and was eventually released.

With this latest setback, officials at Pinkerton Detective Agency headquarters decided that the time and energy invested by its detectives was yielding little in the way of progress on the Fountain case. Sayers and his associates were pulled out on May 16, 1898. Pat Garrett remained the sole investigator.

While the Fountain disappearance attracted most of the headlines and occupied much of Garrett's time and thought, the sheriff's efforts, for the most part, were given over to the mundane duties of enforcing the law. In July 1896, he was given the position of a United States deputy marshal. Around this time, the government was becoming increasingly concerned over the growing smuggling of Chinese laborers from across the Mexican border. Hundreds of Chinese had been employed as laborers during the construction of over one thousand miles of railway throughout Mexico. With much of the work completed, and faced with overt and sometimes violent discrimination, the Asians perceived life would be better north of the Rio Grande. Garrett's appointment was related to facilitating the investigation of any migrant activity in his jurisdiction. In addition Garrett, who was always broke, needed the extra money.

THIRTY-TWO

♦♦♦

Garrett and Lee

More than two years had passed since Colonel Fountain's disappearance, and Garrett, who did more idling than investigating, was no closer to solving the case than when he started. Governor Thornton served out his term and New Mexico had a new reigning bureaucrat in Miguel Otero. Otero was not impressed with the way the Fountain investigation had progressed and he insisted on some action by and results from Garrett. Encouraged, or more likely goaded, by Otero's wishes, Garrett made some moves to seek indictments. The grand jury was set to meet on April 1, and Garrett served notice on prospective jurors in Tularosa. While in town, Garrett stopped in Tipton's Saloon and General Store and encountered Oliver Lee, Albert Fall, District Clerk George Curry, and Tobe Tipton playing poker. When Tipton left the game to attend to business, Garrett took his seat.

What followed was a seventy-hour card game, with Garrett and Lee prodding and verbally sparring with each other. The game grew tense. Garrett and Lee were armed, and neither man was inclined to turn his back on the other.

Lee told Garrett that if he intended to serve papers on him that he knew where he could find him. Garrett said that if that were the case, he would send them to him or have them delivered by Curry. The game finally broke up and Garrett rode back to Las Cruces.

After seizing several hours of sleep, Lee decided to travel to Las Cruces to see if he could determine what action the grand jury had taken. He discovered that the jury met and adjourned without ever having mentioned him or the Fountains. Lee thought this odd, given Garrett's claim to be soliciting jurors. Lee, in fact, had been outsmarted by Garrett. The sheriff knew everyone was certain the grand jury would issue indictments. If they were not handed down, Garrett was convinced confusion would reign. And, the sheriff believed, the best time to strike was when there was confusion. Lee was clearly confused. While he was pondering the actions of the grand jury, he dropped off a bundle of clothes at a cleaning establishment and bought a train ticket to El Paso.

The next morning, April 2, Garrett approached Judge Frank Parker and asked for bench warrants for the arrest of Oliver Lee, Jim Gilliland, Bill McNew, and Bill Carr. In his deposition, Garrett promised that the aforementioned men were those who had killed Colonel Fountain and his son, in spite of the fact that no bodies had ever been recovered. Major Llewellyn and Thomas Brannigan lent their authority to a second deposition stating that on February 3, 1896, they found evidence in the form of tracks and other signs indicating that the Fountains had been murdered.

The following day Garrett surprised both Carr and McNew by showing up unexpectedly and arresting them. Both men were so startled at the move that they offered no resistance whatsoever. They were held without bond in the Las Cruces jail.

Garrett appeared to be a bit more reluctant about arresting Lee. The rancher had returned to Las Cruces from El Paso, and while picking up the clothes he left at the cleaners learned of the arrests of Carr and McNew. He traveled on to his Dog Canyon ranch without being encountered by Garrett.

A few moments after arriving at his ranch, Lee was carrying his belongings into the house when he noted the approach of a posse of ten deputized men. Apparently Garrett preferred to have a contingent of others arrest Lee than take on the job himself. The posse reined up several yards beyond Lee's front porch. The rancher merely stood his ground and glared at the riders for a moment, then stepped inside.

Without doubt, the members of the posse were intimidated by Oliver Lee, a man known to be fearless and to have killed others. They huddled for a moment to discuss their next move. One of them suggested they enter the house and place Lee under arrest. Most of them, however, wanted to return to Las Cruces. As they were debating their next move, Tom Tucker, a Lee cowhand, stepped out onto the porch to address the posse, telling them that Lee was not at home. Clearly unsure of themselves, and unsettled as to what to do next, the posse men turned and rode back to Las Cruces. Later that day, Lee returned to El Paso, where he was interviewed by a newspaper reporter. He stated that he had no intentions of being arrested and placed in a jail in Las Cruces.

Lee was certain Garrett did not possess enough evidence to convict him of anything. It is likely Lee was convinced, or at least suspected, that he intimidated Garrett. Lee was a powerful rancher and well connected politically. Garrett, on the other hand, had made little to no progress in the investigation of the Fountain disappearance and was suffering the displeasure of the governor and citizens alike. Lee assumed that the sheriff would try to elicit a confession from him.

Lee was more concerned that his cowhands—Carr and McNew—now languishing in jail, would tell Garrett more than Lee wanted revealed. Lee worried that Garrett might offer either or both of the ranch hands a deal wherein they would be set free if they provided enough information to convict Lee. It turned into a waiting game that both Garrett and Lee were perfectly capable of playing.

Albert Fall finally realized what Garrett was up to. Despite Fall's patronization of Garrett, he was much closer to Lee when it came to politics and power. It is also probable, based on research, that Fall was complicit in the disappearance of his archenemy Fountain. Fall initiated the process wherein he hoped to have Carr and McNew released from jail as soon as possible. Within a few days, Fall managed to schedule a preliminary hearing for the two men. This strategy worked in Fall's favor, for if the two men were to remain in jail, the prosecution would have to show its evidence, and Fall and Lee were desperate to know what they had.

The hearing got underway during the first week of April 1898. A man named Jack Maxwell was introduced and settled into the witness chair. Maxwell was intended to be Garrett's star witness. It is not clear why Garrett selected Maxwell, for he turned out to be a poor choice and came close to destroying the sheriff's case against Lee.

Maxwell testified that he was at Lee's house on the day that Fountain disappeared. He stated that Lee, Gilliland, and McNew were not present but arrived much later on trail-weary horses. Maxwell further testified that the three men appeared to be deeply concerned about something.

Maxwell was nervous and unsure of himself on the witness stand, and Fall sensed this. Like a shark going after a wounded fish, Fall attacked Maxwell. His lawyerly pressure was too much for the inarticulate cowhand, and he crumpled under the onslaught. Maxwell testified that Garrett had offered him $2,000 if his testimony would send Lee, Gilliland, and McNew to prison. Fall adeptly turned the hearing into an accusatorial format wherein he implied Garrett was bribing witnesses to provide testimony that would be useful to Garrett, true or not.

By the time Fall finished with Maxwell, the cowhand had done more damage to Garrett and the prosecution than to Lee and his henchmen. The hearing continued for another six days. Garrett, who should have known better, paraded one witness after another before the court. Each provided nothing in the way of evidence or pertinent testimony, only opinions.

As if things weren't going bad enough for Garrett and the prosecution, the evidence gathered at the site of the presumed Fountain abduction and elsewhere along the pursuit route had vanished.

At the end of the hearing, the judge ordered Carr released but determined that McNew must remain in jail without bond. Garrett's spirit was bolstered somewhat by this, for he was convinced that McNew would eventually yield to interrogative pressure in order to be released. Garrett was wrong again. McNew remained locked up for almost a year. During that time he provided not a scintilla of testimony that could have been helpful to the sheriff.

THIRTY-THREE
✦✦✦

Incident at Wildy Well

Pat Garrett's star was dimming. Whatever notoriety and prestige he once possessed had faded and grown tarnished. People have short memories, and their recollections of the days of Billy the Kid's rustling activities and the subsequent pursuit by Garrett, if they had any at all, were now a generation old. Further, Garrett's inability to make any progress on the Fountain case left the impression among many that he was little more than a political appointee and lacked investigative competence. Remaining busy trying to advance his cause with politicians and moneyed citizens, Garrett had little to do with the common folk of Doña Ana County, and most of them cared little to nothing for the sheriff. Months had passed since swearing out indictments for Lee and Gilliland and yet the two men were still at large. The consensus of most of the area population was that Garrett was afraid of tangling with Lee.

Garrett needed to do something to change the momentum, to reposition himself in a positive way in the eyes of the voters. His opportunity was soon to come, one that would have put to rest all of the concerns about his abilities as a law enforcement officer. As it turned out, it was an opportunity he somehow managed to bungle.

In addition to being intimidated by Oliver Lee, Garrett was also cowed by Albert Fall, the astute and successful defense attorney who once professed to be his friend but whose specialty was getting accused felons set free. In his memoirs, Fall claimed to have defended some five hundred criminals, at least fifty of whom were charged with first-degree murder. Of those, he said, he lost only one case.

While Garrett was allegedly investigating the Fountain case, Fall decided to offer his services to fight the Spanish in Cuba. Some have praised the lawyer for wanting to serve his country in such a manner, but it is more likely that the politically oriented Fall wanted to add military service to his resume, at the time an important consideration for many voters.

Fall appeared not in the least concerned that he was leaving his clients Lee, Gilliland, and McNew. His opinion of Lee and his cowhands was higher than that of Garrett, and he felt certain they would continue to elude the incompetent sheriff. After blustering a great deal about his pending dangerous mission in Cuba, Fall said his good-byes to his Doña Ana followers and departed. The truth is Fall never saw a moment of conflict. He ended up stationed at a military legal office and never left the United States.

As McNew occupied a jail cell and Garrett hopelessly awaited a confession, Lee and Gilliland managed to elude the sheriff at every turn. The two men rarely went near the Dog Canyon ranch house, which they suspected was under surveillance. It was rumored they wore disguises, grew beards, and ranged throughout southern New Mexico. They spotted Garrett and his posse on at least one occasion, but none of the lawmen recognized Lee and Gilliland. Print Rhode and W. W. Cox, both of them brothers-in-law to Lee and living in the area, provided the fugitives with supplies and fresh horses when needed.

On the afternoon of July 11, 1898, two of Garrett's men encountered Lee and Gilliland. Deputies Jose Espalin and Clint Llewellyn rode up to a corral in the foothills of the Organ Mountains where the suspects were working with cattle. Instead of a confrontation, the four men, each of whom apparently knew the other, spent several minutes in conversation. During the visit, Lee mentioned that he and Gilliland were getting ready to ride to Wildy Well, where they would spend the night. The cabin, Lee said, was occupied by James and Mary Madison and their children. The Madisons were two of Lee's employees, and they watched over the rancher's cattle at that end of his range.

Before riding away, Espalin warned Lee to be careful, for Garrett was still on the hunt for him. After saying their good-byes, the two deputies then rode immediately to Garrett and informed him of Lee's plans.

Garrett wasted no time in assembling a posse. It consisted of Espalin, Llewellyn, Kent Kearney, and Ben Williams. Kearney was an odd choice for a posse member. He was a schoolteacher and possessed no experience whatsoever with law enforcement or firearms.

Garrett led the posse out onto the trail just before sunset, intending to cover the nearly forty miles to Wildy Well during the dark of night. Wildy Well was a location on Lee's ranch approximately a day's ride south of his Dog Canyon headquarters. Such was consistent with Garrett's tactics—pursuing at night when the quarry was not expecting the arrival of lawmen. By 4:00 AM they were within one mile of Wildy Well. Here they reined up, tied off their horses, and continued on foot toward the cabin.

The cabin was an adobe structure with a roofed wagon port attached. The roof of the port was a few feet lower than that of the house. Nearby were a pump house, a large water tank, a corral, and scattered outbuildings. In the corral, Garrett spotted horses belonging to Lee and Gilliland. In silence, Garrett led his men toward the house.

Garrett, revolver in hand, stepped up onto the porch and put his ear to the door. He could hear snoring coming from inside. Garrett turned the door latch and found it unlocked. Noting that Kearney was standing next to him, Garrett indicated he wanted the deputy to accompany him inside the structure. With that, he pushed the door open, stepped across the threshold, and jammed the tip of his weapon at the first sleeping person he encountered, and shouted that they were all under arrest.

The person in the bed rose to a seated position and screamed. To Garrett's dismay, it was Mary Madison. Within seconds the rest of the room's occupants were awake and confused. They consisted of Madison and her husband James, their two children, and a man named McVey. Garrett demanded to know where Lee and Gilliland were but received no response. He decided he would have to go in search of them.

As Garrett and his deputies searched the outbuildings, he glanced back at the house and noticed McVey attempting to communicate with someone on the roof. The roof was flat, with the adobe walls of the structure projecting two feet above the level to form a parapet. Garrett realized immediately it served as a substantial defensive position. Grabbing a ladder, Garrett carried it to the house and leaned it against one wall. He told McVey to climb the ladder and instruct the men on the roof to surrender. McVey refused. Frustrated, Garrett then gave the same order to James Madison, He, too, refused.

Garrett ordered Williams to take a position behind the water tank. He then instructed Llewellyn to move McVey and the Madisons back into the house and stand guard over them. He, Espalin, and Kearney then used the ladder to climb to the roof of the wagon port. From where they stood, they could see a portion of the house roof but saw no one there. One of the deputies secured a smaller ladder that was lifted to the top of the port and leaned against the wall of the house. Kearney climbed up this ladder a couple of rungs to get a better view of the roof. At the same time, according to Garrett, the sheriff yelled for whoever was on the roof to surrender. When interviewed later, Lee stated that this was not true, that the call for surrender came only after Garrett and the deputies started shooting.

Lee later stated that he "was asleep when fired upon," though it is difficult to believe that he remained asleep with all of the activity taking place below him in the house and in the yard, as well as the screaming of Mary Madison. Lee said, "Kearney fired twice and Garrett also fired before I fired. I heard no commands of 'hands-up,' but Garrett was talking while shooting."

In any event, once Kearney was in a position to see the roof, he fired his revolver. A second later, Garrett sent several shots from his rifle onto the roof. Holding position atop the roof were Lee, Gilliland, and two of Lee's ranch hands including Todd Bailey. As far as can be determined, this is the first time Garrett had encountered Bailey, but it would not be the last.

Two of Garrett's bullets struck the roof close to Lee, scattering gravel, dirt, and twigs. Garrett dropped down from his position just as Lee returned fire. Lee was certain his bullet struck the sheriff. As Lee fired, so did one of his cowhands, the bullet striking Kearney in the shoulder and shattering bone. A second bullet struck the posse man in the groin. He fell from the ladder, rolled across the wagon port roof, and slammed down onto the ground.

Feeling exposed, Garrett jumped from the port roof and, ignoring the severely wounded Kearney, took shelter inside one of the outbuildings. Espalin lowered himself to the ground, but gunfire from the roof kept him confined to a position up against the wall of the house.

While hiding in the outbuilding, Garrett heard Madison yelling at him from the house. He said he wanted to take his family to the root cellar in order to get out of the line of fire. Garrett told him to do so. In his haste, Madison forgot his daughter, no more than a toddler, who was left inside the house.

Deputy Williams was maintaining his position under the water tank, which was supported atop a low platform. From there, he fired at rifle flashes he saw on the roof. His attack was immediately answered, and several bullets tore through the tank, spilling water onto the helpless lawman. Unable to flee, he was forced to remain under the dripping tank in the freezing weather. This left Garrett as the only member of the posse who was in a position to continue the fight.

According to R. L. Madison, the son of James Madison, who was a toddler at the time of the gunfight, Lee called Garrett a bastard and scorned him for shooting at men at the same time he was calling for them to surrender. Garrett asked Lee to lay down his arms and give up, but the rancher refused, saying that he was convinced Garrett was going to kill him if he did.

According to Buck Bailey, the grandson of Todd Bailey, Lee ordered the lawmen to drop their guns and Garrett replied that he was afraid to because the outlaws would then kill them. Lee told Garrett that he was a man of his word and that if he and the deputies dropped their weapons he would let them ride out if they did as they were instructed. Garrett finally agreed.

Garrett then approached Kearney and saw that he was badly wounded, in severe pain, and might not live. From the roof of the house, Lee repeated his order for Garrett and his men to ride away.

Author Leon Metz refers to this "as the most humiliating episode of Garrett's life." Despite the element of surprise Garrett believed he carried into Wildy Well, he and his posse had been forced to surrender to Lee, leave their weapons, and ride away. Much to Garrett's discredit, he chose to leave the wounded Kearney behind.

The lawmen rode a few miles to a location called Turquoise Siding, where they encountered a section line crew. Garrett talked some of the men into taking a wagon to Wildy Well and retrieving Kearney. When the railroad men arrived later, they found Lee and his cowhands with the badly wounded man, talking to him and attempting to make him comfortable. After the railroaders took charge of him, Lee and his men rode away.

Kearney was transported to Turquoise Siding, where Garrett waited. The sheriff had him loaded onto a train and carried to Alamogordo, where he was unloaded, placed in another wagon, and taken to La Luz. Kearney died the following day.

Garrett and his deputies returned to Las Cruces. His mission to arrest Lee and Gilliland was a failure, and the two fugitives were still at large.

THIRTY-FOUR

❖❖❖

Surrender

Doña Ana County Sheriff Pat Garrett had accomplished little in the two years since Colonel Fountain and his son had disappeared save for arresting Bill McNew. That in itself proved inconsequential, since McNew provided absolutely nothing in the way of incriminating Oliver Lee and Jim Gilliland. Governor Otero was growing impatient with Garrett, as were citizens of New Mexico. Meanwhile, Garrett continued to collect a monthly paycheck and assured the voters that he was indeed active in the investigation.

Not only were Lee and Gilliland wanted in relation to the Fountain incident, they were now saddled with an additional charge: the murder of Kent Kearney. Feelings ran high that Lee and Gilliland cared little about surrendering to Garrett because they were convinced the sheriff, at best, could not guarantee their safety, and at worst, wanted them dead. By this time, Albert Fall had returned to Las Cruces from his military service and insisted that arrangements needed to be made to guarantee the safety of his two clients.

To add to the troubles the two fugitives were experiencing, word spread that Gilliland, a boastful sort, was bragging to acquaintances about his role in the killing of Fountain. Fall was concerned that Gilliland was talking too much and feared that if Garrett arrested him, he might reveal too much information, thereby making a courtroom defense difficult.

Fall pondered a number of strategies. He could agree that Lee and Gilliland stood a good chance of evading Garrett forever by hiding out; he could convince them to surrender to the sheriff; he could arrange to have them surrender to law enforcement authorities who were outside of Garrett's jurisdiction. The more he considered these options, the more Fall realized that the latter one stood the greatest chance of success. He also considered that this could best be accomplished if a new county was created, one that could claim legal jurisdiction in the Fountain case.

Fall decided to use his influence and apply his skills, clever and devious as they were. He visited with W. A. Hawkins, an attorney for the El Paso and Northeastern Railroad who had also manifested the desire to see a new county formed, but for different reasons. The railroad company he represented had enjoyed a strong and favorable agreement with Oliver Lee. Lee sold a large portion of his Dog Canyon ranch to the EP & N in 1897 for $5,000. By 1898, the railroad was running through this area from El Paso to Alamogordo. Further, an arrangement was made to construct a system of canals across Lee's ranch to deliver water from the Sacramento Mountains to critical railroad stations along the route.

All of this was located in Doña Ana County, but county officials were less than helpful to the railroad. Roads were poorly maintained, if at all. Communication lines were poor to nonexistent. The railroad argued for a new county and a new county seat and lobbied for Alamogordo. Fall volunteered to assume the responsibility for petitioning for a new county as long as it was agreed that the western boundary would extend to the San Andres Mountains. If this could be accomplished, the new county would thus contain the alleged Fountain murder site and assume legal jurisdiction. Doña Ana County would be removed from the jurisdiction.

The New Mexico politicos who could facilitate such a move were less than enthusiastic when this plan was presented to them. Thomas Catron, a prominent Republican in the territorial senate, saw no reason to support a proposition advanced by Fall, a Democrat, and one he didn't care for anyway. Governor Otero, who was no friend of Catron, even opposed the idea. Further, both Otero and Catron were convinced Lee was behind the killing of Colonel Fountain and were not inclined to do anything that would make his arrest and prosecution difficult.

History suggests that Albert Fall and W. A. Hawkins were considerably more intelligent than Otero and Catron. Knowing well that moves and decisions made by politicians were often, if not mostly, strongly determined by ego, they proposed that the new county be named after the governor. Within hours of having this idea presented to him, Otero decided it would be a good idea to have a new county.

It was no surprise to anyone that Otero's primary opposition to the idea came from Catron, whose own ego was likely bruised by this plan. He acquiesced, however, when everyone involved agreed to lend support to his own proposal relating to establishing a new county in the western part of the territory to be named after President McKinley. Agreements were arrived at and Otero County became official on January 30, 1899. A short time later, George Curry was named sheriff.

While all of these political machinations were being undertaken, Oliver Lee was living in San Antonio, Texas. There, he married Winnie Rhode, a sister-in-law of W. W. Cox, one of Lee's neighboring ranchers. The uniting of the Lee and Cox families was to eventually impact Garrett.

By March 1899, Lee and Gilliland had returned to New Mexico and were living at the home of Eugene Manlove Rhodes in the foothills of the San Andres Mountains. Rhodes was a smaller-than-average man with a speech impediment, but became a noted writer of books about southwestern ranches and ranchers. Rhodes was known to provide sanctuary to men on the run, and Lee and Gilliland were not the first. While Rhodes was sympathetic to Lee and Gilliland, he also was an admirer of Pat Garrett. It was through this unique position that Rhodes was able to arrange for the surrender of the two men. Rhodes contacted Sheriff Curry of Otero County and agreed to turn over the fugitives on two conditions: They would not be placed in the Doña Ana County jail, and they would not be handed over to Sheriff Pat Garrett.

Curry, in turn, contacted Governor Otero and requested advice. Otero agreed that the conditions could be met. Between Rhodes and Curry, it was agreed that the two outlaws would be taken to Las Cruces and surrender to Judge Frank Parker. On March 13, 1899, Lee and Gilliland, both wearing minimal disguises and accompanied by Rhodes, boarded a train at Socorro and headed south. Unknown to them, Pat Garrett and Texas Ranger Captain John Hughes were also riding the same train. Garrett and Hughes, who were old friends, were transporting a prisoner from the prison at Santa Fe to El Paso.

According to Rhodes, Garrett and Hughes entered the smoking car where Lee and Gilliland were seated. For several minutes Hughes thumbed through a magazine as he stood next to the seat occupied by Gilliland. Garrett walked down the aisle and stopped next to Lee, bent down, and stared past the outlaw and out the window. More minutes passed, and the two lawmen, neither of them lingering long enough to enjoy a smoke in the car, turned and walked away.

According to writer W. H. Hutchinson, there is little agreement among historians as to whether or not the two lawmen recognized the fugitives. Gilliland, however, was convinced that they did. He implied that Garrett was too frightened of Oliver Lee to make an arrest, or even say anything. Gilliland may be correct. It is doubtful that the blue eyeglasses worn by Gilliland and the beard worn by Lee were sufficient to fool Garrett, an experienced lawman who had been close to both men on several occasions.

The train eventually arrived at Las Cruces. On stepping out of the car, Rhodes escorted Lee and Gilliland to the home of Judge Parker, where they formally surrendered. Because the Alamogordo jail was still under construction, the two prisoners were installed in the Las Cruces jail in spite of the earlier agreement not to do so. A short time later, Parker agreed to have the two men placed under the authority of Socorro County Sheriff C. F. Blackington and ensconced in the Socorro County jail. Days later when construction on the Otero County jail was completed, Blackington escorted the prisoners to El Paso, where they were loaded onto an EP & N train and delivered to Alamogordo.

Metz relates a humorous event at the train station in El Paso. Blackington left Lee and Gilliland at the train station while he went to a nearby tavern to have a few drinks. After getting drunk and boisterous, Blackington was arrested by Constable Mannen Clements. Blackington tried to explain who he was and that he was on an important mission delivering Lee and Gilliland. Clements did not believe him and escorted the sheriff to the jail. Some time later, the prisoner Lee walked over to the jail and identified Blackington for Clements.

At Alamogordo, Lee and Gilliland were placed in the new jail. As they conferred with their lawyer Fall and awaited their trial, logistical difficulties arose.

THIRTY-FIVE

✦✦✦

Incident at Cox Ranch

As Lee and Gilliland waited in jail for their trial to begin, Garrett went about his duties as sheriff. George Blalock, the sheriff of Greer County, Oklahoma, wired Garrett that a man named Norman Newman, alias Billy Reed, was wanted for murder and was known to be living at the Doña Ana County ranch of W. W. Cox. On October 7, 1899, a warrant was issued for Newman's arrest. Joined by Sheriff Blalock, who arrived by train, and Deputy Jose Espalin, Garrett left Las Cruces bound for the Cox Ranch. Garrett and Blalock traveled in a buckboard while Espalin rode horseback. What ensued at the Cox Ranch was to impact Garrett years later.

One year earlier, Newman and his partner in a farm were returning from the market where they sold their produce. The money was divided, and each man stuffed his share in his pockets. The trip back to the farm took two days, and the men were forced to camp along the route. That night, Newman slew his sleeping partner, crushing his skull with a wagon wrench. After taking the money off the dead man, Newman stripped the clothes off the corpse and dropped the body in a shallow pond where it remained for six weeks before being found.

Following the killing, Newman headed west in search of gainful employment. His journey took him to New Mexico, where he was arrested for some minor infraction. While in jail, Newman met inmate Perry Cox, a brother to rancher W. W. Cox. Several weeks later, Perry Cox helped Newman escape. He secured a horse for him and told him to ride to his brother's ranch, explain what happened, and ask for a job.

On arriving at the Cox Ranch, Newman, who was going by his alias, Billy Reed, was put to work in the kitchen assisting Mrs. Cox, who was several months pregnant. In the meantime, a reward for Newman was posted in Oklahoma, and the Greer County citizenry pressured Sheriff Blalock to track down the killer and bring him to justice.

Cox's Ranch was once known as the San Augustine Ranch and was located on the eastern side of the rugged Organ Mountains some twenty-five miles from Las Cruces. In 1850, a man from Indiana named Thomas J. Bull moved onto the property but was convinced to sell out to Warren J. Shedd a few years later. The enterprising Shedd, appreciating the fact that a major transportation route ran through the property and deciding he could make a profit catering to travelers, constructed a hotel, a livery, a gambling parlor, a tavern, a dance hall, and corrals. It was not long before the location grew popular with overnighters.

In addition to serving as a resting place and offering fresh water, Shedd's ranch was a center for prostitution, gambling, and liquor. From time to time, men arrived flashing large sums of money and then mysteriously disappeared. Fistfights and gunfights were common, and not much time passed before the area was littered with tombstones and other grave markers.

During the 1880s, Shedd, by then an old man, sold his property to Benjamin E. Davis, a Welshman who served in the California regiment that occupied the nearby Mesilla Valley in 1862. Davis set out immediately to remove the taint of Shedd's enterprises, and in a short time installed herds of cattle and sheep on the rangelands. The respectable and respected Davis prospered, but life for him in the shadow of the Organ Mountains was trying. His daughter—four years old—died from a rattlesnake bite. Devastated, Davis lost much of his passion for the place and died a short time later. His wife, either incapable of running the ranch or unwilling to, put it up for sale. In 1893, it was purchased by W. W. Cox.

William W. Cox was from Texas, and his life was speckled with hardship and violence. His father was James W. Cox, who held an office with the state police. This agency was installed by the Reconstruction government and was largely despised by the Texas citizenry. Many of the state policemen were little more than outlaws themselves, and often used their position to bully, rob, beat, and even kill those who opposed them. James Cox was killed during an ambush by Karnes County citizens led by the killer, John Wesley Hardin.

W. W. Cox chanced by the scene of the ambush hours later and found his father's body riddled with fifty-eight bullet wounds. Cox swore revenge, took it, and before long there were several warrants out for his arrest. Cox was finally caught, tried, and sent to prison for several years. After escaping, he gathered up his family, left the area, and took jobs on West Texas ranches. In 1890 he arrived in Doña Ana

County. Cox manifested little of his troublemaking youth and became a respected citizen. Three years later he bought Davis's ranch.

Even while working cattle, Cox dressed in a starched white shirt, string tie, and vest; he was rarely seen wearing anything else. He proved an able stockman and was admired by his ranch hands, who were loyal and dedicated to him. Cox was a chain smoker and an inveterate curser; he was seldom seen without a hand-rolled cigarette and rarely spoke a sentence that wasn't littered with several profane words.

Cox and Oliver Lee became brothers-in-law. In spite of the relationship, Cox got along well with Garrett and even assisted, or appeared to assist, the lawman in some aspects of the Fountain investigation.

As Garrett, Blalock, and Espalin neared the Cox ranch house, they decided to hide the wagon and horses and sneak up on foot. Blalock was left to watch the animals behind the shelter of some trees as Garrett and the deputy made their way to a position behind the house. After crossing the backyard and stepping up to the kitchen door, Garrett spotted a man washing dishes. Garrett pointed his revolver at him and asked him if he was Billy Reed. When the man replied that he was, Garrett told him he was under arrest.

Knowing he was face-to-face with a murderer, Garrett, in an odd and careless move, holstered his weapon. One second later, Newman slammed a punch to Garrett's face. Stunned, the sheriff pulled the handcuffs out from under his belt, swung them, and cracked Newman across the head, knocking him to the ground. As Garrett and Espalin fell atop Newman and attempted to cuff him, they were attacked by a large bulldog that charged into the kitchen from an adjacent room. By coincidence, the bulldog belonged to Albert Fall, W. W. Cox's lawyer. Newman fought with the lawmen as they, in turn, tried to fight off the bulldog, all the while cursing and yelling. During the melee, Newman broke free and ran toward the smokehouse located just outside the kitchen. Newman knew that Cox kept a revolver there and was intent on retrieving it. As Newman momentarily stood in the open doorway of the smokehouse, two gunshots sounded and he was shot in the back, one of the bullets tearing through his heart and killing him instantly.

The gunshots frightened the bulldog away. Regaining their composure, Garrett and Espalin entered the smokehouse and pulled Newman's body out. They dragged the corpse to the buckboard, tossed him in the small wagon bed, and returned to Las Cruces.

The next day the body of Newman, aka Reed, was sent to El Paso, where it was embalmed. When it could be arranged, it was then shipped to Greer County, Oklahoma. The following day, an inquest was held wherein Joe Espalin admitted he fired the two shots, one of which killed Newman. Both Garrett and Espalin were judged to have acted within the bounds of the law.

Several days later, Cox returned to his ranch from a trip to Mexico. When he learned of what had transpired in his absence, he expressed his displeasure. He was particularly incensed that his pregnant wife had been subjected to the violence and terror. Cox's anger and irritation, however, was never manifested toward Garrett. Cox, in fact, even lent the perpetually broke Garrett some money a short time later.

While W. W. Cox appeared to have taken Garrett's intrusion into his home in stride, Mrs. Cox's brother, Print Rhode, was outraged. When he learned of what had happened and the stress it had caused his sister, Rhode swore he would kill Garrett.

Print Rhode was a short, muscular cowhand who seldom went out of his way to avoid a confrontation. An adept cowman, Rhode also excelled at fighting. He came to New Mexico with Cox and was one of his most loyal ranch hands.

Garrett, a man who went his own way and followed few rules, had very few friends he could count on. He was better, it seemed, at making enemies. Cox and Rhode represented two more adversaries that would cause the sheriff to keep looking over his shoulder.

THIRTY-SIX

◆◆◆

Trial

As Albert Fall prepared to defend Lee and Gilliland, he determined that it was not likely he would be able to assemble a fair and impartial jury in Otero County. The prosecution wanted to hold the trial in Las Cruces, but it was argued that since that was Colonel Fountain's hometown, most of the jury would be prejudiced. The prosecution fought the objection, but eventually agreed. A compromise was made to hold the trial in Sierra County in the town of Hillsboro.

Hillsboro was a mining town that stretched along a portion of Middle Percha Creek. While today it can be classified as a picturesque small community, it was fairly bustling during the 1890s. It boasted a schoolhouse, a hotel, sheriff's office and jail, and a smelter. Several fine homes belonging to mining officials lent an air of abundance to the area. At the time, Hillsboro also served as the county seat.

The trial commenced on May 25, 1899, and was to last eighteen days. Hillsboro seemed an odd choice as a setting for the event, save for the fact that it likely offered the best opportunity to find impartial jurors. Many residing in the town were unaware of the disappearance of Colonel Fountain and Garrett's efforts to arrest the suspects. Hillsboro had no telegraph and no railroad. A stagecoach came through town once a week.

When the location was announced, Western Union set about stringing wires from the tiny town to Las Cruces, Silver City, and elsewhere. Newspaper reporters were beginning to drift into the little community, and these were soon followed by the curious. In no time at all, the hotel was booked up. A tent community was set up just north of the town. Here, the witnesses for the prosecution were installed. At the other end of town, similar arrangements were created for the defense. Onlookers, friends and family of the defendants and witnesses, and others were forced to find a place to camp in the surrounding foothills.

The impending trial began to take on meaning above and beyond whether or not Lee and Gilliland were guilty or innocent. By this time, feelings were settling in along political party lines. If the prosecution won and Lee and Gilliland were found guilty, most were prepared to interpret it as a victory for the Republicans, and, as such, it would enhance the image and prestige of Tom Catron, who had been appointed as special counsel for the prosecution by Governor Otero. On the other hand, if Lee and Gilliland were successfully defended and found not guilty, it would be viewed as a victory for the Democrats and a significant setback for the Republicans. Fall was determined to rout the Republicans and continue the momentum geared to accelerating his longed-for rise to power.

Catron was affiliated with the so-called Santa Fe Ring. Author Robert M. Utley described the ring as "a band of shrewd lawyers and businessmen [along with] certain territorial officials [who] made up a loose cabal of opportunists." Members of the ring, according to Utley, "enjoyed modest bonanzas by trafficking in old Spanish land grants, the public domain, and contracts for supporting the territory's huge federal establishment, especially Indian agencies and army forts." The membership of the ring consisted entirely of Masons.

Metz argues that the name Catron, as well as the term "Santa Fe Ring," was synonymous with political corruption. Unlike the mostly blue-collar residents of Hillsboro, Catron was a soft, portly man who likely never experienced hard work of any kind. He was perceived as making his living by arranging for taxes on those who did. Catron was not well received in Hillsboro.

By contrast, Fall looked good to the citizens. He was approachable, stopping often to visit and speak with residents as well as newspapermen. While Catron kept himself surrounded by his well-dressed and elegant coterie, Fall, the consummate politician, was shaking hands, slapping backs, and kissing babies. Quickly grasping the tenor of the multitudes, Fall characterized the trial as a contest between the working class, represented by ranchers and farmers just scraping by, as well as miners who labored from dawn to dusk, against the wealthy, the major landowners, and the elite. Fall carefully and cleverly constructed the image of a giant killer, and his enemy was the evil power that wielded a heavy hand over the region.

Into this milieu strode Pat Garrett. Though he was a prominent figure in the trial, he remained somewhat low key. While many recognized him, he was largely ignored, for he represented the establishment.

A short time later came Lee and Gilliland. They were escorted and surrounded by friends, all armed. They were treated as celebrities. Like Albert Fall, they mingled with the citizenry shaking hands and accepting good wishes. The two defendants appeared to be having a good time.

The newspapers reporting from Hillsboro generated an image of Lee quite different from the one he had endured prior to his surrender. Earlier he had been described as calculating and cold-blooded. Now, as Metz deftly portrayed, Lee was regarded as a Robin Hood–type character who fought for the little people against the evils of power as represented by Garrett and Tom Catron. Seeing this, Catron and the rest of the prosecution team began to grow concerned.

At the onset of the trial, Lee and Gilliland were formally charged only with the murder of Henry Fountain. Charges related to the deaths of Colonel Fountain and Deputy Kearney were held back to be filed at a later date. McNew, still residing in the Las Cruces jail, had been granted a change of venue to Silver City. He had been scheduled to go on trial in April, but the charges had been withdrawn by Fall. Fall regarded McNew as insignificant compared to Lee. In defending McNew, the lawyer did not want to tip his hand and reveal evidence that might be better served at the trial of Lee. Even Gilliland was regarded by Fall as expendable. Like McNew, he was just an employee following orders.

Jury selection took place between May 25 and 27. Right from the beginning, the prosecution could only watch as its plans began to crumble. Key witnesses failed to show up. Three Mexicans who claimed they saw the accused ride from the murder scene with bodies strapped to horses were missing. Jack Maxwell, who was a victim of Fall's questioning earlier, had to be retrieved from White Oaks by Garrett.

On May 29 the trial got under way. Todd Bailey, one of Lee's ranch hands, sat up front on one side of the room and another Lee employee sat on the other side. A third employee sat in the back. Each of the cowhands carried concealed weapons rolled up in their saddle slickers.

Former governor Thornton testified that he visited the alleged murder site and shortly afterward offered a reward for the killers. Witness Theodore Heman provided the motive; as foreman of the Lincoln County Grand Jury in 1896, he testified to the cattle rustling indictments handed down against Lee and McNew. Mail carrier Barela related his visit with Colonel Fountain on the road to Las Cruces.

When Jack Maxwell was sworn in, he testified that he had forgotten most of his earlier testimony wherein he stated that he was staying at the Dog Canyon ranch house when Lee, Gilliland, and McNew rode in on tired horses and appeared gravely concerned about some matter. The prosecution, however, possessed a copy of the testimony and read it to the jurors.

Fall objected to the reading of Maxwell's testimony but was overruled. He decided instead to attack Maxwell's credibility. He reminded the jurors that Garrett had paid him $2,000 to testify against Lee. Fall also forced Maxwell to admit he had written a letter to a Lee acquaintance telling him that there was no need to worry and that he would state that Lee was forty miles way when the disappearance occurred.

Maxwell did not hold up well under questioning. Sweating profusely, he appeared to be sick. He folded under Fall's onslaught and appeared unable to recover. When it seemed as though Maxwell had done as much damage to the prosecution as he possibly could, Fall dismissed him.

Fall started out at a relentless and aggressive pace and did not let up on subsequent witnesses for the prosecution. A Dr. Francis Grosson testified he examined an amount of blood-soaked earth near the Fountain wagon and concluded that the blood came from a human. Fall embarrassed him by getting him to admit he could not tell the difference between human blood and dog blood.

At least two witnesses testified that Gilliland had bragged about killing Henry Fountain. Fall managed to bring out the fact that both witnesses were sworn enemies of Gilliland and that their testimonies should not be admitted.

Then Pat Garrett was called to the stand. Garrett testified to his role in the Fountain case from the time he was invited into the affair through his term as sheriff. Fall did his best to unnerve the sheriff but was unsuccessful. In the end, the Garrett and Fall back-and-forth ended in a tie, but ultimately the sheriff was not particularly helpful to the prosecution. Following Garrett, a few more witnesses testified to no particular end. Then, Albert Fall was called to present the defense.

George Curry, the sheriff of Otero County, testified that Maxwell, initially regarded as the principal witness for the prosecution, had told him that Lee, Gilliland, and McNew had been at the ranch during the time Fountain disappeared, thus destroying any credibility Maxwell's testimony may have had with the jurors. Albert Blevins, a railroad fireman, testified that he was at Lee's ranch at the time of the disappearance and all three men were there. Lee's mother stated her son had been home the entire day of the Fountains' disappearance.

When Oliver Lee took the stand in his defense, he stated that since he had never left the ranch, he was not aware that Fountain and his son had gone missing until several days after it happened. Print Rhode, one of Lee's brothers-in-law, testified that Major Llewellyn threatened to blow up Lee's ranch house. This testimony placed the prosecution in a bad light with the jurors. Though Catron and his prosecution team vigorously denied the tactic, few listened to them.

Todd Bailey was called to the stand. He turned out to be an effective witness, testifying that he was working alongside Oliver Lee the entire afternoon of February 1, 1896. He stated that there was no way that Lee could have ridden to Chalk Hill, almost fifty miles away from where the men were working cattle.

The trial plodded on until the defense rested and it was time for the final arguments. Following a short break, Todd Bailey and the two other Lee cowhands assumed their previous positions in the courtroom. Bailey was wearing a saddle slicker. Hidden underneath the folds was a shotgun. Earlier in the day, the barrel and stock were both shortened. The other two Lee employees were also armed.

Years later, Bailey stated that if Lee was found guilty, he and the other two cowhands were to rise up and shoot Garrett, the other deputies, and the prosecuting attorney. Following this, the plan was for them to escort Lee out of the building, and ride to a location outside of town where more Lee hands were waiting. From there, they would travel for several miles with a pair of cowhands splitting off from time to time to confuse the trackers. Lee and Bailey would continue on to Mexico.

In a somewhat odd move, the prosecution selected Richmond P. Barnes to open the final arguments. Fancying himself a much more skilled orator than he turned out to be, Barnes quoted from Charles Dickens's *The Pickwick Papers* and succeeded only in confusing the jurors, assuming they could understand anything he was saying at all. Some of the jurors were Mexicans who manifested very little facility with the English language and Dickens meant nothing to them. They were assisted by an interpreter, but as it turned out he had no more of an idea of what Barnes was trying to say than anyone else. The final arguments for the prosecution were off to a bad start.

Following the wordy Barnes, the prosecution sent in William B. Childers, a much more efficient communicator. Childers argued that the defendants remained at large for three years because they knew they were guilty of the charges, and that the argument that they were afraid Garrett would kill them was unsound. He pointed out that McNew had been in Garrett's custody for months and had gone unmolested. He further argued that Garrett's offer of $2,000 for Maxwell's testimony against Lee was within the ethical bounds of the law.

By the time Childers sat down and it was time for the defense, the jurors looked like they could use a nap. Albert Fall rose and faced them. Fall was eloquent but without the bombast of Barnes. He praised the members of the jury for their good work and lauded the legal system and the manner in which it served those who found themselves in difficulty. He pointed out that Jack Maxwell was a proven liar, that his testimony had been contradicted by no less than eight witnesses.

During his argument, according to an article in the June 15, 1890, issue of the *El Paso Daily Herald*, Fall called Doña Ana County officials "a lot broken down political hacks . . . gathered together, as does the slimy filth on the edges of a dead eddy." This went over well with the members of the jury.

Fall also pointed out to the jurors, mostly poor residents of Hillsboro, that the territory spent a great deal of money, money from their taxes, to prosecute the accused, but that the defendants, salt-of-the-earth working men like themselves, were forced to pay for their defense out of their own pockets.

Fall stated that, despite the charge of killing Henry Fountain, no body had ever been found. He looked the jury in the eyes and said that based on the evidence presented by the prosecution, "you would not hang a yellow dog." When Fall was finished, the entire courtroom, excluding the prosecution, burst into applause that lasted several minutes.

Tom Catron then stood and presented a rebuttal. By this time it was late in the evening and he orated for two-and-a-half hours. It is doubtful that many heard much of what he had to say. Jurors and spectators were tired and some had fallen asleep. By now, the jury was desperate to be excused.

It was not to be. In a brilliant move, Fall, knowing well that the jurors had strong negative feelings about the prosecution and didn't want to allow them time to get over them, moved that they adjourn and render a decision before retiring for the night. It was 11:30 PM. During the eight minutes it took the jury to arrive at a verdict, Todd Bailey and his companions checked their weapons and readied themselves for the final decision.

The jury was called in. Lee and Gilliland, accompanied by Fall, were ordered to stand to receive the verdict. With little in the way of preliminaries, the verdict was announced: Not guilty. The courthouse came alive with applause, cheering, shouting, and laughter. The celebrations lasted for over an hour.

Disheartened and disappointed with the defeat and the implied political failure, the prosecution slunk out of town. Realizing what they were up against with Fall, they elected not to activate the charges against Lee and Gilliland for the killings of Colonel Fountain and Kearney.

The decision was another blow to Garrett, both personally and professionally. In all, he had spent three years at the job of bringing Fountain's killers into a courtroom. His investigation of the case was unimpressive, suffered two years of inactivity, and in the end yielded nothing.

THIRTY-SEVEN

✦✦✦

More Troubles, More Lies

With the Lee and Gilliland trial over and the business of being sheriff settling into dealing with the day-to-day affairs of law enforcement, paperwork, and patronizing the necessary politicians in order to remain in favor with the prevailing powers, Garrett was beginning to grow restless again. An able and capable man-hunter, Garrett was nevertheless regarded as somewhat inept at paperwork and managing the office of sheriff.

Though he longed for the spotlight and enjoyed hobnobbing with the political and social elite, Garrett was clearly out of his element. A man of few social graces who tended toward being abrasive, and bearing the reputation of a drunkard and an unsuccessful gambler who was often away from his family, he was seldom included in the social affairs and activities of Doña Ana County or in those of other New Mexico gentry at the state level. In addition, Garrett, as usual, was broke. He began to cast about for other opportunities, and he looked south toward El Paso, Texas.

A major crossroads, El Paso was experiencing growth and business success. As the city entered the twentieth century, it boasted a population of ten thousand residents, ten newspapers, numerous hotels, two electric plants, and twenty churches.

As was common in dozens of western towns, such growth and prosperity was quickly followed by elements considered to be less desirable. Prostitution was rampant; an entire district of the town, referred to as the Tenderloin, openly provided women for anyone who had the cash. There were dozens of saloons, gambling halls, opium dens, and other diversions. While ministers railed against such activities, these businesses flourished, often assisted by the complicity of the local police force.

Much of El Paso's business came from Mexico. Across the river was Juarez, twice as large as El Paso. Through Juarez came goods, and thriving import-export businesses were established. Large herds of cattle were driven from the interior ranges and purchased by ranchers in Texas and New Mexico. Traffic went both ways. The same attractions found in El Paso could also be obtained in Juarez.

In downtown El Paso and near the border stood a customs house. The responsibility of the government-established customs operation was to oversee the trade of goods and livestock arriving from Mexico. In 1853 it was named the Customs District of Paso del Norte, and its realm of governance encompassed not only all of Texas, but Arizona Territory as well, which included Arizona and New Mexico. The collector of customs was responsible for supervising the imports over nine hundred miles of border. The job paid $2,000 per year, an impressive salary for the time. The collector of customs was in charge of twenty-five employees spread across seven different offices along the border. When Arizona became a state in 1890 and established its own collection district, this number was reduced.

Pat Garrett had long had his eye on the job of collector of customs, a presidential appointment. When Garrett learned that President William McKinley was coming to El Paso, he arranged for and organized a delegation of New Mexicans to meet with him in order to advance the cause of statehood for New Mexico. The group prepared a proposal listing all of the advantages of accepting New Mexico as a state, including an abundance of mineral and agricultural resources, population growth, and the establishment of railway lines across the territory.

Though his intentions were good, Garrett had an ulterior motive: He wanted face-to-face time with the president to present a positive and memorable image for the time when he would campaign for the job of collector of customs. During the meeting, Garrett's delegation asked McKinley to remove Otero from the governorship, claiming he was a liability to statehood. McKinley listened to the proposal, assured the party that he was indeed for New Mexico statehood, but reminded them that he was merely on vacation and would consider such things when he returned to his office in Washington, D.C.

Garrett undoubtedly came away from the meeting with a good feeling. His cause was noble and presented in what he felt was a professional manner, and he felt he had come across well in the presence of the president. He began laying his plans for the future political appointment he felt was in his grasp.

It was all for naught. Less than five months later McKinley was assassinated by an anarchist named Leon Czolgosc. Vice President Theodore Roosevelt assumed the highest office in the land.

During the fall of 1901, however, Roosevelt decided he wanted a new collector of customs installed at the El Paso office. The current collector was H. M. Dillon, who had served in the position for three years, but his record failed to impress the new president. Roosevelt wanted a proven leader, a man unafraid to tackle many of the difficult issues that faced the customs office. The new appointee also needed to be a Republican.

A few of Garrett's political allies sent letters to Roosevelt recommending the sheriff for the job. Roosevelt was dimly aware of Garrett's reputation as a lawman and noted that he was a Republican. The president also began receiving letters from others who opposed the notion of Garrett being named collector of customs. Most of the letters came from men who held grudges against the sheriff or who desired the position for themselves.

Garrett was aware of the dissenters. He approached a number of prominent El Paso businessmen known to hold the lawman in favor and requested they send letters of support to the president. In addition, the chameleon-like Albert Fall and former New Mexico governor Lew Wallace sent messages complimentary of Garrett's abilities. A short time later, Garrett himself made arrangements to travel to Washington, D.C., to meet with the president.

Roosevelt had been led to believe that Garrett was ignorant, illiterate, and a drunk. During their meeting, he found that the sheriff was, in fact, well spoken and could write, at least enough to sign his name. Satisfied with this, Roosevelt asked Garrett to sign an oath stating, "I will totally abstain from the use of intoxicating liquors during my term of office." Garrett signed the document.

Roosevelt nominated Garrett collector of customs on December 16, 1901, and forwarded his recommendation to the United States Senate for approval. The paperwork eventually fell into the hands of the Senate Committee on Finance, which elected to summon Garrett for an interview. During the question-and-answer period, the subject of Garrett's fondness for gambling came up. Though his gambling habit was well known, and his reputation as a loser at cards and horses widespread, Garrett professed ignorance of such things.

It is not known precisely what the Finance Committee discussed after dismissing Garrett that day, but they approved the president's nomination and Garrett was confirmed as collector of customs on December 20, 1901, a two-year appointment. He returned to El Paso by train and set about the business of moving into his new job.

As collector, Garrett encountered a number of obstacles in his first few weeks on the job. Metz described Garrett as having a "grating personality" which did not serve him well in this current endeavor. In addition, Garrett always somehow managed to collect enemies, many of them political, and though he was no longer sheriff and now enjoying a presidential appointment, nothing had changed. Garrett's difficulties began almost immediately.

Cattle coming from Mexico to the United States were assessed a duty of $2 per head for calves one year old or less and $3.75 per head for those older. A government-appointed inspector, one with experience in such things, had the responsibility of determining the ultimate duty assessed. Garrett, however, decided he could handle this job himself. Naive about such things as governmental structure and, for that matter, politics in general, in spite of his long experience with the system, Garrett released the inspector and added the departed employee's duties to his own. Trouble was not long in coming.

During the spring of 1902, the Corralitos Ranch in Sonora, Mexico, shipped four separate herds of young cattle, more than three thousand head, across the border to El Paso. The agent for the ranch was J. D. Campbell. Campbell listed all of the cattle as calves, all eligible for the two-dollar duty. Garrett, however, listed 1,866 of the animals as being over one year old and assessed the $3.75 duty. Furious, Campbell appealed the decision to the Board of Appraisers in New York.

Apparently the El Paso customs office was not a high priority with the Board of Appraisers and a lengthy period of time elapsed with no decision being made. There ensued a heavy traffic of letters and telegrams between El Paso and New York, while the calves were residing in corrals near the border and growing older.

On August 22, the board arrived at a recommendation. From more than two thousand miles away, it somehow determined that a total of 587 of the calves were over one year old, and the subsequent report stated such. Angry at this decision, Campbell nevertheless agreed to it so the matter, as well as the herd, could be processed. Garrett, on the other hand, was enraged at the decision, and perceived the report as a slight and an insult to his abilities to evaluate livestock. He immediately filed an appeal that eventually arrived at United States Circuit Court, where it was either dismissed or ignored. No records of the appeal have ever been found.

The dispute with the Mexican cattle company, along with a number of other complaints against Garrett, began piling up on the desk of the secretary of the treasury, Leslie M. Shaw. Garrett had been attacked from several different directions, and accusations ranged from being unreasonable to being contentious. To many, Garrett was difficult to impossible to do business with. In addition, Shaw was receiving communications related to Garrett's drinking and carousing.

A petition calling for Garrett's dismissal as collector of customs was circulated throughout Juarez by I. A. Barnes, a representative of an import company. The petition lacked teeth in part because the same document recommended that Barnes himself be appointed in Garrett's place.

Garrett supporters claimed that the collector was merely doing his job and that the people being charged duties were unhappy about it. Regardless, the list of anti-Garrett forces was growing. As it turned out, however, Garrett didn't need enemies to have him removed from his office. He was about to do it to himself.

Secretary Shaw was growing weary of dealing with problems created by Garrett. He mailed him a reprimand and suggested he employ good manners and an element of "politeness" in his job as collector. Garrett took the rebuke personally and hurried a letter off to President Roosevelt. Roosevelt gave signs that he was growing nervous about what was turning out to be a controversial appointment, but at the time took no action relative to removing Garrett.

Further annoying and embarrassing Garrett was treasury agent Joseph Evans. Evans had been assigned to El Paso by Shaw to evaluate Garrett's performance. Evans advised Garrett to name George M. Gaither as cattle inspector. Garrett refused, claiming Gaither was unfit for any government job. Responding to pressure from Evans, however, Garrett named Gaither cattle inspector on March 9. The appointment was for thirty days. Garrett placed himself in the position of appearing to work compatibly with Evans. At the end of thirty days, however, he released Gaither, telling him he had no authority to provide him with a full-time job. Gaither, angry and vowing revenge, was added to the growing list of Garrett enemies.

On May 8, Garrett encountered Evans and Gaither on a busy El Paso street. An argument ensued and Gaither punched Garrett. Garrett fought back, and for several seconds the two men were embroiled in a raging fistfight that attracted more than two-dozen onlookers. Garrett and Gaither were arrested, charged with disturbing the peace, and fined five dollars each.

A report of the incident reached Secretary Shaw's desk a few days later. In a bizarre move, Shaw responded by designating I. A. Barnes of the earlier self-aggrandizing petition as a special investigator of the encounter between Garrett and Gaither and instructed him to submit a report. By all accounts, Barnes submitted an unbiased statement, terminating it with the comment that the citizenry of El Paso regarded the episode as a "disgraceful affair."

On May 14, the secretary sent a letter to Garrett, stating, "You are directed to submit a prompt and full report upon the subject, and you are advised that such conduct upon the part of a person holding the office of Collector of Customs is regarded as indefensible and deserves censure in the strongest terms." Garrett responded to Shaw's letter, admitting that he was wrong but that there were extenuating circumstances. Garrett was growing uncomfortable with the constant and growing pressure placed on him by Shaw.

Another letter from Shaw was not long in coming, and it took the form of another reprimand. It informed Garrett that the secretary of the treasury was convinced the collector was not performing his duties appropriately in fixing the correct market price of cattle coming across the border. Shaw stated "there was too much laxity in the admission of cattle."

Shaw apparently knew which buttons to push to get under Garrett's skin. A more astute man would have simply acknowledged Shaw's concerns and gone about his job. Garrett, on the other hand, was proud and stubborn. Unwilling to modify his confrontational nature, he decided to argue with the secretary. He fired back a letter claiming that too much was being made of "trivial discrepancies" and that the reports submitted by Evans to Shaw were generated "for the purpose of causing conflict."

Barnes continued to file reports denigrating Garrett's performance. One of them could have been regarded as funny if the consequences of the accumulating documents were not so serious: While Shaw was concerned about Garrett overvaluing the cattle, Barnes charged the collector with constantly undervaluing them. Garrett charged Barnes with being in league with cattlemen who wanted Garrett terminated.

As Garrett's position as collector of customs was being threatened, he began spending time with an old acquaintance, Emerson Hough. Hough was a writer and had professed some interest in doing a book with Garrett, a rewrite of *The Authentic Life of Billy the Kid.* Garrett told Hough that the first book contained many errors, an odd comment from the man who was listed on the book as the author. Garrett, however, saw this new version of the book as an opportunity to make some money and he grew excited about the notion. Hough, on the other hand, eventually decided against it and instead concentrated on a manuscript dealing with the Lincoln County War. This idea was also eventually abandoned, and Hough decided to work on a manuscript that was to be part of a series entitled *The Story of the Outlaw.* He invited Garrett to read the piece, make any necessary corrections or changes, and provide advice and insight on any part of the manuscript that dealt with Lincoln County. Garrett agreed to the proposition and did the necessary work. During the final editing, most of Garrett's contributions were deleted.

Garrett had counted on making money from the project and was convinced he and Hough had a verbal contract related to such. The relationship between Garrett and Hough, however, grew strained. While no records exist relative to whether or not Garrett received any money from the project, the assumption is that, if he did, it did not amount to much.

Garrett also took to hanging around with another friend. Tom Powers was the owner of El Paso's Coney Island Saloon. Powers had only one eye that worked, was an occasional brawler, and developed a reputation as a gambler. It was said that games of chance took place on a nightly basis at the Coney Island, and through the doors wandered Pat Garrett at every opportunity. Powers was known throughout El Paso as disreputable. He claimed that Garrett gave him the revolver that he used to shoot Billy the Kid, but many doubt the provenance. A handful of researchers suggest it was more likely that Garrett lost a revolver to Powers in a card game.

Powers convinced Garrett to take him to the 1905 Rough Riders convention in San Antonio. Garrett agreed, but explained to Powers that he was to pose as a cattleman, since hanging around with a gambler was not going to ingratiate him with Roosevelt, largely because of the oath Garrett had signed in the president's presence.

At the reunion, Garrett introduced Powers to Roosevelt and the three men posed for photographs. At least one of the photos was published in a local newspaper. At the same time, Roosevelt learned that Powers was not a cattleman, but a gambler and tavern owner, and felt he had been duped and lied to by Garrett.

The subterfuge was exposed, and El Paso newspapers printed the story. Editorial comments predicted that Garrett's reappointment as collector of customs was in jeopardy. Garrett, realizing he had been caught in his lie, sent an apology to the president. When he did not receive a reply, Garrett began making plans to travel to Washington to seek an audience with Roosevelt. In a move many regard as stupid, Garrett invited Powers to go with him. The politically inept Garrett reasoned that if the president got to know Powers, he would find many things to like and admire. Garrett also brought with him a stack of endorsements and recommendations from El Paso businessmen and government appointees. Roosevelt refused to meet with Garrett. On December 13, 1905, Garrett was informed he would not be reappointed as collector of customs.

Garrett turned to Emerson Hough for some last-minute assistance. He knew that Hough and Roosevelt were acquainted and pleaded with the writer to help him get reappointed. During subsequent correspondence between Hough and the president, it was learned that Roosevelt was persuaded to consider another man for the position of collector of customs as a result of the reports he had received from Treasury Secretary Shaw. Had the president held any reservations whatsoever, Garrett's deception tipped the scale. Hough also noted that the president was well aware of Garrett's huge gambling debts and "that his habits were bad."

In a somewhat interesting footnote to this sequence of events, Tom Powers and Theodore Roosevelt subsequently became friends. Powers, undeterred by the setback created by Garrett at the 1905 Rough Riders convention, shipped Roosevelt a bear cub he had trapped while on a hunting trip in Mexico. Roosevelt, an avid outdoorsman and lover of wildlife, was delighted with the gift and often posed for pictures with the cub. Newspapers referred to the cub as Teddy's bear. An enterprising doll maker began manufacturing likenesses of the animal and named it a "teddy bear."

On March 15, 1911, Roosevelt arrived in El Paso on a visit and was greeted by none other than Powers. In fact, the two had a photograph taken together standing side by side and smiling.

With his job over, Garrett retuned to Doña Ana County. The previous two years had not been good to him. While he had had a job with a decent salary, the stress created by his own inability to get along was beginning to show. Furthermore, he drank more than ever and he had accumulated even more gambling debts. Once again, Pat Garrett was broke.

THIRTY-EIGHT

◆◆◆

Deeper in Debt

From the time Pat Garrett first arrived in New Mexico in 1878, he found himself in debt. From the time he first arrived in Lincoln County until he was killed in 1908, he appeared to pile debts one atop the other. Never competent at handling what money he had, Garrett's lifestyle, which included gambling, drinking, racing horses, and consorting with prostitutes, drained much of his income. Amazingly, he found enough money to purchase ranches at various times and support a wife and family of eight children. The notoriety Garrett received as a result of his version of the shooting of the southwest's most famous outlaw, Billy the Kid, never catapulted the lawman into the realm of fortune and respect he craved. His book, *The Authentic Life of Billy the Kid*, was an unmitigated financial disaster, as was just about everything else Garrett attempted.

Historians have expressed wonder at why Garrett, on being removed from his duties as collector of customs in El Paso, returned to his ranch located on the eastern slopes of the San Andres Mountains. Though no records have been found, it is believed he purchased the ranch in 1898. The list of Garrett's enemies, political and otherwise, in Doña Ana County had grown, and on the surface the location did not take on the appeal of a comfortable place. The truth was Garrett had no options; he had nowhere else to go.

Some speculation existed that Garrett wanted to reopen the investigation of the Fountain murders and that he would solicit funds from interested and concerned parties to finance the effort. Since Garrett must have known that he had clearly bungled the earlier investigation, and that the public knew this as well, this appears somewhat unlikely.

Garrett's ranch had abundant water, and he stocked it with beef cattle, dairy cows, and horses. For a time, Garrett supplied beef to a Las Cruces butcher and sold milk to the families of the miners living at Gold Camp and Oro Grande. His passion, however, lay with his horses. Enlisting his teenage son Poe, named after his former deputy, to work as a trainer and occasional jockey, Garrett's horses were commonly seen at racetracks throughout southern New Mexico, parts of West Texas, and even Mexico.

The horses became a problem for Garrett's neighbors. Because boundaries between ranches during this time were not extensively fenced if they were fenced at all, livestock of different owners often mingled. Ranchers who desired the tough working horses so necessary in the rugged terrain of this part of New Mexico were not happy with their mares mixing with Garrett's stud racing horses. Racehorses boasted long, slim legs and were built and bred for speed and not for hard work.

Years earlier, in May 1899, Garrett had acquired Bear Canyon in the San Andres mountain range, a parcel of land adjoining his ranch and located seven miles from his house and north of Black Mountain. The canyon was desirable for its dependable spring of cool, clear water. A small rock cabin and corral had been constructed near the mouth of the canyon, and Garrett intended to use the location to raise his racehorses. He also suspected that a mineral survey might locate valuable ore in the canyon.

Garrett's property was near Gold Camp. Today little remains of the town, but in the late 1800s it was regarded as the wealthiest mining district in all of southern New Mexico. Silver and copper were dug from rich deposits. Investing what little money he had, Garrett acquired some interests in mining claims in the area, but none ever yielded a profit. He was hopeful that similar deposits of ore might be found on his Bear Canyon property, and he delegated his son Poe to investigate every promising outcrop. Ore was found and mines excavated, but the yield was so poor that Garrett was never able to cover expenses. Garrett eventually came to the conclusion that the people who were making money in mining were not the miners and mine owners, but rather the speculators who sold mining investments. He decided to try his hand at the enterprise.

Garrett was not a newcomer to such things. While he was serving as collector of customs, he occasionally led investors from the east into Mexico to investigate ranching and mining potentials. At the time, such activity was not popular with Secretary of the Treasury Shaw, who reprimanded him about being away from his office for great stretches of time.

Presently, Garrett, along with W. H. H. and Clinton B. Llewellyn, formed the Alabama Gold and Copper Mining Company. Garrett was named secretary of the corporation. The stated objective of the company was to acquire and operate gold and silver mines in the area of Oro Grande, forty miles northeast of El Paso, but as with many ventures that involved Garrett, it was a lie. The three men did nothing related to the prospecting and excavation of ore. Instead, they issued stock for sale in their cooked-up enterprise. So inefficient were the three men in peddling their worthless stock that the company disbanded within two years. With his hopes of making a killing in mine speculation having vanished, Garrett once again found himself broke.

During his time as a speculator, Garrett came to the realization that the few people who made any money at all in the mining business were the lawyers who represented the companies. They were paid handsomely and on time. The lawyers of Garrett's acquaintance, including A. B. Fall, Thomas Catron, and others, all lived well, drove expensive buggies, and appeared to have abundant discretionary money. The notion of becoming a lawyer, therefore, appealed to him.

With no experience or education, but with the payment of a modest fee in Mexico, Garrett became an attorney. His practice, however, could only be conducted below the Rio Grande. A few weeks after making it known that he was now a lawyer, Garrett was hired to defend a murderer.

Santa Rosalia rancher O. E. Finstead shot and killed two men and wounded another during a poker game at his home. Finstead claimed he and his company had been attacked by bandits intent on robbing them. No money was missing; the poker pots were still on the table and an open safe containing a great deal of money was untouched. Furthermore, according to the police, there were no boot or hoof prints in the snow outside of the house. Finstead was charged with murder. He wasted no time in hiring Garrett to defend him.

Garrett's efforts went for naught and Finstead was convicted and sent to a prison in Chihuahua to serve a life sentence. He was released a few years later during the Mexican Revolution when the city was taken over by the Villistas.

Realizing his talents did not lie with defending criminals in Mexico, Garrett returned to his ranch. He realized little income from his defense of Finstead, and his travels and living expenses in Mexico ate that up rapidly. When he returned to Doña Ana County, he was turned away from the grocery store where he usually purchased his provisions and supplies. He had a bill at the store that had remained unpaid for months and grocer L. B. Bentley refused him any more credit.

From time to time, Garrett found himself in civil court over his debts. He still owed Tom Catron the $500 he had earlier borrowed. During the intervening time, Garrett had not reimbursed Catron a penny. Repeated letters from Catron to Garrett went ignored. Catron pondered legal action against Garrett but eventually determined it would come to no good end. Instead, Catron asked El Paso business-man W. G. Walz "to discount the note to a local bank, send him what he could get, and ask the bank to collect from Garrett." Walz went to several banks on this mission but was turned down at each one. As it turned out, each of the banks already had notes against Garrett and were themselves having difficulty collecting.

Catron wrote Garrett another letter admonishing him about his debts and explaining to him that it would be in his best interest to take care to repay people to whom he owed money. Catron stated that the time might arrive when Garrett would find himself interested in a political appointment, but that with banks and businessmen against him he would have a difficult time appearing worthy. Garrett did not respond to Catron, nor did he make any effort to satisfy his numerous creditors. Garrett had acquired the reputation of a deadbeat in and around Doña Ana County.

Back in 1890, the Albuquerque Bank of Commerce lent $1,000 to a trio of applicants: George Curry, John Eubank, and Pat Garrett. There is no record of what the money was to be used for and no collateral was advanced. The paperwork on the loan stipulated that the money was to be repaid within six months. The time passed and the bank had received not a single payment on the note. By this time, Garrett had moved to Uvalde.

When Garrett returned to Doña Ana County in 1896, the bank notified him that he was required to repay the $1,000 loan plus inter-est. Oddly, no such claim was made to Curry or Eubank. Having no money, Garrett was unable to pay a cent on the debt. On September 18, he was summoned to the Second Judicial District Court to explain his refusal to repay. Garrett ignored the summons. In December, a civil suit was filed against him requiring repayment of the amount in full plus interest and damages. Garrett argued that the statute of limita-tions relative to such things had expired and requested that the entire case be dismissed. The judge rejected his proposal and ordered him to appear in court. Garrett again refused, and on January 28, 1898, the court ordered that the bank had the right to collect on the full sum, interests, court costs, and attorney fees plus damages amounting to almost an additional $1,000. The final amount was negotiated, revised, and settled on at $1,733.18. The court provided for the seizure of Garrett's property and ordered Doña Ana probate clerk José R. Lucero to carry out the order.

On February 7, clerk Lucero returned the unserved paperwork stating that, at the time, Garrett did not own any land and his personal property amounted to only $565.65. As it turned out, two men already held legal notes on Garrett's ranch: Martin Lohman and W. W. Cox.

Nothing happened with regard to people trying to collect on debts from Garrett. Garrett kept pleading that he had no money and requested people give him more time to pay off the notes. In spite of his professed and apparent destitute condition, however, the former lawman managed to acquire two ranches and then, using them as collateral, borrowed additional money from Lohman in the amount of $3,567.85. The note included the ranches, houses, improvements, thirty head of cattle, and one hundred fifty head of horses. The note also required Garrett to repay it in one year. Convinced he could convert some of this newfound money into a greater fortune, Garrett became a regular at the gambling parlors in the area. As usual, he lost more than he won. In addition, he purchased a number of blooded horses figuring they would enhance his winnings at the racetracks. They never did.

Two years went by and Lohman never received a payment from Garrett on the note. On April 9, 1904, Lohman had a second note written in almost the exact same language as the first. One more year passed and Lohman began to despair of ever receiving a payment from Garrett. He then sold the note to W. W. Cox for $2,000. Cox, like Lohman, was unsuccessful in collecting a payment from Garrett. He pondered the notion of seizing Garrett's ranches, but instead extended the note for another year.

The Albuquerque Bank of Commerce had not forgotten the debt owed to them. In September 1904, the bank undertook measures to seize Garrett's ranches, but on learning that Lohman and Cox held mortgages, it was unable to do so. Following a series of meetings with lawyers, the bank convinced a judge that they held the first rights to the Garrett property based on an 1898 claim against him, a claim that predated any of the subsequent mortgages. The court ruled in the bank's favor. On May 14, 1906, José Lucero, the former clerk who had since been elected sheriff, was provided the authority by New Mexico Supreme Court Justice Ira A. Abbott to seize Garrett's ranches, all buildings and livestock, and place them up for sale at auction.

Lucero's duties as sheriff kept him busy with law enforcement matters for two weeks before he was able to travel to Garrett's ranch to serve the papers. On learning of the decision to seize Garrett's property, W. W. Cox gathered up his cowhands and rode to the ex-lawman's ranch. There, they rounded up all of the livestock they could locate and transferred it to Cox's ranch. When Sheriff Lucero arrived, he could find only twenty head of cattle that had been overlooked by Cox and his men.

On July 28, in a strange move, two of Garrett's neighbors—J. H. Bonney and J. C. Thompson—were directed by the court to go to Garrett's ranch and make an appraisal of the property, the land, and the springs. The one hundred sixty acres of ranchland, including the buildings and corrals, were valued at an astoundingly low $225. The spring was valued at $250. The appraisal included neither the Bear Canyon portion of the ranch nor the livestock. Following the appropriate filing of a notice, Garrett's properties and livestock were then auctioned off. The Albuquerque Bank of Commerce outbid all others and assumed ownership of the Garrett properties for $1,000. According to the prevailing laws of the time, Garrett was given one year to repay all of his debts before he was forced to vacate his property. Though no details have ever surfaced, Garrett was able to accommodate the bank and remain on the ranch, where he lived for what remained of his life.

Instead of putting the former lawman at ease, securing ownership of his ranch was only the beginning of a new set of troubles. Though he had owned the property for six years, he had never paid any taxes. Doña Ana County notified him that he owed $922.72. If not paid by August 1906, the county would seize Garrett's stock and auction it off in order to satisfy his tax obligations. Most of Garrett's stock, it will be recalled, had been relocated on the ranch of W. W. Cox.

Cox, to whom Garrett still owed money, decided he was not going to relinquish the animals. On August 17, Cox pressured Garrett to sign a bill of sale for the entire herd of cattle for "one dollar and other valuable considerations." When Sheriff Lucero arrived at the Garrett ranch to conduct the auction, all he and his men could locate were the few stray cattle that Cox had missed during his original roundup and transfer.

The sheriff seized everything Garrett owned, including personal possessions, and sold it at auction for a total of only $6.50. Garrett was allowed to keep his so-called blooded horses. Since it appeared that no more money was forthcoming from any Garrett source, the county deemed the tax obligation fulfilled.

Following the auction, the Albuquerque Bank of Commerce reentered the affairs of Pat Garrett. The bank filed a suit against the Doña Ana County commissioners maintaining that they had auctioned property that was legally theirs. Garrett, in hope of recovering some of his land and belongings, also filed a suit against the sheriff for selling property that legally did not qualify for seizure. Mentioned were a suckling calf, a bay horse, a sorrel mare, and a dun mare, the total value of which he estimated at $200. Garrett stated he would settle for the amount to compensate him for his losses or $100 in damages and court costs along with the return of his property. The case was not provided a high priority and was still pending when Garrett was killed two years later.

Garrett was still counting on some kind of payment for his assistance to Emerson Hough in the writing of *The Story of the Outlaw*. In early February 1906 he undertook communications with the writer. The two exchanged missives, and on March 8 Garrett wrote that he was "suffering great distress of mind and soul."

In a return letter, Hough explained to Garrett that the manuscript had been withdrawn from the earlier publisher and placed with another. As a result, and on the instructions from the new publishers, Hough had to rewrite the entire manuscript.

When Garrett replied, he stated that he hoped the book would sell well and inquired about the status of royalties due him. Hough informed Garrett that he had received an advance of $300 but that he, personally, had spent over $1,000 during the time he was researching the book. Hough stated that he had recommended to the publisher that he provide at least $200 to Garrett. In Garrett's case, an addendum to the contract stated that if the book did not experience decent sales, the $200 would have to be returned. Hough also expressed the notion to Garrett that he did not believe the book was going to meet everyone's expectations.

In a subsequent letter, Garrett wrote to Hough and detailed his financial troubles. He told the writer that he planned on planting a large vegetable garden and, with the few head of cattle he had left, would attempt to rebuild the herd.

Garrett finally received some copies of *The Story of the Outlaw*. He wrote to Hough that "there are some parts of it that are not up to what I expected" and told the writer that he would like to discuss them with him. Hough never wrote back.

THIRTY-NINE
✦✦✦

Enter Wayne Brazel

Pat Garrett was not an easy man to get along with, nor was he an easy man to like. During the waning years of his life, his troubles continued to worsen. He owed money to prominent people and institutions throughout the area, and his abrasive personality, often fueled with alcohol, helped matters not one whit.

Garrett's list of enemies had grown longer. He had gone from being mildly disliked by many in Doña Ana County to being completely despised. When he came to town he was, as Metz described, "quarrelsome and insulting, brawling drunkenly in the streets." Garrett threatened people, and provoked fistfights. The tall and experienced lawman was often victorious, but now and again he was thrashed by smaller, sober opponents.

Metz believed Garrett's "most deadly feud" was with W. W. Cox. Garrett seethed at the notion that Cox still maintained control of his herd of cattle and intended to continue doing so until the mortgage on his ranch was paid off. Garrett explained that without the cattle he was unable to make any money. Cox would not yield. Garrett's rage against Cox grew by the day.

Garrett gathered up his family and moved to Las Cruces. It was a matter of a short time before George Curry, as a result of the decision by President Theodore Roosevelt, would assume the mantle of governor of New Mexico. Garrett was confident that Curry would appoint him to be the new superintendent of the territorial prison at Santa Fe. It is unclear why Garrett believed such an appointment would be forthcoming. In any event, Curry was apparently of a different mind, for he never had contact with Garrett again. In order to make some money to support his family, Garrett moved himself to El Paso, where he took a job with a real estate firm.

Shortly after arriving in El Paso, Garrett moved in with a woman known only as Mrs. Brown. Though no details are known, Mrs. Brown was regarded as a prostitute. The two were often seen in the dining and drinking establishments and riding through town in a buggy. It is believed Garrett and Mrs. Brown had known each other well during his tenure as collector of customs, and that some believed she was, in part, responsible for Garrett losing his job.

It is not known how much real estate Garrett sold while living in the border city, but it was clear that he was spending a great deal of money on liquor. While he was gone, son Poe was managing the responsibilities of the ranch. In Garrett's absence, Poe signed off on an arrangement with a Doña Ana cowboy named Jesse Wayne Brazel to lease the Bear Canyon ranch for five years. The papers were signed on March 11, 1907.

Brazel was to figure prominently in the life of Pat Garrett for the next eleven and a half months. Brazel was born in Kansas in 1876. His family moved soon afterward to Lincoln County, New Mexico, and then to Gold Camp, not far from Garrett's ranch and bordering Cox's ranch. As a youngster, Wayne worked as a cowhand on the Cox ranch. Cox was so fond of Brazel and so appreciative of his hard work and loyalty that many thought the two men were related. In turn, Brazel saw Cox as a mentor and an inspiration.

Though extant photographs of Brazel lend him the appearance of a simpleton, he was regarded as a hardworking, dependable, and uncomplaining cowhand who did not drink, and was adept at breaking horses. At the time, Brazel was courting Olive Elizabeth Boyd. Boyd was living in the home of W. W. Cox's brother-in-law, A. P. Print Rhode. While working as a teacher at the Gold Camp school, Boyd also served as a private tutor for Rhode's children. Metz writes that Brazel married Boyd in 1907. Other references as to when they got married have cited the years 1909 and 1910.

Married or not, Brazel cast about for ways to make more money than he was earning as a common cowhand for Cox and a sometime swamper in a Las Cruces saloon. Following some consultations with Rhode, Brazel decided money could be made raising goats. Goats were greeted with mixed reactions by traditional cattlemen. On the one hand, they competed with cattle for grass, often ruining pastures for cattle grazing. On the other, they were a low-maintenance and high-profit livestock. Brazel and Rhode looked around for a suitable location on which to place their goat herd. They decided on Bear Canyon, a part of the Garrett ranch.

A major drawback to leasing Bear Canyon was Garrett. The former lawman and Print Rhode despised one another, a hostility that stemmed from the earlier fight with and killing of Norman Newman at the Cox ranch house. Rhode was also aware that Garrett hated goats. Knowing that Garrett was living in El Paso and that son Poe was managing the ranch, Brazel approached the younger Garrett to work out the details of the lease. Rhode's name was not mentioned, for Poe was aware of the animosity between him and his father. Brazel also withheld the information that they were going to raise goats on the property. The terms of the lease called for Brazel to pay Poe ten heifer calves and one filly colt.

During July and August of 1907, Brazel and Rhode began stocking goats on the Bear Canyon property. On discovering what the two men intended, Poe alerted his father in El Paso. A man of quick temper, the enraged Garrett raced back to the ranch to put an end to the lease and drive the goats off of his land. On returning home, he learned that Brazel was running the goats in partnership with longtime enemy Print Rhode. Based on Garrett's personality, his plan may have been to bully Brazel off of the land, but the alliance with Rhode gave him second thoughts. Rhode was no pushover, and it may be that Garrett harbored a touch of fear of the man. Further, he learned that Brazel had borrowed the money to undertake the goat-raising operation from another enemy, W. W. Cox.

Garrett attempted to prove that the contract between Brazel and Poe implied that cattle were going to be placed on the Bear Canyon land. Lawyers examined the contract and found that it did not specifically state how the land was to be used. Garrett argued that the approved payment in cattle and a horse implied that the land would be used for those kinds of livestock.

When Garrett got nowhere with this line of reasoning, he invoked an old territorial law that made it illegal to graze livestock near a domicile. The house in question, Garrett maintained, was the rock cabin located in Bear Canyon. He filed the complaint with the Organ, New Mexico, justice of the peace, Charles M. Anthony. Knowing well Rhode's penchant for violence, Anthony decided not to serve the warrant. Instead, he contacted Hence Rhode, a brother to Print, and convinced him to arrest him and bring him in to Anthony's office.

Somehow Brazel learned of the arrangement, and in an attempt to protect Print, turned himself in to Anthony. Around the same time, Hence brought Print into Organ. A short time later, Garrett was informed of the arrest of both Rhode and Brazel and the date of the impending trial in the tiny town.

When the time for the trial was posted, a large crowd gathered in Organ. In spite of their arrest, Rhode and Brazel strolled the streets wearing their revolvers. Garrett voiced his opposition to allowing the two men to go around armed, and Sheriff Lucero ordered them to relinquish their weapons. Both men handed their handguns to Hence Rhode, who stuck them in his waistband.

Organ had no courthouse and the law was processed at whatever available location that could be scheduled. On that afternoon, the local butcher shop was chosen. Because of the cold weather, the doors remained closed, and the smell of raw meat filled the crowded building.

Garrett raged and paced and badgered Anthony to get the trial underway. It did not help matters that Print Rhode constantly taunted Garrett, even challenging him to a fistfight.

It turned out to be impossible to gather an impartial jury in Organ. Furthermore, Anthony refused to serve as an arbitrator. He was well aware of the divided opinions that existed in the small town and knew that whatever decision he rendered would antagonize at least half of the citizenry. He decided to call a recess for several months in the hope that tempers would cool and a reasonable solution could be determined.

In the meantime, a dark and somewhat elusive character arrived in El Paso, one who had strong connections with Garrett's enemies. James P. Miller, better known as "Killin' Jim" Miller, had earned a living and built a reputation as a professional assassin. His first victim was one of his own brothers-in-law, and it was estimated that he had killed at least forty men since then. His weapon of choice was a shotgun.

Miller was a brother-in-law to cattleman Carl Adamson. The two men claimed to have over one thousand head of cattle in Mexico that they wanted to move to a ranch in Oklahoma. Before doing so, they needed to get the stock across the border and herd them to a location where they could be fattened up before the long journey. They spoke with a number of ranchers in the area but were turned down for a variety of reasons. On learning about Garrett's Bear Canyon property, Miller and Adamson arranged a meeting with the former lawman-turned-real estate dealer in El Paso.

Garrett was attracted to the arrangement and saw the chance for some easy money from the lease of the land. He told Adamson and Miller that he was willing to make a deal, but that the property was currently leased to a goat herder. Garrett explained that if the lease could be broken and the goats moved elsewhere, then he would be amenable to stocking the cattle on it. Miller requested a meeting with Brazel, who came to El Paso to discuss the matter.

Brazel was not inclined to cancel the lease. He did agree, however, to consider such a move if he were paid $3.50 for each animal. He told Miller he had twelve hundred goats on the land. Miller agreed to the deal, summoned a lawyer, and a contract was executed.

In a subsequent meeting with Garrett, Miller offered him $3,000 for the Bear Canyon property. If Garrett would agree to the terms, Miller said he would also employ Garrett to drive the cattle from Mexico to the Bear Canyon location and oversee them on the ranch until such time as they could be shipped to Oklahoma. Anticipating the pending sale of the property and the herding arrangement, Garrett began to dwell on his newfound luck and potential income. He immediately left his job with the real estate firm, traveled to Las Cruces, and moved his family back onto the ranch. Garrett, who somehow had a penchant for tumbling into bad luck, was unprepared for the difficulties that were soon to follow.

A short time after returning to the ranch, Garrett was notified by Wayne Brazel that he had misquoted the number of goats on the property. Instead of the twelve hundred figure that he provided Miller, he informed Garrett that there were, in fact, eighteen hundred of the animals. Brazel also told Garrett that unless he was paid for every one of the animals he would not agree to withdraw from the lease. Miller was not pleased with these new conditions and informed Garrett that the agreement they made would likely be canceled.

Life for Garrett continued its downward spiral. In desperation, he wrote a letter to Governor Curry and asked to borrow $50. In spite of the fact that Garrett already owed Curry money and that it was unlikely it would ever be repaid, the governor sent a check in return mail.

On Friday, February 28, Carl Adamson arrived in Las Cruces. There, he leased a two-horse buggy to make the four-hour trip to the Garrett ranch. Adamson's journey set a deadly momentum in motion.

FORTY

✦✦✦

The Killing of Pat Garrett

On arriving at the Garrett ranch house late on the afternoon of February 28, Adamson was greeted by the former lawman and his wife. For reasons never explained, Adamson aroused the suspicions of Mrs. Garrett, who remained nervous around the short, stocky rancher. Following a brief visit, the two men walked around the adjacent property, Garrett pointing out various features. During the stroll, Garrett commented that he had been awakened the previous night by his dogs barking at what appeared to be some kind of intrusion. That morning, Garrett sent ranch hand Frank Adams to investigate. In a nearby arroyo, Adams found the tracks of two men and horses.

Mrs. Garrett expressed her concerns about Carl Adamson to her husband. Garrett found her fears amusing, and explained to her that Adamson was the key to their future financial independence. Garrett had a message sent to Wayne Brazel indicating the necessity of a meeting the next day with him and Adamson in Las Cruces.

The following morning after breakfast, Garrett and Adamson boarded the buggy and set out for Las Cruces. Garrett had tied his horse to the back of the buggy for the return trip. In an interview with Leon Metz, daughter Pauline Garrett related that as they drove out of the yard, her mother informed her that, although it was a relatively warm day for February, her father had failed to take his topcoat and told the daughter to carry it to him. Grabbing the garment, Pauline climbed onto her mare and raced down the road toward the departing buggy. As the vehicle slowed down on approaching a gate, Garrett heard Pauline's approach and told Adamson to stop. Garrett stepped onto the ground, picked Pauline from her horse, and carried her over to the gate to unlatch it. He took the topcoat, kissed his daughter, placed her back on the mare, and told her he would bring her a present from Las Cruces. It was the last time any of his family saw him alive.

The road followed by Adamson passed Gold Camp, into and across San Augustine Pass, and through the tiny village of Organ. A short distance out of town, Adamson pulled up at a livery stable owned by Russell Walter. As Adamson guided the horses toward a water trough, Garrett spotted Willis Walter, the son of the proprietor. According to an interview provided by Willis Walter in 1968, Garrett asked him if he had seen Wayne Brazel. The question seems an odd one, since Garrett and Adamson were expecting to meet Brazel in Las Cruces.

Willis Walter told Garrett that Brazel had been there but rode away only minutes before the arrival of the buggy. Willis pointed down the road at a column of dust that had been stirred up by Brazel's horse. Adamson pulled the horses back from the trough and headed them back onto the road to Las Cruces. He hied the animals on, but not at a pace such that he anticipated catching up with Brazel.

South of Organ the road forked, the two routes extending for a couple of miles before rejoining. One of the roads was known as the Mail-Scott Road and the other called the Freighter's Road. Freighter's Road was more suitable for handling the traffic from the heavy ore wagons that traversed it. It was shorter but rougher, thus most travelers preferred Mail-Scott Road. As Adamson neared the junction, Garrett spotted Brazel some distance down Mail-Scott Road in conversation with an unidentified man on horseback. In a moment, the stranger rode away.

Historians suggest the unidentified man was Print Rhode. This is, at best, a poor guess. If the men in the wagon were able to identify Wayne Brazel at that distance, then Rhode, who was well known to Garrett and likely to Adamson as well, would have been easily recognized. Accumulating evidence strongly points to the notion that the rider was Todd Bailey, Oliver Lee's nephew and ranch hand.

Minutes later, Adamson and Garrett caught up with Brazel. Garrett and Brazel did not like each other, and the two men did little more than acknowledge each other's presence with a nod. According to articles in the *El Paso Herald* and the *Rio Grande Republican*, Brazel sometimes rode ahead of the buggy and at other times behind it. When the road was wide enough, he traveled alongside the vehicle. At one point during the trip, Adamson asked him if his goats were kidding.

Finally, Garrett asked Brazel why he originally stated that he had twelve hundred goats and later changed the number to eighteen hundred. Brazel replied that he miscounted.

The difference between twelve hundred and eighteen hundred goats should strike any competent researcher as dramatic to the point of being unbelievable, but this disparity has never been treated by historians during the more than a century since Pat Garrett was killed. The fact that the goat herd was claimed to be one-third larger than it was earlier should not be disregarded. The actual number of goats originally placed on the Bear Canyon range would surely have been known by Brazel, Rhode, and Miller. Even allowing time for kidding, it remains unlikely that the herd would have grown to such a size in the amount of time that the goats had been at Bear Canyon. The question must be asked: Were these numbers cooked up in order to delay or obviate Garrett's opportunity to place Adamson's cattle on the range? Was Garrett being set up the entire time? What was Adamson's relationship with Oliver Lee?

Following the brief exchange between Brazel and Garrett, Adamson chimed in with the comment that he and Miller would not pay for eighteen hundred goats and that the deal might be canceled. Adamson further stated that he didn't want any of the goats, that he had only purchased them in order to secure the lease. Brazel replied that he would sell all eighteen hundred of the goats or none.

As Adamson steered the buggy along a portion of the road that passed between a low ridge on his left and Alameda Arroyo on his right, he slowed, then pulled to a halt, claiming he needed to urinate. He handed the lines to Garrett and then climbed down and walked to a position in front of the horses. The conversation between Garrett and Brazel had progressed to an argument. Brazel told Garrett that he was probably going to retain the lease. Garrett replied that he would get Brazel off the land one way or another.

At this, Garrett, according to Adamson, picked up the shotgun he brought with him and climbed out of the buggy. Walking to the rear of the vehicle with the shotgun in his right hand, he turned away from Brazel, removed the glove from his left hand, and unbuttoned his pants. He had just begun to urinate when a bullet tore through his cranium. Garrett spun and fell to the ground, his head pointing toward the ridge, his feet toward the arroyo. A moment later a second shot sounded and a bullet tore through his abdomen.

Pat Garrett, once a famous lawman but now regarded as a deadbeat drunk, was dead.

FORTY-ONE

◆◆◆

The Trial of Wayne Brazel

Who killed Pat Garrett? For years, the death of the lawman, a man whose life was linked to controversial events such as the alleged killing of Billy the Kid and the disappearance of Albert Jennings Fountain was mired in controversy. Published history records that Wayne Brazel was tried for the murder and that he was found not guilty on the basis of self-defense. Some few historians, along with a host of enthusiasts, point out that in addition to Brazel, at least four other men could be considered suspects: Carl Adamson, W. W. Cox, Jim Miller, and Print Rhode. Some have tried hard to make a case for the notion that Miller was the assassin, and a few prefer Rhode. Other than author Metz, no one who has spent any time at all in close examination of the particulars of this event believes Brazel pulled the trigger on Garrett. New evidence that surfaced in 2013 makes a strong case for the killer being a man never considered by the historians.

Following Garrett's death, Brazel and Adamson hurried to Las Cruces. Brazel approached Deputy Felipe Lucero and confessed to him that he had just killed Pat Garrett and told the deputy to lock him up. He handed Lucero his Colt .45 revolver. Brazel informed Lucero that Adamson was present at the killing and would testify that it was done in self-defense. Brazel claimed Garrett was about to shoot him with his shotgun. Brazel was placed in a cell. According to Metz, Lucero then assembled a coroner's jury and rode to the site of the killing. Following an examination by Dr. W. C. Field (sometimes spelled Fields), Garrett's body was loaded onto a wagon and transported into town. It was determined that a bullet had struck Garrett from behind, entering the back of his head and exiting through his right eyebrow. A second bullet had struck Garrett as he lay on the ground, entering at the stomach and ending up near one of his shoulders at the top of the rib cage.

Also visiting the site of the killing was former New Mexico militia-man W. H. H. Llewellyn. In a telegram sent to New Mexico Governor George Curry at 2:22 PM on March 4 from Las Cruces, Llewellyn stated, "Wayne Brazel killed Pat Garrett about noon five miles from Las Cruces on Organ road. Garrett and Miller were in buggy, Brazel on horseback. Brazel in jail here."

Llewellyn's telegram provides two additional mysteries for the Gar-rett killing. If, as some historians allege, Llewellyn, who was in Las Cruces, visited the site of the killing, there is no way he could have returned to Las Cruces in time to send a telegram at 2:22 PM. Fur-thermore, Llewellyn's mention of "Miller . . . in buggy" could only be a reference to "Killin' Jim," the only Miller involved in the ever-widening web of Garrett entanglements.

Did Llewellyn simply make a mistake and state Miller instead of Ad-amson? What did Llewellyn hear that caused him to mention Miller's name? And from whom? Was Llewellyn privy to information that history missed? The answers to these questions may never be known.

On March 3, Brazel was escorted into the courtroom of Justice of the Peace Manuel Lopez. When asked how he wished to plead to the charge of murder, Brazel appeared confused and was described as hav-ing a blank stare on his face. He asked that the question be repeated. This done, he pled not guilty, "then resumed his vacant staring."

That same afternoon, a hearing was arranged for Brazel. The pros-ecuting attorney for Doña Ana County was Mark Thompson. He was assisted by New Mexico Attorney General James M. Hervey. Hervey and Governor George Curry, along with a New Mexico mounted policeman, Fred Fornoff, had arrived from Santa Fe to attend the funeral of Garrett and take part in the proceedings. The defense team representing Brazel consisted of Albert B. Fall, Cox's personal attorney, along with Herbert B. Holt, William A. Sutherland, and Edward C. Wade. In an ironic twist, Holt had long served as Garrett's attorney. W. W. Cox arrived and remained at Brazel's side throughout the entire ordeal.

When Adamson was called to testify, he stated that when he stopped the buggy to urinate, Garrett reached over and took the lines. While he was standing near the horses, Adamson said he heard Garret say to Brazel, "Well, damn you. If I don't get you off one way, I will another." During this conversation, according to Adamson, Garrett was in the buggy and Brazel was on horseback near the left side of the buggy. Adamson said his back was turned to the pair.

When the attorney asked Adamson if he had seen Garrett standing upright, he replied, "I think when I seen Garrett, the first shot had been fired and he was staggering," and that he fell "about two feet from the side" of the buggy. Brazel was still on horseback where he had been, but now holding a revolver.

The attorney asked who fired the second shot. Adamson only replied, "One of my horses started to run and I grabbed the lines and wrapped them as quickly as I could around the hub of the wheel and went back to where Mr. Garrett lay."

Dr. Field was called to the stand. He stated that Garrett had no glove on his left hand and that his trousers were unbuttoned. It was clear to Field that Garrett was urinating at the time he was shot in the head. Field stated that a .45 caliber bullet struck Garrett in the back of the head and exited at his right eyebrow. The second bullet, according to the physician, struck Garrett in the stomach and ranged upward into the shoulder. In Field's opinion, the evidence pointed to murder in "cold blood and in the first degree."

Attorney General Hervey set Brazel's bond at $10,000. In a short time, W. W. Cox made his way through town raising money from businessmen, cattlemen, and private citizens. He had no trouble coming up with the money.

On April 13, the grand jury indicted Wayne Brazel for murder. His trial was not held until one year later on April 19, 1909. Brazel testified that Garrett had threatened him with the shotgun and that he had no choice but to shoot first. In contradiction to Field's testimony that Garrett was shot in the back of the head, he stated that Garrett was facing him when he fired his revolver.

According to Metz, the "case was prosecuted with appalling indifference and incompetence." Adamson, the only witness of record at the scene of the shooting, was not called on to testify. Adamson was, in fact, in jail for smuggling Chinese laborers into the country. It was learned that following the killing of Garrett, telegrams were sent back and forth between Brazel, Adamson, Cox, Miller, and Rhode. The communications were subpoenaed but never produced in evidence.

Attorney Thompson attempted to make a point that had Garrett intended to kill anyone, he would have loaded his shotgun with buckshot and not the birdshot it carried. He also suggested Garrett would have likely fired from the buggy seat rather than climbing down to the ground.

The case was given to the jurors at 5:30 PM. Fifteen minutes later they returned with a verdict of not guilty. That evening, a huge party was held for Brazel at the Cox ranch.

FORTY-TWO

✦✦✦

Suspects

Again the question: Who killed Pat Garrett? Before answering that, it is incumbent on the investigator to respond to an equally important one: Who did *not* kill Pat Garrett. The suspects, according to the prevailing wisdom, included Carl Adamson, Wayne Brazel, W. W. Cox, Jim Miller, and Print Rhode.

Members of the Garrett family were convinced that Carl Adamson was the killer for no reason other than that those who knew Brazel insisted that he did not possess the mentality or wherewithal for killing. Therefore, that left the only other person at the scene—Adamson. Added to this suspicion was the fact that when Adamson arrived at Garrett's ranch house to deliver him to the meeting in Las Cruces with Wayne Brazel and Jim Miller, Mrs. Garrett had an uncomfortable feeling about him.

Adamson is, in truth, the easiest of the known suspects to dismiss. Despite what the Garrett family might have claimed, there exists not a single shred of evidence that he killed Garrett. Adamson was an acquaintance of W. W. Cox and Oliver Lee, and it has been established that he was involved with the ring that was smuggling Chinese laborers across the U.S.-Mexico border. Once the immigrants were across, the smugglers needed a place to house the illegals before shipping them to Colorado, where he contracted with mining companies to supply workers. Garrett's Bear Canyon property would have served as an ideal location. The truth is, however, that Adamson and Garrett got along well and there had never been any animosity between the two men.

Could W. W. Cox have killed Pat Garrett? It has been oft alleged (but never proven) by some who claim to be historians that a secret meeting took place in El Paso, Texas, at the St. Regis Hotel wherein those in attendance discussed ways to get rid of Pat Garrett. The names of those suspected of being at the meeting include Carl Adamson, Wayne Brazel, Mannen Clements, W. W. Cox, Albert B. Fall, Oliver Lee, Bill McNew, and Jim Miller. It was rumored that Cox called for the meeting. Attributed to Cox were the following motives: He wanted Garrett's land and water; he hated the former lawman for the disturbance at his ranch that was created when Norman Newman was killed; and he and his trusted friend and close relative Oliver Lee were concerned that Garrett was on the verge of solving the Fountain mystery.

One story that made the rounds had Cox agreeing to pay someone for killing Garrett. Another story had Cox deciding that the best way to get rid of Garrett was to provoke him into placing himself in a position where he could be easily killed. Related to this, Cox supposedly came up with the idea of having Brazel place goats on his ranch, thus creating a dispute wherein Brazel would then have a good reason to kill Garrett. Brazel would take the blame for killing Garrett in self-defense and subsequently be found not guilty, but the actual killing would be accomplished by someone else.

A man named W. T. Moyers once practiced law in New Mexico around the time of Garrett's assassination. Years later after moving to Colorado, he claimed he conducted research into the killing and was finally convinced that W. W. Cox had shot and killed Garrett. Moyers passed his revelations on to one Fred M. Mazzulla, a collector of old west photographs, and suggested he write up the story and sell it for $5,000, which they would split. Nothing ever came of the project, and if Moyers ever possessed incriminating evidence regarding Cox's role in the death of Garrett, it has never surfaced.

There exists no evidence, however, that such a meeting between Cox and the others ever took place. It is entirely probable that this event was concocted out of whole cloth and repeated enough times to the point where some history buffs accepted it as fact. It remains nothing more than hearsay, and until something resembling evidence can be uncovered indicating that it might have happened, it must be dismissed as a fiction.

Cox's alleged motives for having Garrett killed require a second look. The notion of Cox wanting Garrett's land as a motive is absurd. In the first place, Cox could have acquired Garrett's properties ten years earlier had he wanted, because he held notes that would have provided the proper legal mechanisms for doing so. In the second place, Garrett's ranch had been described as "poverty-stricken." It is doubtful Cox could have longed for such a property when he already had his hands full with his own extensive holdings. In the third place, by the end of 1908, Cox simply wound up taking possession of Garrett's ranch anyway based on the notes. It is believed he provided some money to Mrs. Garrett to facilitate her move off of the ranch.

The alleged ploy to install goats on Garrett's property to provoke him into what was intended to be a life-ending dispute is fraught with nonsense. If such were Cox's plan, he would have been willing to fund the goat operation, which he did not. The truth is that Brazel borrowed money from Cox and signed a promissory note to repay it in a year. With Brazel's difficulties related to his trial, as well as trying to tend to his goat herd, he was unable to pay it, so Cox extended the debt until such time as Brazel would be able to repay him. Almost a year after lending Brazel the money, Cox lent him another $300 so attorney fees could be paid. The terms stated that this loan had to be repaid in ninety days with a 10 percent interest. After four years of holding Brazel's debts and not receiving any money, Cox filed suit to collect. It was all for naught. Brazel clearly could not pay the debts and Cox finally withdrew from all of his efforts to collect them.

It must also be pointed out that the so-called goat herd scheme to lure Garrett into a position such that he could be murdered would have been a terribly inefficient and expensive way to handle the matter. Cox was smarter than that, and there existed a number of other more efficient and logical ways to get to Garrett.

No evidence of any kind exists that links Print Rhode to the shooting of Pat Garrett. It is true that Rhode had despised Garrett for a long time, and his distaste for the lawman went back ten years earlier to the disturbance at the Cox ranch when Newman was killed. Why would Rhode have waited ten years to do away with Garrett? Further, the Newman-related event hardly seems like a sufficient reason to kill a person, even for a hothead like Rhode. It is also true that Rhode was involved with Brazel in the goat-ranching operation, but the complications of that scheme have already been discussed and eliminated. Besides, there would have been no logical reason for Adamson to lie for Rhode. And why would Brazel agree to take the blame for something his partner did? No aspect of Print Rhode as a suspect in the killing of Pat Garrett carries with it any logic or credibility whatsoever.

Historians and outlaw enthusiasts love to point the finger at Killin' Jim Miller as the assassin of Pat Garrett. Miller had been a notorious, colorful, and attention-generating character. As a suspect, Miller deserves, even requires, close examination.

Miller posed as a cattleman and a rancher, but no records exist to indicate he was either. The Miller-as-assassin enthusiasts employ this connection as a ruse he used to get close to Garrett. This is an unreasonable assumption. If Miller had been the killer, why employ an involved tactic such as this when all that was needed was to hide behind a bush and shoot a man while he was urinating? Furthermore, if Garrett and Miller were, in truth, on the verge of arranging a business deal that, on the face of it, appeared to be beneficial to both men, what reason would Miller possibly have to kill him?

According to Metz, the "attempt to place Miller at the death site is based on the discovery of a Winchester cartridge case along with horse tracks and droppings in the murder area." It is difficult to impossible to discern any tangible links to these observations and Jim Miller. For one thing, Miller's long-preferred weapon was a shotgun. Since the road taken by Garrett, Adamson, and Brazel was well traveled, it should come as no surprise that someone might encounter horse prints and droppings. Further, the .45 caliber shell casing found by examiner Field could have come from anybody and could have been fired as a result of a hunting venture long before Garrett, Brazel, and Adamson arrived at the location.

Another thing that enthusiasts like to quote when presenting and promoting the Miller-as-assassin position is his alleged confession of the deed just before he was hanged in Ada, Oklahoma, on April 19, 1909. Such a thing never happened. Walter Gayne, who was Miller's jailer when the killer was dragged from his cell and strung up from a barn rafter, stated that Miller mentioned neither Garrett nor his role in much of anything before he died. According to author C. L. Sonnichsen, Gayne said, "I ought to know because I hung him."

This leaves us with our final suspect, Wayne Brazel. In spite of the absurdities associated with Brazel's role, his confession, and the trial, author Leon Metz writes, "A thorough examination of the many theories, all the evidence now obtainable, leads one to the inescapable conclusion that [Brazel] was, indeed, the killer of Pat Garrett."

To this day, many people are convinced Brazel killed Pat Garrett, in large part, based on Metz's published statement. But Metz was mistaken; Wayne Brazel did not kill Pat Garrett. By the time Metz's book on Pat Garrett was published in 1974, a "thorough examination of the many theories" had not been conducted, by Metz or anyone else, although a number of cursory examinations had been conducted, some by Metz himself. Metz was a competent writer, but when it came to research he tended to be disorganized and incomplete. To Metz, as well as many others who regard themselves as historians, research amounted to little more than looking something up and repeating it. Nowhere in Metz's book on Pat Garrett can one find an example of where Metz had conducted an in-depth investigation, a deconstruction, an analysis, and a reconstruction. He only repeated what others wrote and took what they penned at face value.

Metz was further handicapped by two things. He only had at his fingertips, as he stated, "the evidence now obtainable." Since his book was published, additional evidence has come to light. It is also clear that Pat Garrett was a kind of hero to Metz, one who demanded to be glorified rather than exposed for what he was, that he was a man to be admired for his many alleged accomplishments. Metz emphasized this stand in print and in a number of presentations and conversations throughout the years.

Why should Wayne Brazel be dismissed as Pat Garrett's killer? Brazel testified in court that he shot Garrett in the head while he was facing him. Dr. W. C. Field, the head of the coroner's jury and a man experienced in such things, observed that Garrett had been shot in the back of the head just below the hat line, the bullet traveling on a straight plane, and exiting at the right eyebrow. Fields noted that graying brown hair from the back of Garrett's head had been carried into the skull and mixed with the destroyed brain matter.

The term "hat line" is rather arbitrary, and in this case meaningless. No one knows how Pat Garrett was wearing his hat at the time he was shot. It could have been tipped up in front, pulled down in front, or even cocked to the side.

Garrett had climbed down the off-side of the buggy. He took at least a couple of steps, removed the glove from his left hand, and turned toward Brazel, who was still on horseback on the left side of the buggy. As the argument continued, he unbuttoned his trousers and was facing Brazel as he was urinating. Beyond Brazel was the low ridge. Behind Garrett was a shallow arroyo. The shot came from behind Garrett. The first shot, the one that killed Pat Garrett, was not fired by Wayne Brazel.

After the bullet tore through his skull, the force of the impact caused Garrett to wheel around and fall to the ground onto his back, his head toward the buggy. A second bullet entered Garrett's stomach and plowed at a shallow angle through his upper body and finally ended its journey near the left shoulder. Brazel did not fire this shot either. For him to have accomplished this, he would have had to dismount, walk around the buggy, kneel near the foot of Garrett's body, and, holding his revolver at a nearly horizontal level, shoot the already dead man in the stomach. Brazel did no such thing.

Brazel testified that Garrett was about to shoot him with his shotgun when he, Brazel, drew his revolver and shot first. Garrett's shotgun was allegedly loaded with birdshot, hardly the kind of ammunition one would load into a shotgun if his intention was to kill someone. In addition, during the act of urinating, Garrett was hardly in a position to shoot someone with a shotgun. Further, when the party consisting of Sheriff Lucero, Dr. Field, and others arrived from Las Cruces, they found Garrett's shotgun on the ground about three feet from the body. It was noted that the weapon appeared to have been placed in its position as opposed to having been dropped or thrown by the mortally wounded Garrett, for the sand around the weapon had not been disturbed. On inspecting the shotgun, Sheriff Lucero found that it was still encased in its scabbard and was unloaded. With the shotgun still in its scabbard, it seems unlikely that Garrett could have placed Brazel in a position such that he would be forced to plead self-defense.

The only "inescapable conclusion," as Metz put it, should be that Brazel did *not* kill Pat Garrett. This sequence does not even demand a "thorough examination," as Metz suggested he had conducted. Even a cursory examination of the events reveals that Brazel could not have shot Pat Garrett. None of the so-called evidence leading to Brazel being the shooter carries any logic whatsoever. Indeed, the evidence is strongly *against* Brazel being the killer.

Why, then, did Brazel admit to killing Garrett when he clearly did not? Given the circumstances related to the shooting of Pat Garrett, taken in context with subsequent events, it becomes clear that Brazel, who did not pull the trigger, was nevertheless part of a plot to do away with Garrett. Evidence suggests the plot involved Oliver Lee, W. W. Cox, Jim Miller, Print Rhode, and the assassin. Brazel was set up to take the fall, for all involved knew that he, more than anyone else, would stand the best chance of being found innocent of the charge of murder and would never serve a day in prison.

FORTY-THREE

---◆◆◆---

The Plot

Fred Fornoff was serving as a captain in the New Mexico Mounted Police when Pat Garrett was assassinated. Born in Baltimore, Maryland, in 1859, Fornoff traveled west as a young man and found work as a miner, a brick maker, and day laborer. He served in the Spanish American War as one of Theodore Roosevelt's Rough Riders. On returning stateside, Fornoff became the city marshal of Albuquerque. Following that, he held positions as a deputy United States marshal, a Secret Service agent, and a special investigator for the Justice Department. As a lawman, Fornoff earned a reputation as a solid investigator and man hunter.

On March 1, 1908, Fornoff accompanied Governor George Curry and New Mexico Attorney General James M. Hervey to Las Cruces for the funeral of Pat Garrett. Governor Curry was one of the pallbearers.

Fornoff visited the Garrett murder site. Later, responding to orders from Governor Curry, Fornoff conducted an investigation into the killing as well as the circumstances leading up to the death of Pat Garrett. Fornoff's handwritten notes were given to Page B. Otero, the Mounted Police office clerk, for typing. It was titled "The Fornoff Report," and in August 1908, Fornoff presented the report of his findings to Curry, who in turn handed it over to Attorney General Hervey for his comments.

The *El Paso Herald*, on learning of the existence of the Fornoff Report, requested a copy of it. The newspaper was refused by Hervey, who claimed that the report was to be used at Wayne Brazel's upcoming trial and until that time must remain confidential. In fact, it was never entered into the trial proceedings and Fornoff was never asked to testify relative to any part of his investigation.

A short time after Brazel's trial, Attorney General Hervey resigned his post to return to private practice. When he moved out of his office, he took all of his personal papers along with several marked confidential. One of those was the Fornoff Report. Hervey passed away in 1953. His law partner, Charles Brice, assumed ownership of Hervey's papers until his own death in 1963. Most of Brice's law office papers, along with Hervey's, went to Brice's family. The materials meant nothing to them and they carried them to the Roswell City dump and burned them. It is believed that the only extant copy of the Fornoff Report was among them.

During the 1960s, the last living member of the New Mexico Mounted Police was living in Cimarron, New Mexico. Fred Lambert told an interviewer that he had read Fornoff's field notes and Page Otero's draft of the report. When the interviewer asked Lambert to reveal what was in the notes, the old policeman replied, "Let it be. The families of those men are respectable now. Let the closets stay closed."

During a series of subsequent interviews, however, Lambert revealed portions of Fornoff's report. Lambert also revealed that sometime in 1912, he and Fornoff discussed the murder of Pat Garrett.

Lambert said that starting just before Wayne Brazel's trial and continuing on through 1913, certain lawmakers invested a great deal of time and energy in an attempt to abolish the New Mexico Mounted Police. The attempt failed, but the force was cut to half. Lambert stated that during the upcoming 1913 meeting of the state legislature, the opponents to the police would have finally gathered enough votes to eliminate the force for economic reasons. Lambert asked Fornoff why the lawmakers wanted to eliminate the police. Fornoff replied, "They know I know about the Garrett plot and the big money interests behind the Fountain killings. As long as the police exist, they are in danger. [If there are] no police, [then] there's less danger of any new evidence seeing daylight." Fornoff then outlined for Lambert a plan and motive that likely resulted in the death of Pat Garrett. The original idea, according to Fornoff, was to ruin Garrett financially, take his property, and then force him to leave the area. This scheme, he suggested, generated a momentum that eventually led to his murder. Fornoff was only partly correct.

During his years as a deputy U.S. marshal and Secret Service agent, Fornoff established a number of close relationships with high-level federal officials. These same officials informed him that they were involved in building a case against a group of men involved in smuggling illegal Chinese laborers out of Mexico, through the state of New Mexico, and on to the mines and farms in southern Colorado. Involved in this plot were Oliver Lee, W. W. Cox, Carl Adamson, Print Rhode, Mannen Clements, and probably others including Jim Miller.

The information relating to the smuggling operation came from
none other than Dr. W. C. Field, the man who led the coroner's jury
in Garrett's inquest and conducted the autopsy on the body. Field had
treated one of the smuggled Chinese for some ailment while he was
housed in the county jail at Las Cruces. The prisoner revealed to Field
the smuggling arrangements and named the suspects. Field wrote a
letter containing this information to U.S. Marshal Creighton Foraker,
who in turn passed the letter to other federal agents. It was at this
point that Fornoff undertook his investigation.

Fornoff learned that during the movement of the illegal Chinese
through New Mexico after crossing the Mexican border, the smugglers
needed a remote and safe place to hold them until such time as they
could transport them northward to Colorado. Garrett's Bear Canyon
ranch was considered ideal for this purpose. As it turned out, Wayne
Brazel and Print Rhode were already utilizing the site for the goat
ranch operation. The fly in the ointment was that Garrett made it
known that he wanted the goats off his property because he believed
Carl Adamson and Jim Miller desired it for cattle they were allegedly
bringing up from Mexico. The truth was that Adamson and Miller had
no cattle. They wanted the place to hide the Chinese.

It must have been clear to Adamson and Miller that Garrett would
soon realize no cattle were forthcoming, and they must have considered revealing their plans to the old lawman and offering him a piece
of the action. The only problem was that when Garrett learned that
his longtime enemies Oliver Lee and Print Rhode, as well as men to
whom he owed money, such as W. W. Cox, were involved in the plot,
he would not only refuse to be involved but would likely alert law
enforcement officials. An even greater danger lay in thus achieving
a level of revenge against men who had tormented him in the past,
some of whom he owed a lot of money. There was only one solution.
Because the Bear Canyon property was so necessary to the smuggling operation, and because Garrett was in a position to expose the
operation, he had to go.

Fornoff was convinced the masterminds behind the plot to get
Garrett out of the way were brothers-in-law Oliver Lee, W. W. Cox,
and Print Rhode. At one time, Garrett had connected Lee and Cox to
the killing of Colonel Fountain and his son Henry. Cox provided the
money to finance the killing of Pat Garrett. People would have to be
paid off, and it seems reasonable to assume Wayne Brazel was one of

them. Brazel was convinced by Cox to confess to the crime with the assurance he would not go to jail. To assist in this part of the plot, Cox contacted his own personal lawyer to represent Brazel at the trial. That lawyer was Albert B. Fall.

Oliver Lee provided the gunman for the assassination. It was a man who had long proven his loyalty and devotion to the rancher: his nephew and trusted ranch hand, Todd Bailey.

FORTY-FOUR

Reenter Todd Bailey

harles Lewis Bailey was born on July 12, 1879, in Buffalo Gap, Texas, to Rutha Altman and John Wesley Bailey. A younger sister gave him the nickname "Todd." Bailey's mother, Rutha, was the older half-sister of New Mexico rancher Oliver Lee. Todd's older brother, Oliver, was named for Oliver Lee's father. Brother Oliver was killed in a wagon accident when he was seven years of age. Todd was two years old at the time. Rutha died two years later, leaving Todd and his two siblings to be raised by their father. Shortly after moving the family to Commerce, Texas, one account has John Bailey dying from a heart attack and the children placed with a neighbor. According to the Bailey family, however, John simply dropped the children off at the home of their uncle Charlie Hass and his wife and rode away. Todd was not yet six years old.

Life with Hass in Commerce was unpleasant. He worked the children from dawn to dusk and treated them poorly, often whipping them. Todd despised his uncle, but options were few for the orphan.

From New Mexico, Mary Lee, Oliver Lee's mother, learned that her grandchildren were being treated poorly by their guardians. She sent her son Oliver to Commerce to retrieve them and bring them to the New Mexico ranch. Oliver made the journey to Commerce, but succeeded in returning only with one of them, Mamie.

On July 6, 1890, six years after depositing his children on the doorstep of Charlie Hass, John Wesley Bailey rode up to the Commerce home. He unsaddled his horse, walked over to the front porch without a word to anyone, threw the saddle to the ground and then lay down, using the saddle for a pillow, and died.

One afternoon when Hass thought young Todd was not working hard enough, he lashed him with a horsewhip, opening cuts on his face and chest. The boy fell against a wagon wheel where he was pinned, unable to flee. Hass continued to lash him. Todd tried to roll away and wound up on top of a pitchfork as the whip laced across his back. He was certain his uncle was trying to kill him.

From the ground, Todd seized the pitchfork and thrust it upward, hard, and plunged it into Charlie's stomach and deep into the rib cage. Hass fell down, blood pouring out of his wound and puddling on the hay-covered ground. Through his tears, Todd Bailey watched his hated uncle writhing on the ground, moaning. He turned and ran. He stopped at a shallow creek some distance away long enough to ponder what he had done. He realized he could never go back, so he continued running.

Todd fled to Abilene (near Buffalo Gap) in hope of finding some Altman and Lee relatives, only to learn that they had moved to New Mexico. Somehow, the youngster made his way across seven hundred miles of arid West Texas and New Mexico landscape and arrived on their doorstep, nearly dead from starvation. Here he was reunited with Mamie, and the two were raised by their loving grandmother, Mary.

Todd Bailey went to his grave believing he had killed his uncle Charlie Hass. Hass, though badly wounded, recovered. Years later he moved to Victoria, Texas, where he lived out the rest of his life.

As he grew up, Todd Bailey learned ranching and cowboy skills from his uncle, Oliver Lee. Todd became one of the ranch's most competent and dependable hands, and he worked as an agent for Lee, selling horses for him from time to time. There was never a ranch hand more devoted and loyal to Oliver Lee than Todd Bailey. When Lee went to Hillsboro to stand trial for the killing of Henry Fountain, he developed a plan whereby if he was found guilty, some of his ranch hands in the courtroom would rise up and open fire on the judge and others. Without a second thought, Todd Bailey volunteered. Years later, when Oliver Lee needed someone to shoot and kill Pat Garrett, he turned to his half-nephew, Todd Bailey.

According to the plot, Carl Adamson was to transport Pat Garrett to the location along the Mail-Scott Road where he would be killed, a location that had been selected by Oliver Lee. Following a brief stop outside of the town of Organ, Adamson and Garrett spotted Wayne Brazel some distance up the road ahead of them. Brazel was in conversation with a man on horseback historians thought was Print Rhode. It was Todd Bailey.

A short time later, Wayne Brazel, loping along on his horse, joined Adamson and Garrett and rode with them, sometimes ahead, sometimes behind, and where the road was wide enough, alongside the

buggy. Todd Bailey had ridden ahead and guided his horse up the
eastern spur of the low ridge that paralleled the road. From a point
near the western end of the ridge, Bailey, sitting atop his horse, looked
down the north-facing slope and spotted a location where the road
crossed another. From his position, Bailey could also observe the road
from Organ and pick out travelers. A moment later, he spotted the
buggy transporting Adamson and Garrett with Brazel riding along.

As the buggy got closer, Bailey guided his horse down the south slope
of the ridge and out of sight from the road. At the bottom, he tied the
animal to a low-growing mesquite tree. From a leather scabbard, he
withdrew a .30–.40 Krag, a lightweight lever-action carbine made
by Winchester with a twenty-two-inch barrel, one employed by the
U.S. Army since around 1892. Loaded and ready for shooting was a
.30–.40 smokeless powder cartridge popular with hunters.

Rounding the western spur of the ridge on foot, Bailey made his way
across the flat, brush-covered desert toward the road, crossed it, and
proceeded another 130 feet to Alameda Arroyo. Bailey found an ideal
location in the shallow arroyo wherein he had a perfect field of fire.
Brush and junipers lined the bank and grew thick in places between
it and the road, but at the point where Bailey stood there were no
obstacles between him and the place where Adamson would stop the
buggy. While he waited, he lit a hand-rolled cigarette and sat down
on the bank to await his target.

Before long, Bailey could hear the jingle of traces and the clop of
horse hooves on the road. From his position, he spotted the buggy a
short distance away. Wayne Brazel was on horseback and maintaining a position to the left of the vehicle near the rear. Bailey could hear
Garrett and Brazel arguing. At the designated point, Adamson reined
the buggy to a halt, stating that he needed to urinate. After climbing
down from the vehicle, Adamson walked to a spot next to the head
of the horses. This placed him in a position to keep the animals from
bolting when the planned-for shot was fired. Brazel remained in his
position on the left side of the buggy.

When Pat Garrett climbed down off the buggy, unbuttoned his trousers, and began urinating, he was facing Brazel as he continued his
argument. From his position near the bank of the arroyo, Todd Bailey
had a clear line of fire; Brazel was positioned a sufficient distance to
the left and Adamson was far to the right near the horses. Garrett was
between them.

Bailey rose to a standing position just below the low bank of the arroyo, took aim, and fired. The bullet entered the back of Garrett's head not far from the left ear, tore through his brain, and exited at the right eyebrow. He was spun around, flailing his arms as he did so, and dropped to the ground on his back. Bailey said later that when Garrett hit the ground, the sound was "like you had dropped a sack of potatoes."

Garrett's head was toward the wagon, his feet toward Bailey. Bailey ejected the shell, inserted another, took aim at the prone Garrett, and fired a second shot. The bullet entered Garrett's lower stomach, proceeded at a low angle through the torso, and came to lodge near the left shoulder.

Pat Garrett, whose life was a mix of fame and shame, was dead.

Todd Bailey, the assassin, continued to work for Oliver Lee on his ranch for many years, eventually retiring to southwestern Arkansas and southeastern Oklahoma. Though Bailey's role in the killing of Pat Garrett was well known to many in New Mexico, and subsequently to his family and descendants in Oklahoma and Arkansas, he somehow managed to escape the notice of historians in spite of the fact that he was involved in a number of significant events that affected Pat Garrett. Portions of Bailey's life and his relationship with Oliver Lee were detailed in the book *The Pioneers of 1885 in New Mexico* by George McNew. For additional information on Todd Bailey, see appendix III.

FORTY-FIVE

✦✦✦

Conclusion

Pat Garrett holds a significant place in the history of New Mexico and America's outlaw west. As a lawman, Garrett accomplished some positive things. During a time when it was necessary to hunt down criminals and bring them to justice, Garrett had important skills and managed a few successes.

Garrett is known primarily, some would argue entirely, for an act that, in the final analysis, he did not perform: The killing of the outlaw Billy the Kid. Garrett lied, and he rode that lie to a significant level of fame and recognition. Because Garrett was a documented liar, perhaps a pathological one, and because he suffered from a number of character flaws and vices that rendered him largely unfit for and unacceptable to polite society as it existed in southern New Mexico and elsewhere, he was largely rejected and ignored by those groups and affiliations he wished to be part of as well as those in power who could have had a hand in advancing his career. Garrett's fame, brief as it was, receded. Throughout the remainder of his post-Billy-the-Kid life, Garrett experienced flashes of success, all short lived. He died broke, deeply in debt, and despised by nearly all but his family.

It can be argued that Garrett was more of a criminal than was Billy the Kid, the man he claimed he shot and killed. The evidence presented here provides a strong case for this. Garrett did not rustle cattle and horses like the Kid. He did kill men, and may have killed as many or more than the Kid and not necessarily in the context of enforcing the law. Garrett's criminal talent and pursuits were more related to his orientation toward deceiving people: He deceived men into investing in mining schemes that he knew were dishonest; he borrowed money, great sums of it, from men who once were friends, but never paid any of it back; he deceived the public into believing he was attempting to solve the disappearance of Colonel Fountain and his son when he was

200

merely collecting a paycheck. In the end it turned out he wasn't nearly as smart as the Kid. The Kid survived; Garrett was murdered by his enemies, and he had many. Garrett's ego, his ill-perceived notion of his imagined power and influence, and his lack of ability to see beyond his own self-serving interests worked to bring him down.

The image of Pat Garrett as hero is a canard. The image was and is based on a lie, one perpetuated by Garrett himself, and then further perpetuated by men purporting to write and record history. It has become clear that these writers were more interested in relating the accepted version of a popular tale by repeating the hoax and maintaining the historical status quo, the myth, than to invest the time and energy required to learn the truth. Perpetuating a myth is easy; digging for the truth is difficult and time-consuming work.

Cold cases are difficult to investigate under the best of circumstances, but not impossible. As sometimes occurs, undiscovered evidence can show up decades later that sheds light on old and long-unsolved mysteries. With the development of new investigative techniques, along with the myriad ways in which the Internet can assist in research and analysis, this is being proven on a daily basis.

Historical interpretations are subject to change in response to new and legitimate evidence, new questions asked of the long-standing evidence, and new perspectives gained with the passage of time. Revisionism is what makes history dynamic. It is also a necessary process in the quest for the truth.

Revisionist historians and others have applied their investigative skills toward unraveling mysteries and/or providing new and different interpretations pertinent to a number of topics including religion, politics, government diplomacy, economics, and society. The field of western history, one that is replete with a colorful and dramatic mythology, is ripe for investigation and reinterpretation by revisionists.

Prevailing notions about western American outlaws, lawmen, and associated events invite a legitimate scholastic reexamination of the existing "knowledge." Indeed, a number of the orthodox views on evidence, motivation, decision making, and published accounts surrounding such historical events are long overdue for challenge.

A principal obstacle to such challenges exists in the form of the reigning clique of outlaw/lawman enthusiasts who resist departure from the orthodox thinking. One who transgresses, who refuses to repeat the same old tired and unproven historical clichés, is regarded as an outsider, perhaps even a troublemaker. Such attitudes inhibit serious contributions to the history and lore of America.

Dismantling Pat Garrett's status as hero and exposing him for the fraud, the liar, and the con man that he was provides no satisfaction. There are men who will rage against the contention that Garrett was a deceiver, a charlatan. Many will be disturbed that their perceptions have been impugned by a new truth. No doubt some negative reaction will emerge from those who embrace the status quo. To those who feel outrage, to those who take issue with the evidence presented in this book, please challenge the findings, confront the evidence, and provide credible alternative proof. The subsequent debates, should there be any, might prove fruitful. After all, the quest is to determine the truth, not to avoid it.

What does provide some satisfaction, however, is the knowledge that a dedicated and honest attempt has been made to research, to investigate, to study, to analyze, to generate hypotheses and null hypotheses, to reconstruct, and to present to the reader the resulting truths, ones that are supported by an array of evidence that can be backed up with confidence.

In the end, all you have is the truth.

APPENDIX I

―――――― ◆◆◆ ――――――

William Henry Roberts, aka Billy the Kid

While investigating a contested inheritance in 1948, a paralegal named William V. Morrison learned of an eighty-eight-year-old man living in Hamilton County, Texas, whose few close acquaintances insisted was the outlaw Billy the Kid. Morrison tracked him down, interviewed him over a period of two days, and came away convinced that the man, William Henry Roberts, was indeed the famous outlaw. At the time, Roberts was going by the alias Oliver L. Roberts, one of many he had used throughout his life, including Henry McCarty, Henry Antrim, and William Bonney.

Morrison invited noted author, historian, and folklorist Dr. C. L. Sonnichsen to assist him with the investigation of William Henry Roberts, aka Billy the Kid, and write a book. The Harvard-educated and well-respected Sonnichsen agreed. He, like Morrison, interviewed Roberts and became convinced of the old man's identity. In 1955, the University of New Mexico Press released Sonnichsen and Morrison's book, *Alias Billy the Kid.* The response from the community of western and outlaw aficionados was hostile; negative criticism rained down on the authors, and the two men even received death threats. It turned out that those steeped in outlaw lore did not take contradictions or challenges to their perceptions lightly.

Sonnichsen and Morrison presented a remarkable array of evidence indicating Roberts was Billy the Kid, and while those committed to maintaining the historical status quo railed against this notion, none of them came forth with substantive rebuttals relative to the thesis that Roberts was *not* the Kid. Before he passed away, Sonnichsen professed his belief in Roberts and the Kid being one and the same and suggested more work needed to be done to convince the naysayers.

Concentrated research and investigation followed. During the ensuing decades, an array of evidence that accumulated related to

Roberts's claims as the Kid and to his life for the sixty-nine years following the alleged killing by Pat Garrett proved he was telling the truth. This evidence consisted of researching Roberts's genealogy (the names Antrim, McCarty, and Bonney were all family names); verifying his claims; and, most dramatic of all, a photo analysis.

There have been a number of photo comparison studies on men who claimed to be Billy the Kid, including Roberts. All of the analysts claimed that the studies showed Roberts could not have been Billy the Kid. The truth, however, is that none of these photo comparison experiments could claim any statistical validity. They were more akin to an elementary school project. In 1992, the only statistically valid photo-comparison study technique available in the world was obtained from the Federal Bureau of Investigation and applied by engineers at the University of Texas to comparable images of William Henry Roberts and Billy the Kid. The results: they were images of the same man. Conclusions from a study such as this are admissible in court and the technique has been used not only by the FBI, but the Secret Service, the CIA, Scotland Yard, Interpol, and progressive law enforcement agencies around the world.

The result of the photo-comparison study, as well as all of the other evidence associated with numerous aspects of Roberts's life as the Kid were reported in the book *Billy the Kid: Beyond the Grave* (2005). The book was well received by credible historians, garnered positive reviews, and generated a number of television documentaries. Those opposed to the notion of Roberts being Billy the Kid, however, forwarded criticism, engaged in name calling, and, inexplicably, provided more death threats. Those people took their myths seriously and would not permit a truth to sway their positions. In spite of the criticism, not a single person came forward with any substantive research or information that contradicted the evidence presented in the book.

In 1949, Roberts was subjected to a series of taped interviews oriented toward gaining information on his life as Billy the Kid and after. During the early 1950s, the tapes were listed as lost, and numerous attempts to locate them proved fruitless. Then, in 1989 the missing interview tapes surfaced. They had been stored at the bottom of a wooden chest of items that had once belonged to Roberts and was in the possession of a step-grandson living in Temple, Texas. The tapes were transcribed and published in their near-entirety in *Billy the Kid: The Lost Interviews* (2012). The tapes provided insight into a number of events in the life of Billy the Kid and other related occurrences in remarkable detail from a man who was clearly at the scene and a participant. The tapes indicate without a doubt that Roberts, an illiterate man who could barely read and write, knew more about the history of Billy the Kid and associated figures, as well as the Lincoln County War, than the historians.

The interview tapes, the genealogy, the research and investigation into verifying Roberts's story, along with the photo-comparison study yield the conclusion that William Henry Roberts was, indeed, the outlaw Billy the Kid.

APPENDIX II

✦✦✦

Crime Scene Investigation
The Washstand

On July 31, 2004, a forensic investigation team consisting of lawmen Steve Sederwall and Tom Sullivan, forensic consultant Calvin Ostler, crime scene assistant Kim Ostler, chief emeritus of the Connecticut State Police Forensic Laboratory Dr. Henry Lee, David Turk of the U.S. Marshal Service, and Mike Haag, a firearm examiner from the Albuquerque Police Department, arrived at the residence of Manny Miller in Albuquerque, New Mexico, to examine pieces of evidence once in the possession of Pete Maxwell. One item selected was the washstand that stood in Maxwell's bedroom on the night Pat Garrett claimed to have shot and killed the outlaw Billy the Kid.

The washstand measured 28¾ inches long, 16 inches deep, and 30 inches tall. Visual examination of the external surfaces of the washstand revealed two holes, one in each side panel. Microscopic examination of these holes indicated they were consistent with bullet holes. On the night of July 14, 1881, the washstand was positioned in Maxwell's bedroom such that the right side panel was against the wall opposite Maxwell's bed. The hole on the left side panel is consistent with a bullet entrance hole. The hole on the right side panel is slightly deformed and there is a small chip of wood missing, consistent with an exit hole. Sodium rhodizonate, used in testing for lead, was applied to the holes. The results were positive.

A laser was set up to reconstruct the angle of trajectory of the bullet that passed through the washstand. The laser was placed approximately twenty feet from the left side panel and adjusted to project a beam directly through that hole as well as the exit hole on the right side panel. The bullet path from left to right had a slight downward angle determined to be 4.47 degrees.

The conclusion was that the person, determined to be Pat Garrett, who shot the holes into the washstand did so from a position that likely involved being on both knees with one hand on the floor for support while the opposite hand fired the revolver.

APPENDIX III

Todd Bailey

Todd Bailey resided for well over a century in the nooks and crannies of published history. Those who wrote what passed for New Mexico history, the life of Pat Garrett, the disappearance of Colonel Fountain, and the life and times of rancher and politician Oliver Lee, chose, for reasons known only to them, to ignore this quiet, competent, yet dangerous figure.

Todd Bailey first came to my attention on November 11, 2011. I received an e-mail from a man named Buck Bailey, who was living in Wickes, Arkansas. Mr. Bailey said he had seen me on a History Channel program wherein Pat Garrett and Billy the Kid were discussed. Bailey mentioned his grandfather, Todd Bailey, and his connection with Oliver Lee. Bailey also stated that Oliver Lee had Pat Garrett killed and that Todd Bailey was involved.

Following a series of e-mail conversations over the following weeks, I learned the details of Todd Bailey's role in the assassination of Garrett, his participation in the disappearance and killing of Colonel Fountain and his son, and his role in Lee's trial. During the time I was communicating with Bailey, investigator and writer Steve Sederwall was working on the Fountain case and making plans to write a book. I put him in touch with Buck Bailey.

What followed was another series of communications between Sederwall and Bailey in which a wealth of pertinent information and insight into the killing of Pat Garrett and the disappearance of the Fountains was revealed.

As an old man, Todd Bailey, living out his final years in southwestern Arkansas, related numerous aspects of his past to his children and grandchildren. Thus was revealed his role in the killing of Pat Garrett, Colonel Fountain, and more. Todd Bailey's past was handed down in his family via the oral tradition. The tales were never in the form of boasting, merely a telling of the facts of what occurred. They never changed. Buck Bailey became a reservoir for the story of Todd Bailey, and it was this knowledge he shared with Sederwall and me.

So intrigued was Sederwall with this font of valuable information that in March 2013 he made a trip from his home in Capitan, New Mexico, to Wickes, Arkansas, to visit with and interview Buck Bailey. In addition to Buck, Sederwall interviewed Mike Bailey, a cousin. Buck and Mike had not seen each other in thirty-five years, but they came together to meet with Sederwall to reveal a long and closely guarded family secret. Sederwall was the first person outside the family to hear the stories of Todd Bailey, stories that came down through two different branches of the family, stories that Buck and Mike shared for the first time, but stories that were identical in substance. The following day, Sederwall traveled to Oklahoma to interview Buck Bailey's sister, Brenda, who provided even more insight and information pertaining to Todd Bailey. In the end, Buck Bailey, his sister, and his cousin assisted us in solving both the murder of Pat Garrett and the mystery surrounding Colonel Fountain.

As much as was possible, we checked out Todd Bailey's stories as related by Buck Bailey and found them to be remarkably accurate. Though Buck Bailey had never been to the site of Garrett's assassination, his descriptions of the road, the ridge, the arroyo, the logistics, and the field of fire were accurate down to the inch. A visit to the site was followed by a precise walk-through of Bailey's descriptions. The geography was exact; the setting for the logistics related to the ambush was on the mark. Even the mathematical calculation relative to the angle the second bullet entered and traveled through Garett's body pinpointed Todd Bailey's position when he fired the shot some one hundred thirty feet away.

Buck Bailey is a retired lawman with thirty-seven years of experience. Bailey knows the truth when he sees it. If there was any hokum associated with the stories Todd Bailey told to his relatives, Buck would have known it. Bailey is as credible a witness as one could find. By the time we finished dissecting and investigating Buck Bailey's versions of what occurred, we found him to be far more credible that Pat Garrett.

APPENDIX IV

The Unfolding Years

Following the death of Pat Garrett, and thus the elimination of a thorn in the side of many, life continued to unfold in New Mexico and elsewhere with considerably less drama than the citizens were heretofore used to experiencing. Life for the participants in a number of the region's greatest mysteries, murders, and other events settled into a pattern of routine, with a few, such as Oliver Lee, branching out into politics, and others simply vanishing without a trace.

OLIVER LEE

Though Oliver Milton Lee undoubtedly played a prominent role in the abduction and killing of Colonel Albert Fountain and his young son Henry, he spoke little about the affair during the remainder of his life. Further, though he, along with others, was responsible for the assassination of Pat Garrett, he never revisited the subject.

Lee continued living in his Dog Canyon home, operated his ranches, and enjoyed some success. During this time he was regarded as a prominent cattleman. He became acquainted with a man named McNary, a prominent El Paso, Texas, banker. McNary convinced Lee to manage the large Circle Cross ranching operation, with headquarters near Tiburon, New Mexico. At the time, it was regarded as the largest ranch in that part of the state. Months later, however, McNary's bank failed, financial difficulties ensued, and Lee found himself idled.

In 1919, Lee accompanied racecar driver Johnny Hutchings on a cross-country competition from El Paso to Phoenix. The race was well publicized, as was Lee's presence. Thirty miles out of El Paso, an observer, Army Major William F. Scanland, fired a shot into the car, striking and mortally wounding Hutchings. Scanland was arrested and sent to prison. Rumors following the shooting suggested that Lee had been the intended target.

Lee maintained a residence in Alamogordo, and there served as director of the Federal Land Bank. He ran for and was elected to several terms in the New Mexico state legislature from 1918 to 1930, thrice as a representative and thrice as a senator. In 1932 he ran for New Mexico State Land Commissioner on the Republican ticket and was soundly defeated.

In 1941, Lee suffered a stroke at the age of seventy-six. He died on December 15 of that year. Several descendants of Oliver Lee continue to live and ranch in New Mexico today.

JIM GILLILAND

According to clear and abundant evidence, Jim Gilliland was a member of the party that abducted and killed Colonel Fountain and his young son. The recently uncovered evidence also shows that Gilliland killed nine-year-old Henry Fountain by grabbing his hair from behind and slitting his throat with a pocketknife. Later, Gilliland as much as admitted his role. For the rest of his life, he experienced nightmares relative to his role in the killings. He cried openly when he talked about it, and he drank heavily in the hope that it would help him forget.

Members of Gilliland's family let it be known that he had kept a diary that contained the details of the Fountain kidnapping and killing, with special attention to his participation in the events. Further, a story has been related that Gilliland confessed his role to a Las Cruces lawyer who wrote it down and notarized it. The diary and confession, believed to be in the possession of family members, has never been made public.

Twenty years after the killings, Gilliland, who helped to bury the Fountain bodies in a remote canyon in the San Andres Mountains, grew worried that the gravesite would remain unmarked. Whether out of guilt or some other and unknown reason, Gilliland traveled to the site and denoted the graves with a large rock.

Late in life, Gilliland moved to Hot Springs, New Mexico. There he and a man named Butler Oral Burris, nicknamed "Snooks," became friends. Before he died, Gilliland gave Burris a "Masonic pin with an Odd Fellows link on the bottom." He claimed he took the pin off of the body of Colonel Fountain. Gilliland instructed Burris to turn it over to

Albert Fountain Jr., after he was dead. When Gilliland died on August 8, 1946, the pin was turned over to members of the Fountain family, who identified it as having belonged to the colonel.

WILLIAM McNEW

William McNew, a longtime employee of Oliver Lee, was described as being "tough as rawhide" and having "ice-blue eyes." By all accounts, McNew was the meanest, most murderous, and least forgiving of the trio consisting of him, Oliver Lee, and Jim Gilliland.

McNew remained a rancher for the rest of his life. He moved northwest to San Marcial, Socorro County, New Mexico. The town was destroyed on two occasions as a result of flooding from the nearby Rio Grande and again as a result of fire. Today it is a ghost town. As his family grew, McNew moved to the community of Ancho in Lincoln County.

Leon Metz related an odd story regarding William McNew. During the late spring of 1937, he suffered a stroke and, as no heart beat or breathing was detected, was thought dead. He regained consciousness after he was laid on the mortician's table preparatory to being buried. When he was able to talk a few days later, he related to family members a strange dream he had during the time he was unconscious. McNew said that he had been in hell and was "standing up to his knees in molten lava." A short time later, June 30, McNew experienced another stroke from which he died. Just before he passed away, however, it was reported that his lower legs had manifested severe blisters and the skin peeled away as though it had been burned.

BILL CARR

Bill Carr, along with William McNew, was investigated relative to the disappearance of Colonel Fountain and his son Henry. Both men were eventually released from custody at a formal hearing. Following this, Carr was said to have had a conversion at a tent revival and allegedly became overtly religious. Shortly thereafter, Carr would advance to the pulpit of many a subsequent revival or church service and deliver testimonials that reportedly revealed his role in the kidnapping and killing of the Fountains. Hearing of this, Oliver Lee, William McNew, Jim Gilliland, and others began to grow concerned and debated whether or not something needed to be done about their former partner. As it turned out, Carr was regarded by most who heard him testify as half-mad and few paid any attention to his incoherent ramblings.

ALBERT BACON FALL

With help from former courtroom opponent Thomas Catron, A. B. Fall was elected as a Republican to the United States Senate in 1912 and reelected in 1918. In the Senate, Fall served as chairman of the Committee on Expenditures in the Department of Commerce and Labor. In March 1921, he was appointed secretary of the interior by President Warren G. Harding. Harding saw to it that Fall's department assumed responsibility for the Naval Reserves land at Elk Hills and Buena Vista, California, and at Teapot Dome, Wyoming.

In April 1922, Fall granted two of his friends—Harry F. Sinclair of the Mammoth Oil Corporation and Edward L. Doheny of the Pan-American Petroleum and Transport Company—the rights to drill for oil on Naval Reserve land. Fall permitted no open bidding for said rights. During a subsequent congressional investigation of what was to be called the Teapot Dome Scandal, Fall was found guilty of conspiracy and bribery. According to documents, Fall was paid $385,000 by Doheny. It was the first time a cabinet member was convicted of a felony and sentenced to prison. Fall served nine months of a one-year sentence.

After being released from prison, Fall returned to his home in the Tularosa Basin. A short time later, Doheny's corporation foreclosed on Fall's property as a result of unpaid loans. Following a long illness, Albert Fall died on November 30, 1944, in El Paso, Texas.

CARL ADAMSON

A short time after the killing of Pat Garrett, Adamson, who was at the scene, was arrested for "conspiracy to smuggle Chinese into the United States." He was convicted and sentenced to eighteen months in prison. Following his release, Adamson went to work for a New Mexico sheep rancher named, ironically, Garrett, but who was no relation to the deceased lawman. Adamson died on November 1, 1919, in Roswell. He was fifty-two years of age.

KILLIN' JIM MILLER

James Brown Miller, best known as "Killin' Jim," was also occasionally identified as "Deacon Jim" Miller because of his avoidance of alcohol and tobacco and his habit of attending church every Sunday. Miller was said to have killed forty men, but extant evidence can only verify twelve.

Throughout much of his life, Miller made his living as a Texas Ranger, a deputy sheriff, a town marshal, a professional gambler, and a professional assassin. In 1909, he was hired by two men and an accomplice to kill an Oklahoma cattleman and former United States deputy marshal, Gus Bobbit. It was believed the men had a personal grudge against Bobbit, but they were also desirous of his ranch.

Using a shotgun, Miller killed Bobbit on February 27, 1909, in Ada, Oklahoma. He immediately fled to Texas. Before he died, Bobbitt identified his killer. Miller was arrested a short time later and extradited to Oklahoma to stand trial for murder. On the morning of April 19, 1909, a mob of thirty to forty men stormed the Ada jail and removed Miller, along with the others involved in the killing. The prisoners were dragged to an abandoned livery stable behind the jail and hanged. Miller was placed on a box while a noose was fastened around his neck. Before he could be pushed from the box, Miller allegedly shouted, "Let 'er rip!" and jumped.

W. W. Cox

William W. Cox continued to operate and add to his ranch holdings via acquired homesteads, railroad lands, and squatters' rights. His property eventually exceeded 150,000 acres on which he ran several thousand head of cattle and one hundred mares for breeding range horses. In 1910, Cox and his family moved to Las Cruces so his children could attend New Mexico A&M College (now New Mexico State University). Cox died in 1923.

During the 1950s, most of the Cox ranch was acquired via condemnation by the United States government for use as part of White Sands Missile Range.

WAYNE BRAZEL

Following Wayne Brazel's trial in the killing of Pat Garrett, the life of the young ranch hand and goat herder became a mystery, one that has gone unsolved to this day.

In October of 1909, six months after being found not guilty of the murder, Brazel came into possession of Harrington Well, located several miles west of Lordsburg, New Mexico, and close to the Arizona border. Brazel filed to homestead 160 acres surrounding the well and moved onto it with Olive Boyd, who was either his fiancé or his wife. In 1911, Olive gave birth to a son.

Olive Brazel's pregnancy had been difficult, and for the next six months she fought to recover her health to no avail. She finally succumbed to pneumonia. Wayne, the widowed father of a six-month-old child, was devastated by the loss of his wife and, according to what little information is available, never got over it.

Brazel sold his ranch in 1913. Soon thereafter, charges of perjury related to a former homestead claim were filed against him by the federal government. For reasons unclear, the charges were dropped in May 1914. Within a few weeks, Wayne Brazel made arrangements for the care of his son and then vanished. He left no word of his plans or destination with friends or relatives and to this day no one knows what happened to him. Reports filtered in over the years that Brazel died a natural death, or that he was killed. The reported places of his demise included more than one dozen locations scattered across New Mexico and Arizona. None were ever substantiated.

In his book, *The Strange Story of Wayne Brazel*, author Robert Mullin reported that Brazel's son hired El Paso attorney H. L. McCune to investigate his father's disappearance and attempt to learn what happened. McCune concluded that the "probable explanation" was that Wayne Brazel journeyed to South America to seek ranching opportunities there and was subsequently killed by the "Butch Cassidy gang."

Attorney McCune no doubt collected a fee for his alleged investigative work and the final determination, but provided little to nothing in the way of substantiating his claim. Further, prevailing evidence shows that while in South America, Butch Cassidy led no such gang and only partnered with his friend, Harry Longabaugh, known as the Sundance Kid. Further, nothing was ever heard from or about Cassidy in South America after November 7, 1908, a bit over eight months following the killing of Pat Garrett and approximately six years before Wayne Brazel disappeared.

BILLY THE KID

Billy the Kid, whose given name was William Henry Roberts but who went by numerous aliases including William Bonney, Henry McCarty, and Henry Antrim, fled to Mexico following the shooting in Pete Maxwell's bedroom. He lived there off and on over the next twenty-five years. In the company of two other men, he owned and operated a horse ranch there. When things became difficult during the Mexican Revolution, Roberts returned to the United States. During the subsequent thirty years, he lived under a variety of aliases, found employment as a lawman, rode wild horses in Buffalo Bill's Wild West Show, and served in the Cuban campaign led by Theodore Roosevelt.

Though known to be the outlaw Billy the Kid by a few close friends, Roberts led a relatively reclusive life until 1948 when his true identity was discovered. Subsequent investigation and research has verified that he was, in fact, the famous bad man. He died from a heart attack in Hamilton County, Texas, on December 27, 1950.

TODD BAILEY

Todd Bailey remained with Oliver Lee for a short time after the killing of Pat Garrett. Lee sent him to Haynesville, Louisiana, a small town near the Arkansas border. There, Bailey met with one of Pat Garrett's brothers. The reason for the meeting was never documented, but Bailey family lore claims it had to do with determining whether or not there would be any hostile reaction from the Garrett family relative to the murder. A short time before Garrett was killed, he was having cattle shipped to New Mexico from Louisiana and Arkansas by his brother. The brother told Bailey there would be no response to the killing of Garrett.

While in Louisiana, Bailey went to a dance across the Arkansas border in the tiny community of Ravanna, where he met his future wife. Bailey returned to New Mexico long enough to be sent to El Paso to kill Mannen Clements, who threatened to expose Albert B. Fall, W. W. Cox, Oliver Lee, and several others in the plot to kill Garrett. He returned to Louisiana and married on April 12, 1909.

On April 19, Bailey was back in New Mexico during the trial of Wayne Brazel. Oliver Lee was concerned that Carl Adamson would arrive to testify and feared his former accomplice could not be trusted to assist the defense. Bailey had orders to shoot and kill Adamson on the road into town. Adamson, who was in jail for smuggling Chinese laborers across the Mexican border, declined to testify.

After Brazel's trial, Bailey returned to Louisiana, and shortly thereafter he and his wife moved to Doddridge, Arkansas, a short distance from Ravanna. Around that time the country was hit with the Great Depression. Bailey and his family moved to Broken Bow, Oklahoma, forty miles northwest of Doddridge. There, he ran cattle, operated a butcher shop, and made illegal whiskey. Todd Bailey passed away on August 3, 1949, in Broken Bow.

Bibliography

BOOKS

Ball, Eve. *Ma'am Jones of the Pecos*. Tucson: University of Arizona Press, 1969.

Bartholemew, Ed. *Jesse Evans: A Texas Hide Burner*. Houston: Frontier Press of Texas, 1955.

Brothers, Mary Hudson (with Bell Hudson). *Billy the Kid: The Most Hated, the Most Loved Outlaw New Mexico Ever Produced*. Whitefish, MT: Kessinger Publishing, 2007.

———. *A Pecos Frontier*. Albuquerque: University of New Mexico Press, 1943.

Brown, Dee. *Bury My Heart at Wounded Knee*. New York: Holt, Rinehart and Winston, 1970.

Clark, Mary Whatley. *John Chisum: Jinglebob King of the Pecos*. Austin, TX: Eakin Press, 1984

Cline, Donald. *Alias Billy the Kid: The Man Behind the Legend*. Santa Fe, NM: Sunstone Press, 1986.

Curry, George. *An Autobiography*. Albuquerque: University of New Mexico Press, 1958.

Dykes, J. C. *Billy the Kid: Biography of a Legend*. Albuquerque: University of New Mexico Press, 1952.

Earle, James H. *The Capture of Billy the Kid*. College Station, TX: Creative Publishing, 1989.

Etulain, Richard W., and Glenda Riley. *With Badges and Bullets: Lawmen and Outlaws in the Old West*. Golden, CO: Fulcrum, 1999.

Fall, Albert B. *The Memoirs of Albert B. Fall*. Edited by David B. Stratton. Southwestern Studies Series, Vol. IV, No. 3, Monograph No. 15. El Paso: Texas Western Press, 1966.

Fulton, Maurice G. *History of the Lincoln County War*. Edited by Robert N. Mullin. Tucson: University of Arizona Press, 1968.

Garrett, Pat F. *The Authentic Life of Billy, the Kid, the Noted Desperado of the Southwest, Whose Deeds of Daring and Blood Have Made His Name a Terror in New Mexico, Arizona, and Northern Mexico, by Pat F. Garrett, Sheriff of Lincoln County, N. Mex., by Whom He Was Finally Hunted Down and Captured by Killing Him*. Santa Fe: New Mexican Print and Pub. Co., 1892.

Gibson, A. M. *The Life and Death of Colonel Albert Jennings Fountain*. Norman: University of Oklahoma Press, 1965.

Glenn, Skelton. *Pat Garrett as I Knew Him on the Buffalo Ranges*. Robert N. Mullin Collection. Midland, TX: Haley Memorial Library and History Center, nd.

Hamlin, William Lee. *The True Story of Billy the Kid*. Caldwell, ID: Caxton Printers, 1959.

Hertzog, Peter. *Little Known Facts about Billy the Kid*. Santa Fe: New Mexico Press of the Territorian, 1964.

Horn, Calvin. *New Mexico's Troubled Years*. Albuquerque, NM: Horn and Wallace, 1963.

Horwitz, Tony. *A Voyage Long and Strange*. New York: Henry Holt and Company, 2008.

Hough, Emerson. *The Story of the Outlaw*. New York: Outing Publishers, 1907.

Hoyt, Henry. *A Frontier Doctor*. Boston: Houghton Mifflin Company, 1929.

Hutchinson, W. H. *A Bar Cross Man: The Life and Personal Writings of Eugene Manlove Rhodes*. Norman: University of Oklahoma Press, 1956.

———. *Another Verdict for Oliver Lee*. Clarendon, TX: Clarendon Press, 1965.

Hutchinson, W. H., and Robert N. Mullin. *Whiskey Jim and a Kid Named Billie*. Clarendon, TX: Clarendon Press, 1967.

Jameson, W. C. *Butch Cassidy: Beyond the Grave*. Boulder, CO: Taylor Trade Publishing, 2012.

———. *Billy the Kid: The Lost Interviews*. Clearwater, FL: Garlic Press, 2012.

———. *Billy the Kid: Beyond the Grave*. Boulder, CO: Taylor Trade Publishing, 2005.

Kaldec, Robert F. *They Knew Billy the Kid*. Santa Fe, NM: Ancient City Press, 1987.

Keleher, William A. *The Fabulous Frontier*. Albuquerque: University of New Mexico Press, 1945.

———. *Turmoil in New Mexico, 1848—1868*. Santa Fe, NM: Rydal Press, 1952.

———. *Violence in Lincoln County*. Albuquerque: University of New Mexico Press, 1957.

Lavash, Donald B. *Sheriff William Brady*. Santa Fe, NM: Sunstone Press, 1986.

Lingle, Robert T., and Dee Linford. *The Pecos River Commission of New Mexico and Texas*. Santa Fe, NM: Rydal Press, 1961.

Mann, E. B. *Guns and Gunfighters*. New York: Bonanza Books, 1975.

McCarty, John L. *Maverick Town: The Story of Old Tascosa*. Norman: University of Oklahoma Press, 1946.

McCright, Grady E., and James H. Powell. *Jesse Evans: Lincoln County Badman*. College Station, TX: Creative Publishing Company, 1983.

McNew, George Lee, *Last Frontier West*. Self-published, 1985.

McNew, George L., and Elizabeth M. McNew. *The Pioneers of 1885 in New Mexico Who Refused to Be Subdued*. Self-published, nd.

Meadows, John P. (Ed. John P. Wilson). *Pat Garrett and Billy the Kid as I Knew Them*. Albuquerque: University of New Mexico Press, 2004.

Metz, Leon C. *Pat Garrett: The Story of a Western Lawman*. Norman: University of Oklahoma Press, 1974.

Morrison, John W. *The Life of Billy the Kid: A Juvenile Outlaw*. New York: John W. Morrison, nd.

Mullin, Robert. *History of the Lincoln County War*. Tucson: University of Arizona Press, 1968.

_____. *The Strange Story of Wayne Brazel.* Canyon, TX: Palo Duro Press, 1969.

Nolan, Frederick. *The Lincoln County War: A Documentary History.* Norman: University of Oklahoma Press, 1992.

Otero, Miguel. *My Nine Years as Governor of New Mexico Territory.* Albuquerque: University of New Mexico Press, 1940.

_____. *The Real Billy the Kid: New Light on the Lincoln County War.* New York: Rufus Rockwell Wilson, 1936.

Poe, John W. *The Death of Billy the Kid.* Boston: Houghton Mifflin Company, 1933.

Poe, Sophie A. *Buckboard Days.* Albuquerque: University of New Mexico Press, 1881.

Prassel, Frank Richard. *The Great American Outlaw: A Legacy of Fact and Fiction.* Norman: University of Oklahoma Press, 1993.

Recko, Corey. *Murder on the White Sands.* Denton: University of North Texas Press, 2007.

Richards, Colin. *How Pat Garrett Died.* Santa Fe, NM: Palomino Press, 1970.

Rister, Carol Coke. *Fort Griffin on the Texas Frontier.* Norman: University of Oklahoma Press, 1956.

Rudulph, Charles Frederick. *Los Billitos: The Story of Billy the Kid and His Gang.* New York: Carlton Press, 1980.

Scanlon, John Milton. *Life of Pat Garrett.* El Paso, TX: Southwest Printing Company, 1952.

Shinkle, James D. *Robert Casey and the Ranch on the Rio Hondo.* Roswell, NM: Hall-Poorbaugh Press, 1970.

_____. *Reminiscences of Roswell Pioneers.* Roswell, NM: Hall-Poorbaugh Press, 1966.

_____. *Fort Sumner and the Bosque Redondo Indian Reservation.* Roswell, NM: Hall-Poorbaugh Press, 1965.

_____. *Fifty Years of Roswell History.* Roswell, NM: Hall-Poorbaugh Press, 1964.

Shirley, Glen. *Shotgun for Hire: The Story of "Deacon" Jim Miller, Killer of Pat Garrett.* Norman: University of Oklahoma Press, 1970.

Sonnichsen, C. L. *Tularosa: Last of the Frontier West.* Albuquerque: University of New Mexico Press, 1960.

Sonnichsen, C. L., and William V. Morrison. *Alias Billy the Kid.* Albuquerque: University of New Mexico Press, 1955.

Tanner, J. M. *Growth at Adolescence,* 2nd ed. Oxford: Blackwell Scientific Publications, 1962.

Tatum, Stephen. *Inventing Billy the Kid.* Albuquerque: University of New Mexico Press, 1982.

Tuska, Jon. *Billy the Kid: A Handbook.* Lincoln: University of Nebraska Press, 1989.

Utley, Robert M. *Billy the Kid: A Short and Violent Life.* Lincoln: University of Nebraska Press, 1989.

_____. *High Noon in Lincoln.* Albuquerque: University of New Mexico Press, 1987.

Weider, Ben, and David Hapgood. *The Murder of Napoleon.* New York: Congdon and Lattès, Inc., 1982.

Wilson, John P. *Merchants, Guns, and Money: The Story of Lincoln County and Its Wars.* Santa Fe: Museum of New Mexico Press, 1987.

ARTICLES

Adler, Alfred. "Billy the Kid: A Case Study in Epic Origins." *Western Folklore* 10 (April 1951): 143–52.
Avant, Buddy, as told to Arthur Clements. "The Buddy Avant Story." *True West* (June 1978): 10–15, 45–48.
Blazer, Paul A. "The Fight at Blazer's Mill." *Arizona and the West* 6, no. 3 (Autumn 1964): 203–10.
Cline, Donald. "Secret Life of Billy the Kid." *True West* (April 1984): 12–17, 63.
Hail, Marshall. "The San Augustine Ranch House." *Frontier Times* (September 1969).
Hatley, Allen G. "Old West Adventurer John W. Poe." *True West* (June 1999): 12–18.
Hendron, J. W. "The Old Lincoln County Courthouse." *El Palacio* 46, no. 1 (January 1939): 1–18.
Hervey, James Madison. "The Assassination of Pat Garrett." *True West* (March–April 1961).
Metz, Leon C. "Pat Garrett: El Paso Customs Collector." *Arizona and the West* 2, no. 4 (Winter 1969): 327–40.
Smith, William R. "Death in Doña Ana County: A Study of the Facts and Theories in the Fountain and Garrett Murder Cases." *English Westerners Brand Book*, *Part 1*, 9, no. 2 (January 1967), *Part 2*, 9, no. 3 (April 1967).

NEWSPAPERS

Ashenfelter, S. M. "Exit 'The Kid.'" *Grant County Herald.* July 28, 1881.
El Paso Daily Herald. June 7, 1899.
———. June 15, 1899.
El Paso Evening News. May 8, 1903.
El Paso Herald. May 8, 1903.
———. February 29, 1908.
———. March 2, 1908.
———. March 3, 1908.
El Paso Times. May 9, 1903.
———. November 4, 1913.
———. November 3, 1914.
———. "Researcher Discovers Document." August 5, 1951.
Koogler, J. H. *Las Vegas Gazette.* December 28, 1880.
Las Vegas Gazette. May 19, 1881.
New Mexico Sentinel. April 23, 1939.
Rio Grande Republican. April 8, 1882.
———. April 22, 1882.
———. August 8, 1885.
———. May 15, 1886.

———. May 22, 1886.
———. February 21, 1896.
———. October 9, 1896.
———. August 24, 1906.
———. September 14, 1906.
———. September 21, 1906.
———. March 7, 1908.
Santa Fe Weekly New Mexican. December 20, 1880.
Schiff, Stacy. "The Dual Lives of the Biographer." *New York Times.* November 25, 2012.

LETTERS

Dow, Hiram, to John Boylan, July 25, 1963. Jim Earle Collection.
Garrett, Patrick F., to New Mexico Acting Governor W. G. Ritch, July 15, 1881.

ARCHIVES

Thomas B. Catron Papers, University of New Mexico Library, Albuquerque.
W. W. Cox Papers, University of Texas at El Paso Library.
A. B. Fall Papers, University of New Mexico Library, Albuquerque.
Colonel Maurice Garland Fulton Papers, University of Arizona Library, Tucson.
Skelton Glenn Papers, University of Texas at El Paso Library.
Robert N. Mullin Collection, Haley Memorial Library and Historical Center, Midland, Texas.
C. L. Sonnichsen Papers, University of Texas at El Paso Library.

INTERVIEWS

Numerous in-person and e-mail interviews conducted by W. C. Jameson and Steve Sederwall with Buck Bailey of Wickes, Arkansas, Mike Bailey of Broken Bow, Oklahoma, and Brenda McKellar and Orene Bailey Yancey of Duncan, Oklahoma.

Acknowledgments

◆◆◆

Many of the interpretations and conclusions found in this book were arrived at with the help of a number of important people. The late Dr. C. L. Sonnichsen, noted historian and writer of Southwestern matters, provided early encouragement and insight and shared many of his findings. A number of discussions and debates with writer Leon Metz revealed the need for concentrated investigative work related to the lives and times of Pat Garrett and Billy the Kid. The late Fred Bean—writer, detective, and psychologist—located and transcribed the long lost interview tapes of William Henry Roberts, aka Billy the Kid, which yielded important information about the outlaw's relationship with Garrett. Intrepid investigator Steven Sederwall turned over more stones and found more pertinent information and evidence regarding Pat Garrett, Colonel Albert Jennings Fountain, Oliver Lee, Billy the Kid, and others than all of the so-called experts put together. Detailed information regarding Todd Bailey, the killer of Pat Garrett, was contributed by his grandson, Buck Bailey, along with other members of the Bailey clan.

Laurie Jameson, multi-award-wining author and poet, continues to provide inspiration and editorial support for my research and writing endeavors. Agent Sandra Bond always seems to find a publisher for my efforts and is fun to hang around with.

About the Author

◆◆◆

W.C. Jameson is the award-winning author of more than ninety books and hundreds of articles. His work has been the subject of television programs and documentaries. He lives in Texas.